COURT-MARTIAL

COURT-MARTIAL

How Military Justice
Has Shaped
America from the
Revolution to
9/11 and Beyond

CHRIS BRAY

W. W. NORTON & COMPANY
Independent Publishers Since 1923
New York London

Copyright © 2016 by Refer to Chart Productions, Inc.

For information about permission to reproduce selections from this book,
write to Permissions, W. W. Norton & Company, Inc.,
500 Fifth Avenue, New York, NY 10110

For information about special discounts for bulk purchases, please contact
W. W. Norton Special Sales at specialsales@wwnorton.com or 800-233-4830

Manufacturing by RR Donnelly North Harrisonburg
Book design by Helene Berinsky
Production manager: Louise Mattarelliano

Library of Congress Cataloging-in-Publication Data

Names: Bray, Chris (Historian), author.
Title: Court- martial : how military justice has shaped America from the
revolution to 9/11 and beyond / Chris Bray.
Description: First edition. | New York : W.W.Norton & Company, 2016. |
Includes bibliographical references and index.
Identifiers: LCCN 2016002824 | ISBN 9780393243406 (hardcover)
Subjects: LCSH: Courts-martial and courts of inquiry—United States—History.
Classification: LCC KF7625 .B73 2016 | DDC 343.73/01—dc23 LC record
available at http://lccn.loc.gov/2016002824

W. W. Norton & Company, Inc.
500 Fifth Avenue, New York, N.Y. 10110
www.wwnorton.com

W. W. Norton & Company Ltd.
Castle House, 75/76 Wells Street, London W1T 3QT

1 2 3 4 5 6 7 8 9 0

This book is dedicated to the memory of
Sgt. William Walker, 3rd South Carolina Colored Infantry,
and Capt. Silas Soule, 1st Colorado Cavalry

CONTENTS

The object of the civil law is to secure to every human being in a community all the liberty, security, and happiness possible, consistent with the safety of all. The object of military law is to govern armies composed of strong men, so as to be capable of exercising the largest measure of force at the will of the nation.

These objects are as wide apart as the poles, and each requires its own separate system of laws, statute and common. An army is a collection of armed men obliged to obey one man. Every enactment, every change of rules which impairs the principle weakens the army, impairs its values, and defeats the very object of its existence. All the traditions of civil lawyers are antagonistic to this vital principle, and military men must meet them on the threshold of discussion.

—Gen. William Tecumseh Sherman, 1879

—◄O►—

I am forty-two years of age, have about half the period of my life been engaged in military duty, + have hitherto escaped censure in the execution of the various offices I have sustained in a regular progression in rank from a private to the office which I now hold, + the reputation acquired by punctuality + fidelity in the discharge of duty as a military officer being the principal claim to respectability I now hold (for I have no title to influence from wealth) when I contemplate the attack now made on my character by the charges exhibited before you, I feel no disposition to suppress what is indeed a most interesting fact, that the importance of a fair reputation to myself + a young family dependent on my standing in society for their own rank among their fellow citizens, makes the trial which I am now undergoing before you the most serious event of my life.

—Capt. Alpheus Shumway, 1820

INTRODUCTION

THE HISTORY OF AMERICAN MILITARY JUSTICE IS INEXTRICABLY the history of America.

For two and a half centuries, courts-martial and military commissions have directly confronted the great questions that have challenged our society. Among many other things, the armed forces have struggled to make sense of immigration and nativism, African American protest in the name of social equality, and our many debates over the limits of power and the boundaries of dissent. Our military justice tells us who we are—all of us, not just soldiers. Armed forces are inevitably ordered and sustained by discipline, and the characteristics of that discipline reveal the values of the country that gives a military organization its personnel and its rules. A court-martial can't help but tell a rich story about culture and society.

Military justice is separate from civilian justice, but not separate from American society; it's a different forum, but it's not a different country. More than a decade before Rosa Parks was arrested for refusing to move to the back of a city bus in Montgomery, Alabama, the future Brooklyn Dodger Lt. Jack Robinson was tried before a court-martial for a similar refusal on a Texas army post. Robinson's court-martial was a prelude and a rehearsal, and one of many. The military was the site of an extraordinarily vital and century-long prologue to the Civil Rights Movement, one of the important first places where African Americans made clear and forceful demands for equality. Charged with offenses against military law and regulations in segregated armed forces, black soldiers and sailors argued over the meaning of their choices—and developed an important narrative about rights and resistance.

In fact, the court-martial was one of the important first places in many serious societal debates. Who are we? What do we value? What kind of justice will we demand for our soldiers—and for our enemies? With sober meticulousness and real pain, Americans have looked for the meaning of our country in military courts.

Today, as we have a long political debate over military justice reform, we've mostly managed to turn the topic into a cartoon. "Military justice," as the usual joke has it, is an oxymoron. Courts-martial are clumsy and thoughtless, an unfair forum operated on the whim of military commanders. None of that is true. It's a view that overlooks more than two centuries of rich history, complex debate, and serious efforts at modernization.

America's treatment of military captives at Guantánamo Bay reflects a similarly thorny past. Gitmo has grandparents; we've been arguing for a very long time over many of the same questions about justice for military captives, especially in the case of people who weren't captured in uniform while fighting a formally declared war in the name of an established government.

There's a paradox to military justice, because its deep connection to the larger society has existed alongside a set of ineradicable differences. The court-martial is a strange creature, and it delivers a separate kind of justice. Military courts have always judged cases with a set of values, procedural rules, and practical considerations that have no place in other court systems. It's easy to miss how different this system of justice has been. Today—precisely as politicians complain about how backward military justice is—the court-martial looks and works more like civilian courts than it did through most of its history, and the few legal scholars who study the armed forces have debated the limits to the "civilianization" of military justice.

Those developments obscure the reality of a long past in which military courts were nakedly an instrument of command, intended above all to protect the effectiveness of armed forces, and had few rules to speak of.

If you attended a court-martial today, it would look a lot like a trial in your local courthouse: There's a judge, the two sides look like the prosecutor and the defendant with his defense lawyer, and the members of the court look like a jury. But the military judge is a late-twentieth-century development, and courts-martial have been far more procedurally casual through much of our past. At least until the years after World War I, the court-martial was usually made up of a group of officers who had no legal training, and was advised on the law only by an appointed judge advocate—who frequently didn't know anything about the law either. Military justice has always been exemplary, showing all soldiers what happens to one soldier who lacks discipline or refuses to obey: *Don't desert, because we'll shoot you.* The point and the process are practical, and it mostly hasn't looked at all like the justice carried out in civilian courtrooms.

"A court martial was not a court, but simply an agency of the commanding officer," the law professor and former soldier Edmund Morgan wrote, describing military justice before the reforms he oversaw at the beginning of the 1950s. "It was said to be his right hand to help him maintain discipline, and was controlled not by law but by his will. . . . There being no legal standard, there could be no legal error." For more than a century and a half, military courts mostly made military decisions; they focused on combat effectiveness, organizational stability, and the unwritten social expectations of warriors. Commanders never wanted lawyers around the courts-martial they had convened,

Morgan explained, because they worried that people with legal training would "bitch up the thing by telling them some law." They rarely had to worry about that problem.

Today, law and legal procedure are far more important to military courts than they were through most of the American past. But at their foundation, courts-martial are still very much instruments of command authority, and their ultimate purpose is to protect the military effectiveness of the armed forces. The separateness of military justice hasn't simply evaporated as legal reforms have substantially reshaped courts-martial. The values and assumptions of a unique culture, and the organizational needs of a unique institution, can't be driven out of the legal system that imposes discipline on the men and women of the armed forces. Warriors are warriors, and judge each other as the thing they are. It can't be switched off, however hard politicians might try.

THIS BOOK DISCUSSES many kinds of military courts. These are the most common, and the most important:

The *court-martial* is a trial court, convened to consider charges against military personnel that can result in punishment. There are different types and levels: currently, they are **general**, **special**, and **summary** courts-martial. (A **drumhead** court-martial—the term is informal—is any kind of court-martial conducted quickly in the field by an army at war.) General courts-martial try the most serious charges, including capital charges, and can impose the most serious penalties; the special court-martial is an intermediate court; and the summary court-martial is a tribunal for relatively minor charges, able to impose only modest penalties.

Under current military law, many minor offenses can be handled by commanders through modest, nonjudicial **Article 15** punishment that allows for mild punishments like temporary loss of pay, brief confinement to quarters, and small reductions in rank.

Earlier state and federal military laws also established different levels of courts-martial, but used different language to describe them. The most serious kind of trial has always been conducted by a general court-martial, but earlier forms of lower courts in the armed forces were **brigade** or **regimental** courts-martial.

The *court of inquiry* is an investigative tribunal that can call witnesses and examine evidence. A court of inquiry has often been convened as a prelude to a court-martial, making a recommendation to a commander about whether or not an incident merits charges and a trial.

A *military commission* is a tribunal staffed and run by the military to conduct trials of people who are usually not military personnel, or at least not the personnel of the military conducting the trials. In the 1840s, Gen. Winfield Scott used them in Mexico as an instrument of military occupation and political stability. During the Indian wars of the late-nineteenth century, military commissions conducted mass trials for Sioux and Modoc warriors who had killed soldiers and settlers. Later, military commissions tried and condemned German infiltrators who snuck into the United States during World War II with plans to sabotage military production. In our own moment, military commissions have been convened at Guantánamo Bay to conduct trials for Taliban and al-Qaeda captives taken off the battlefield in Afghanistan.

Four systems of law have defined the operation of military courts. Until 1951, law in the US Army (and, briefly, the newly independent US Air Force) came from the **Articles of War**. In the US Navy, the **Articles for the Government of the United States Navy** served the same purpose in the same period. The Marine Corps was subject to either, depending on where—and under what command—marines were serving. In 1950, Congress replaced both sets of law with the **Uniform Code of Military Jus-**

tice, which took effect on May 31, 1951. It's the single system of federal military law in place today.

The fourth set of laws is discussed much less often, but it was extremely important well into the nineteenth century: **state laws** for the control of the militia. Today, state military codes still govern National Guard personnel who haven't been ordered into federal service.

ALL OF THESE MILITARY COURTS tell us a story about America and an important system of justice, but above all they tell us an important story about our shared human experience. The court-martial is a vivid record of the things people do in conflict and under pressure, and sometimes in the face of agony and horror.

A military trial grows from a moment of decision. That single moment can echo for decades: The sergeant in the 3rd South Carolina Infantry who laid down his weapon and refused to pick it up until the army paid him the same wage as it paid white soldiers—even as his regimental commander told him he was forfeiting his life. The captain of a warship who decided to execute sailors without waiting for a lawful court-martial, because he believed it was the only way he could avoid losing his ship to a mutiny. The Marine Corps drill instructor who decided to toughen up his indolent and undisciplined platoon by leading it into a treacherous tidal creek in the darkness. Lives were at stake; these decisions mattered.

The court-martial opens a unique window onto the history of American military institutions and the larger American society, and shows us the ways that ordinary people managed big social and political pressures in the face of sweeping changes. It shows us men, and later men and women, in the most serious moments of their lives, making their way through the world that we've inherited from them. The records of military trials take us beyond abstractions and ideas to a history of the actual—the past as it felt, in the moment, to the people who had to answer hard questions in real time.

Courts-martial have taken up deeply political questions at precisely the moments that related controversies have torn at the fabric of the larger American society. But they have managed the resolution of those larger debates with a mixed set of values that are both connected to the larger American culture and unique to an internal warrior culture. Military courts are connected and separate, joined to the nation they serve and animated by a set of beliefs and expectations that are not as widely shared.

That paradox is also the riddle of the law itself, and of the idea of the rule of law. What do our social expectations and cultural values do to the set of rules formally set down in a statute or a regulation? How do we shape the law as we live it? We usually believe that the military is the easiest place to answer these questions, as a place where obedience is simply expected, hierarchy is absolute, and the rules are perfectly clear.

It has never been that simple.

PART ONE

CITIZENS AND SOLDIERS

—◄◦►—

*The Early Republic
to the 1850s*

The Minuteman quit.

If there's one thing Americans know about the years that followed the Revolution, it's the fact that the new nation feared the dangers of a standing army. So the founding generations decided to mostly rely on the militia as their first line of defense, expecting nearly the entire population of white men to serve as a military force that could arise from the whole body of the people—farmers rushing from the fields to fight for their communities, their states, and their shared republic.

After 1792, federal legislation defined the structure of the militia precisely, and set out the rules for calling it to action. A country that didn't believe in a standing army was building its alternative from the old foundation of the colonial and Revolutionary militia, the system of armed force that it would use in case of a threat or invasion. Today, the legacy of the militiaman is who we are, a fundamental part of our national DNA; in one of our most American images, the statue of the Minuteman in Concord, Massachusetts, shows a farmer holding a musket in one hand while his other hand reaches back to hold the plow. There would be no powerful army set apart from the rest of the population, because the people would mostly be their own army, armed for themselves in the common defense.

But it didn't work. Militia rolls withered. Many states didn't bother to send annual militia returns to the War Department, leaving the national military leadership with little to no idea how much armed force it could hope to summon in an emergency. Mandatory training days became an open joke. By the 1820s, the complete collapse of the American militia had become too obvious to ignore, and Secretary of War James Barbour convened a board of officers to examine the failure of the institution. The "Barbour board" proposed answers that Americans debated for years, but never bothered to implement. State legislatures shrugged and gradually did away with the system of militia fines that could be imposed on men who failed to appear for training and inspections.

The early American militia gives us a political case study for the absolute failure of an idea that was supposed to be universally popular. Americans hated standing armies, widely favored the militia as the replacement for a professional military force—and destroyed the thing they all supported. Everyone wanted it, so it died.

The court-martial helps to make sense of this collision between the ideal and the reality. Military trials show us where people argued and dissented; they show us the places where order broke down. In the case of the militia, they reveal two problems that plagued the idea of universal militia service among the white men who were fully regarded as citizens of the new republic.

First, the glorious idea that every citizen walking behind a plow was also a soldier slammed into the unpleasant possibility that every citizen was subject to military law and discipline. Men found themselves standing before military courts for their actions as neighbors and members of society, deeply shocked to be on trial as soldiers.

Second, it wasn't clear to anyone what the militia actually was. Time and time again, men in the early republic expressed the view that they had joined together with their friends and neighbors in the common defense, freemen voluntarily associating for a common purpose; the militia, they believed, was subject to the will of communities and the limits of local values. State officials consistently responded that the militia was a government organization, subject only to orders from above. Men were punished over that conceptual schism.

Part One is about a contest between coercion and cooperation. It describes the death of an idea: the universal obligation of all citizens to provide for the common defense, as neighbors who were willing warriors whenever they needed to be. Then it discusses the coercive models of military service that were the early American opposite of that ideal.

I

"ALMOST A BLASPHEMER"

Citizen-Soldiers as Neighbors in the Early United States

THOMAS BEVINS DIDN'T DENY THE ACCUSATION: HE REALLY DID say those things to his company commander. But it didn't matter, he added, because he wasn't a military officer when he spoke.

"I distinctly admit," Bevins told his Connecticut court-martial, "that in the evening of the 31st of August named after the officers were dismissed I did say in answer to Capt Isaac Beach's remark to me that I was a d-d Irish buggar—that he was not fit to command a company any more than my dog. If this be abuse of Capt Isaac Beach I have abused him. But I beg leave to remark that this was in the evening after we were dismissed, + when as men + gentlemen, we were on the same footing."

Who are you, and when? If, in a society that intends to defend itself with a militia, every farmer and clerk and merchant is an occasional member of the armed forces, then when does the man set aside his identity as a citizen and take on his identity as a soldier? More important, when does he *not?* On that August day in 1814, Ens. Thomas Bevins trained all day under Capt. Isaac Beach; then the militia was dismissed and they sat down to dinner together, and they began to trade insults. But who was trading those insults—Captain Beach and Ensign Bevins, or Mr. Beach and Mr. Bevins? An important implication follows, and it was one that militiamen constantly contested: Who can punish you, and for what, and when do they have the power do it?

Through a long round of witnesses, the court-martial trying Bevins pursued exactly this point. A subaltern had cursed his superior, but they may not have occupied those military identities at the moment of their fight; what was the moment when they went from being one thing to being the other? Two often-repeated questions shaped the trial: Had the sun set? And had candles been lit for the evening meal? If a group of militia officers had been dining together at night, the training day was over; maybe they were citizens again, and only that, and maybe they could call one another whatever they wanted without implicating military jurisdiction.

"Question by the court," the transcript of the trial says, halfway through the testimony of Capt. David Baldwin, a witness to the exchange. "On what account did he call him a D-d rascal, was it in respect to his military or private capacity?" Baldwin couldn't answer, unable to identify the precise portion of Beach's collective identities Bevins had intended to curse. The handwritten transcript of the trial makes the captain's answer emphatic: "Answer. I cannot say!" A portion of Isaac Beach had been damned as a rascal, but no one was sure which portion.

It was a distinction men actually tried to draw in practice. Another captain also witnessed the angry exchange between Beach and his most junior company officer; after they had cursed each other, Capt. Eldad Bradley testified, Beach warned Bevins that he was still expected to turn out for training, and Bevins replied without hesitation: He "said he would obey him on all such days," Bradley told the court. A subordinate insulted a superior but drew a line against refusing to honor the official authority of the man he had insulted: *You're unfit for command, and I honor your command authority without question.*

Over and over again in the records of early militia courts, we can watch men try to figure out where the citizen ends and the soldier begins. The distinction mattered for many reasons, making neighbors into commanders and subordinates, but one was most important: When a man became a soldier, he became liable to military authority.

The persistent blurring of that boundary made men like Jonathan Meredith wild with irritation. In 1808, the prominent Maryland Federalist stood up at a private dinner and offered a toast to his fellow gentlemen: "Damnation to Democracy." But Meredith was also the adjutant of the state's 39th Regiment, and a court of inquiry was convened to determine whether he should face military charges for the expression of treasonous sentiments. Other gentlemen present at the dinner filed a statement with the court, insisting that the adjutant "appeared as a *private* citizen, and not in a *military* character." A man could talk politics at dinner—and end up in front of a military tribunal.

Cleared of wrongdoing—he had, he explained, intended to damn *French* democracy, the bad kind—Meredith resigned his commission in disgust. If an officer could be dragged before a military court on such thin allegations, he told the court, then men of little status had been given the power of "condemning before an unauthorized and illegal tribunal, any officer who may chance to differ from them in political opinion." It wasn't enough that the court had cleared him; it had been convened to police political statements made at a private dinner, and should never have existed. Looking back, it's hard to argue that Meredith was wrong.

Relying on the militia for their defense, the citizens of the early republic were supposed to be imposing restraints on power. There wouldn't be a substantial group of men who had a greater ability to deliver coercive force than the rest of society; strength would be balanced and diffused, a common property managed by consent and mutuality. The late colonial militia had purged

Loyalist officers in standing companies and regiments to prepare for a confrontation with British central authority, with men
choosing the officers they would and wouldn't follow. Obedience
had been a choice. In other instances, starting over, men had
"covenanted" to form their own military organizations: "militias
of association," created by the authority of neighbors with signatures on subscriber lists. As political tension turned to open war,
militiamen in Pennsylvania formed a committee of privates to
negotiate the terms of their service with higher authority. Men at
the lowest levels of the militia expected to obey rules, and commanders, that first won their consent.

Though it was a vision limited by racial exclusion, the Revolutionary military idea shared authority as widely as the values
of the moment allowed—and far more widely than it had usually been shared. It was deeply republican: founded on shared
rights and duties, with a structure that preserved social order as
it restrained power. As British regulars approached Lexington
on the morning of April 19, 1775, the historian David Hackett
Fischer writes, the town's militia commander, Capt. John Parker,
greeted each of his subordinates on the town green as his "neighbor, kinsman, and friend." The militia gathered as men who
knew one another, a community convening to meet a common
emergency. "The men of Lexington did not assemble to receive
orders from Captain Parker, much as they respected him," Fischer
writes. "They expected to participate in any major decision that
was taken. Their minister wrote that the muster was first and
foremost to '*consult* what might be done.' They gathered around
Captain Parker on the Common, and held an impromptu town
meeting in the open air." A cultural premise was at work: Sturdy
men would fight together for their shared causes and values,
by choice, following well-chosen leaders only in moments that
demanded firm and immediate command decisions.

But a dark irony gradually emerged in the lives of militiamen:

To make every man a soldier was to extend a form of official power throughout society. The militia could become a kind of speech police, patrolling politics. A man could become a *military subordinate* as he walked down the street, or lifted his glass at the dinner table. In court-martial records, we can still see the surprise of men who discovered this threat in their own lives.

Perhaps no one was ever more surprised than Robert Cranston. In August of 1817, the captain of Rhode Island's Newport Artillery was brought before a court-martial over a private choice at a community reception. Like Meredith, Cranston was exactly the kind of publicly prominent figure who was most at risk, as courts martial reached into every aspect of a man's personal life. He was an elected official, and a frequent political contestant who could be attacked in military courts by partisan enemies. In Newport, he would cycle through a series of public offices, serving as sheriff, postmaster, tax collector, mayor, state representative, and congressman. He was a climber, busy in the act of climbing, and so he was an officer in the local military company. And so he was a political target.

Cranston's trial was serious, but his offense was laughable. The day before a statewide election, he had agreed to lead an unofficial dockside reception for a visit from the governor. His brother, also an artillery officer and future congressman, borrowed a band from the local US Army commander, and Robert took charge of it—in civilian clothes, and without orders placing him on military duty. As the governor's ship pulled into the dock, Cranston asked the band to play a Rhode Island favorite. But the regular army band wasn't made up of men from Rhode Island, and they didn't know the song. So he called out for someone to just play something military, and the drummer did exactly that: He began to beat the signal for a retreat. Then Cranston called out the name of another song, and they began to play that one instead.

But it was too late. The Federalist governor saw a prominent local Republican greeting his ship, just before an election, with a signal that marked a battlefield disaster. He decided that he was being publicly mocked. More important, he decided that he was being publicly mocked as the commander in chief of the Rhode Island military, by an artillery captain from a state-chartered company who was his subordinate. The legislature agreed, and called on the governor to convene a court-martial. A military trial would follow a trivial political insult.

Accused, the citizen was horrified to discover himself a soldier. Standing before his court-martial, Cranston argued that the whole thing had been an accident—but never mind all that, because he wasn't in uniform, hadn't been ordered to duty, and wasn't officially leading troops. In short, he wasn't a military officer when the governor arrived. He was just Robert Cranston, down at the docks.

This is why his court-martial became a serious matter. Cranston warned the officers who had gathered to judge his case that they couldn't actually conduct a trial without causing themselves direct personal harm. A militia officer ordered into service, he argued, "is at all times, while so situated, subject to the authority of superior officers"; but at every other moment, "he is not a soldier, though liable to become one." Until that moment, Cranston said—until a militia officer was officially ordered to duty in a plainly military role—"martial law and Courts-Martial have nothing to do with him. If they have any thing to do with him, then every able-bodied male citizen, from the ages of 18 to 45, are subject to martial law; a thing they never dreamed of."

Cranston had given precise voice to the threat that hung over the militia: Every citizen could be subject to military law and courts, without having dreamed they could be. In theory, at least, every man who owed occasional militia duty could see his entire life brought under the threat of military punishment. A whole population of citizens could be silenced, forced to enter the public sphere as subordinates in a martial structure. Politicians would become commanders; politics would become an army. You could wander down to the docks to greet the governor, dressed as the citizen you thought yourself to be, and find yourself on trial in the military.

The members of the court saw the point quickly enough, and declined to return a verdict. Their decision on the charges was, instead, that "the jurisdiction thereof be not sustained." Confronted with an absurdly overwrought attempt to govern ordinary political speech, the militia declined to turn itself into a corps of full-time conscripts, subject at every moment of their lives to the hierarchy and regulation of armed forces. Military jurisdiction had found its limit. Captain Cranston couldn't insult the governor, but Robert Cranston could.

But just a few weeks later, up the coast in Salem, Massachusetts, Lt. Joseph Peabody Jr. was convicted on charges of disobedience and unofficerlike behavior after a voluntary ceremony to honor visiting dignitaries. The officers who wrote the complaint against Peabody, mortified that he had argued with superiors and stormed around a parade field in the presence of President James Monroe, told the lieutenant's court-martial that it didn't matter whether Peabody was really on duty: "We consider all the different corps who join together voluntarily at a parade, + all who compose them as subject to the same rules + principles while actually on parade as if the meeting was under the militia law, and that the charges are equally supported whether the meeting of the 8th July was voluntary, or strictly under the militia law."

A militia officer could be liable to military jurisdiction while not on duty, *as if* an event was "under the militia law." Men were citizens at times, soldiers at times, and potentially always subject to a form of justice that had no clear boundaries at all. Military law extended even to places where it didn't officially extend.

These were not just questions for the part-time soldiers of the militia. The early republic had a small regular army, a widely scattered frontier force that added up in its entirety to about a single contemporary brigade. But the country's very few thousand career soldiers struggled over the same questions about the boundary between the personal and the official. The contest was especially evident among officers, who regarded themselves as gentlemen of significant personal substance. The petty routine of military regulation—the chickenshit of army life that Paul Fussell later wrote about with such contempt—seemed far beneath them.

Political superiors provoked misery and resistance when they tried to apply niggling rules to the lives of prominent officers. Two of the most improbable courts-martial in the early American republic conducted two trials of the same officer, over the same subject, because of one of those efforts. Both required military courts to look for this hazy boundary between personal choice and military regulation, in a confrontation with authority that only ended because the protagonist died.

In the years leading up to the Revolution, after a Puritan rejection of long hair as showy and decadent, many American men came to find it fashionable again. As the historian Donald Hickey has written, the choices men made with that long hair had everything to do with class and status. Poor and middling men let it hang loose, but many men of the higher social ranks spent time nurturing their elaborate queues, fussy ponytails that took regular care. And so the Continental Army had sheltered a group of men who emerged from the Revolution as the fathers of their country—powerful and connected military leaders and men of substance—who powdered their braided ponytails. In the army, the waxed and powdered queue became a symbol of the old-line Federalist officer, men who had fought to make the republic. Note the connection: Long hair equals prominent Federalist.

Then came the election of 1800, and the ascension of the

first Republican president. Thomas Jefferson sought to remake the army in many ways, purging Federalist leaders and bringing his own supporters into the officer corps. Long hair became evidence of recalcitrance and atavism, a symbol of the prominent Federalist in a Republican era. The officer Jefferson appointed to run the army, James Wilkinson, issued an order that was publicly premised on hygiene and good order while also twisting the knife in the political opponents of the new administration. In the army, Wilkinson ordered, "hair is to be cropped." Haircuts were politics. Federalist officers were to start looking like Republicans while they served a Republican commander in chief.

The Federalist officers—the longstanding core of the regular army—understood the real point of the order. It was an insult. In places, "the order was greeted with loathing and disgust that bordered on mutiny." In Tennessee, Col. Thomas Butler declined to take notice of the new regulation, and managed to win a temporary exemption as a wartime hero and a senior officer. But when his exemption was withdrawn in 1803, he still refused to cut off his queue; he was still proudly and defiantly a prominent old Federalist warrior in a Republican army. Butler wrote to a family friend, Andrew Jackson, a Federalist elitist reaching out to the personal symbol of early American democracy; Jackson wrote back that the order was "too near . . . Despotism," unsuited for the regulation of an American army. "In his defense," Hickey writes, "Butler argued that hair length was a personal matter not subject to military regulation." If you're on an army post today, find a sergeant major and read that sentence to him.

Butler was convicted of disobedience and reprimanded. Wilkinson expected him to cut his hair.

When Butler appeared to take command of troops in New Orleans in the summer of 1804, though, he showed up wearing a waxed and powdered queue. Now, Wilkinson wrote, the colonel was no longer simply disobedient; now he was engaged in "wilful, obstinate and continued disobedience" that bordered on "Mutinous Conduct." A second court-martial followed. In Tennessee, prominent men circulated a petition in defense of Butler's queue, and sent it to Congress. When the court-martial met in the summer of 1805, Butler argued again that Wilkinson's order intruded on the realm of personal choice, in an area that military regulation couldn't properly reach. And again, his argument failed. Convicted of disobedience a second time, Butler was suspended from the army for a year—but died of a sudden illness before the sentence could be carried out.

On his deathbed, Butler supposedly asked his friends to cut a hole in his coffin so he could he buried with his queue sticking out, defiantly on display. No one has ever proved that story, but it asks the question that Butler took to his grave: What are the limits of an army's authority over a soldier's own body?

WITHOUT CLEAR BOUNDARIES, the personal lives of citizens were sometimes policed as military business. The same pieces of a man's life could be subject to overlapping jurisdictions. A drunk neighbor could be construed as a disorderly soldier; a neighborhood quarrel could become military disobedience.

This is just what happened to David Whitney, a major general in the Vermont militia. As the eighteenth century came to an end, Whitney was a man without an apparent sense of personal decency. He beat his wife, "debauched" a friend's wife, and brushed aside demands that he make good for a shabby attack on an old man. In the intimate setting of a small New England town, he wasn't terribly subtle about any of it, and revealed himself over and over again in the company he kept: a motley collection of "riotous and disorderly persons" who were too appalling to be named in writing by the men who would complain about his behavior. But then his neighbors showed up to fix the problem, and Whitney made the damning choice that finally cost him his commission.

In the years after the Revolution, civilian courts recorded a sharp decline in wife-beating trials. That change was the result of an emerging conception of privacy—as the historian Ruth Bloch puts it, "the revolutionary delegitimation of government intervention in what was increasingly conceived as the 'private' family." It took time for this new idea to turn into our contemporary conception of personal privacy, but the white men of the early republic found more and more space as heads of households to keep their family conflicts to themselves and out of their local courts. In the new republic, what happened in a man's home was increasingly that man's business, and no one else's.

But not entirely, and this is where the court-martial changes the story. Expanding privacy in the arena of civil justice didn't mean that wife beaters and other men of low character weren't being watched, judged, and regulated. Freed from the threat of criminal charges as a citizen, the militia officer David Whitney ended up in front of a military tribunal as a bad neighbor and a terrible husband.

Something else had to happen first, though, a final step that made a private matter worthy of a military trial. The general first had to fail his encounter with one of the other forms of alternative justice for eighteenth-century reprobates, the shaming parade known as skimmington. As two of his subordinates wrote in a letter to the governor, Whitney was "taken and placed by two or three persons astride a pole, or rail, between two horses, with a rope around his neck holden by a boy." This is what we mean when we talk about a mob riding someone on a rail. In the American tradition of social punishment, a man's privacy indoors ended when his degeneracy became unavoidably obvious out in the street—and so that's where the punishment took place, public shame chastised by public shaming.

This is the moment Whitney fully ceased to be a soldier in the eyes of his fellow militia officers, because he let it happen. As his subordinates complained in their letter, the general "meanly, cowardly, and tamely submitted himself, and without any resistance" to the crowd, which then marched him "in open day, several miles, through the public streets of Addison." He had shown that he could beat a woman, but he wouldn't fight other men. A boy held the rope that was tied around his neck; a leader of warriors was unmanned in the public street.

So David Whitney had *privacy*: He didn't have to worry about being taken down to the local courthouse as a wife beater. But he still wasn't safe from his neighbors—and he wasn't safe from the judgment of his fellow militia officers. A court-martial quickly found the general guilty on charges of unofficerlike behavior, and sentenced him to be stripped of his rank and command. He was publicly shamed as a neighbor and then publicly shamed as an officer, paraded as a degenerate and then deprived of his honorable military status. And all of this happened at exactly the historical moment that the rate of civil wife beating trials had gone into a freefall. New forms of personal privacy met new forms of social policing. The court-martial filled in for retreating civil courts; a military forum solved a neighborhood problem.

The malleability of military jurisdiction didn't go unnoticed. The state's Council of Censors, an elected watchdog committee, attacked the trial in its annual message. The citizen David Whitney may have done shameful things, but they had nothing to do with the occasional military duties of Maj. Gen. David Whitney. Both the governor and the members of Whitney's court, the censors warned, had "assumed to themselves new and unheard of jurisdictional powers . . . by arraigning a citizen before an unconstitutional military tribunal, subjecting him to an illegal trial, and passing an ignominious martial sentence upon him, for crimes and misdemeanors, not one of which are even alledged to have been committed while he was acting in his Military capacity, and for which of consequence he could only be amenable before a civil tribunal."* But no one seems to have been listening, and the boundary between military and civil jurisdictions would go on being worn down by practical considerations that had nothing to do with legal structure. There were people who wanted to have the weapon of the court-martial to use against their licentious neighbors.

Sometimes militia officers struck at their opponents in a local controversy by filing complaints, but they also could offer more immediate resistance to men of low character. When they did, the court-martial would follow along behind the event to adjudicate a social dispute in the officer corps. Whole organizations could descend into virulent social conflict, torn apart by status rivalry and contests over personal honor.

The urgency of wartime military needs wouldn't even slow down a really determined social fight, like the kind Connecticut's 17th Regiment nurtured for several years. In 1812, the company officers of the regiment successfully petitioned the legislature to block their new commander's attempt to appoint his own inexperienced younger brother as the regimental major. To Lt. Col. Lucius Smith, the petition amounted to a declaration of war against his family, and he struck back with a series of calculated personal insults directed down the chain of command.

Finally, in 1814, still escalating his conflict with the officers he commanded, Smith appointed Isaac Sheldon as the regimental adjutant. Sheldon was the local eccentric, frequently drunk and loudly heterodox in his social and political views—and now he had authority over other men, who were expected to offer their submission as soldiers to a man they disdained as citizens. They

---

*Throughout this book, court-martial records and historical correspondence are quoted as I found them, with their original spelling and grammar.

instantly, unanimously, and entirely refused; every company officer abandoned the regiment, leaving the parade fields empty on
the days designated for training and inspections. The 17th Regiment had gone on strike. Seething, Smith ordered the arrest of
every one of his company officers. A whole regiment of Connecticut militia effectively vanished—during the darkest days of a war,
with the White House in ashes.

They didn't deny their commander's charges. "It is a fact admitted that not a single commissioned officer of the 17th Regiment
appeared on parade for Battalion Inspection + review on the 22d
of Sept. last," Capt. William Beebe told his court-martial. But they
had been left with no choice. Sheldon was "a profane swearer,
almost a blasphemer, + a drinking man." He was a "vicious, profane + intemperate person." He was "a profane drinking young
man." And so on, in the usual flood of local vituperation directed
against social outliers in early New England. The officers of the
17th Regiment couldn't obey a man like that, whatever the costs
or consequences—it just wasn't possible. "Were we under obligations to obey the Col. and tamely submit to be dragged about by
any creature whom the Col. should please to appoint over us?"
Ens. Henry Whittelesey demanded of his court-martial.

They were seething, in a fit of rage that still shines through
the records of their many trials. "If we tamely submit to every
thing of this kind," Whittelesey's defense statement concludes,
"we should at once forfeit the confidence + respect of our soldiers, they would no longer consider us as worthy their trust +
confidence. If our rights + those of our soldiers are not to be
respected, if we must give up all because a superior officer says
so, then farewell peace, farewell liberty, farewell every thing that
is dear to man. When these rights + privileges are taken from us,
we have no desire any longer to continue in public stations, we
will then resign the trust that has been reposed in us + retire to
private stations in life."

The officers of the 17th Regiment weren't merely debating the limits of their obligation to military authority; they were arguing over the whole structure of their social world. Men of substance, honor, and decency didn't submit to men of dismal character, regardless of military status or hierarchy. Personal identity trumped. And the point was taken. This great social cataclysm— and the serious military disruption associated with it—ended with the barest whimper. Convicted, the officers of the 17th Regiment were sentenced to mild punishments; reviewing their trials, Gov. John Cotton Smith remitted most of the sentences with a mild rebuke. Beebe, identified as the ringleader, was briefly suspended from his company command.

A whole regiment's worth of line officers had walked away from their companies during a war, and were hardly punished at all. The governor didn't explain his decision, but the implication isn't obscure: Everyone knew they had really been provoked, and everyone understood their response. Isaac Sheldon could not be a military officer, and no one could expect order to prevail if someone was foolish enough to make him one. The best way for a man to discover what other men thought of him was to accept an officer's commission.

These trials over David Whitney's behavior with a friend's wife and Isaac Sheldon's unfortunate personal habits were neighborhood discussions, deeply intimate and aggressively local. A court-martial was appointed once, to try charges against one man or a very few, and then it was dissolved. Court members were militia officers, leaders who trained a few days a year, usually unfamiliar with detailed military regulation and untrained in any system of law. In an era when travel was difficult, and a system in which trials were conducted within local regiments or brigades for less serious offenses, and divisions for more serious offenses, the men appointed to militia courts were also usually from the same area, and arrived knowing one another and everyone else in the room: accuser, defendant, witnesses, spectators.

In the 1822 Connecticut court-martial of Lt. Jacob Robinson, the court finished the trial, cleared the room for their private deliberations—and then swore one another in as witnesses and offered their testimony to themselves: "Major Ethelbert Benham, on oath declared, that while he was some years ago captain over the accused, the accused was generally backward in his duty as an officer and a gentleman. He was intemperate." The men trying Robinson on charges of disobedience and neglect of duty already knew among themselves that the defendant was guilty, because they already knew the defendant. They usually did.

There were also no military courthouses, so a state official ordering a court-martial to convene had to choose not just who would serve on it but also where they would meet. Since they needed a public place with plenty of chairs, that usually meant militia courts-martial met in taverns and coffeehouses, or the occasional living room at a general's house. So: men who knew one another, sitting around a barroom, conducting a trial for which they mostly had no formal training or guidance. They usually talked through their cases like neighbors sitting around in a tavern, the very thing that they were.

Sometimes it was even more intimate than all that, and the record of a military trial can look like a particularly painful family gathering.

In October of 1814, at a late moment in the War of 1812, the men of the state-chartered Newport Artillery were taking turns on guard duty at a coastal fortress, protecting the town against the possibility of a British attack. But the duty was mostly uneventful, and so it was mostly dull. Men began to lose their patience for it. One night, rebuked by the sergeant of the guard for his poor performance, a private named Richard Hazard Jr. replied with contempt. The sergeant told him he was under arrest. And then, the record of the event says, Hazard "loaded a gun primed and cocked it; and declared he would shoot the sergeant; and when in the act of taking aim, the gun was wrested from him." Witnesses to the incident would later testify that Hazard hadn't just been gesturing at violence—they were sure he had intended to kill the man who had scolded him and placed him under arrest. The thing that most surprised them all: Private Hazard had tried to kill Sergeant Hazard. A soldier had nearly killed his brother.

There was, and is, no such thing as a company-level military court. But that was exactly the kind of court that assembled to consider Richard Hazard's offense. The records of the "court of inquiry" convened to examine the incident don't appear with other militia court proceedings in Providence, where the state keeps its military records; instead, the court's deliberations and conclusions show up among other company business in an orderly book at the Newport Historical Society, mixed in among the Newport Artillery's votes on the lengths of their plumes— nine inches—and the choice of their officers.

Among the first items of recorded business is the court's acknowledgment that it wasn't a court, and shouldn't have been meeting. The commander of the Newport Artillery should properly have presented the matter to his chain of command, the court agreed, so that a proper court-martial could be called, "whose proceeding might have been governed by the rules and articles of war." But in a real military trial, they went on, "the life of the accused might have atoned for the enormity of his offences." So they decided not to have a real military trial.

The Newport Artillery controlled its own membership rolls, and very much conceived of itself as an association of gentlemen. The presence of the Hazard family name on their rolls argues in favor of that premise, since the Hazards were among the town's founders and leading men. The orderly books record the deliberation of gentlemen members over the composition of the company: who may be allowed to join, who should be forced to leave. On September 17, 1817, without recording the reasons, the company would eject three privates, "it being considered incompatible with the honor and interest of the company that they be any longer continued members of the same." In Hazard's case, the unofficial company court proceeded on just those premises, gentlemen soldiers examining a fellow gentleman soldier over questions of their shared honor.

They found him wanting, "particularly as the person against whom he lifted the deadly weapon was his own Brother." Hazard was absolutely without "sorrow and contrision," and the panel delivered the verdict it had no authority to deliver: Pvt. Richard Hazard Jr. was to be dismissed from the company—and barred from rejoining, as a guarantee that "they may never again be disgraced by having his name (by any accidental circumstance) upon their Roll." And they kept going, recommending that the company commander issue an order forbidding Hazard to set foot inside Fort Greene while the Newport Artillery was responsible for its security.

Finally, they delivered their most devastating sentence, a purely social punishment that makes an artillery unit look more like a men's club than a military organization: "And further, that it be recommended to the Members of the company, not to associate with the said Richard Hazard junr." For a series of dire offenses that ended with an attempt to break arrest and kill a superior and a brother, Hazard was in no danger of harsh martial punishment. He wouldn't be shot by a firing squad, or flogged, or have his head shaved and be marched out of camp to the sound of the "Rogue's March." He was free to leave, unharmed and facing no further legal jeopardy.

Instead, Private Hazard had been sentenced only to social death, excluded from the company and status of Newport's gentlemen. For a military offense that revealed his poor inner character, he would be punished on the streets and in the private front parlors of his neighbors: ignored when possible, actively shunned when necessary, a man of no standing or consequence. He died nine years later, at the age of twenty-seven, his death in Newport briefly noted up the coast in a Massachusetts newspaper. Tried and convicted by a military court that didn't exist, he was no gentleman. And that was the worst verdict of all for a soldier.

THESE CONTESTS over personal character and the meaning of discipline had serious military effects. With neighbors on trial for wife beating and adultery, and sentences of social shunning, the early American militia was two irreconcilable things at once: a government organization, managed down a chain of command, and a neighborhood association, managed by mutuality and consent. Men announcing that they wouldn't be dragged around by the likes of Isaac Sheldon because of his mere military authority were declaring a set of premises that set the militia in a context of community and social values. Formal regulations couldn't overcome the demands of manhood, decency, and personal honor. Militiamen were armed neighbors, managing their own role in the common defense. In Rhode Island, the state-chartered Kentish Guards took that conception of military authority even further: What right, they wondered, did the state have to give them orders at all? The state regarded them as part of its militia forces; the members regarded themselves as an independent military association, a voluntary gathering of gentlemen.

The Kentish Guards were—and still are—an exceptionally proud organization, a leading example of the militias of association formed in 1774 as the atmosphere of confrontation grew in Great Britain's American colonies. "Deeply impressed with a sense of the shameful Neglect of military Exercise and being willing and desirous to repair and revive that decayed and necessary spirit of regular Discipline, at this alarming Crisis," they wrote, "We the subscribers do unanimously join to establish and constitute a military independent company." The colony's militia didn't work well or serve the needed purposes, so they just made their own. Kent County's new military organization had a subscriber list, a set of signatures on an agreement; they made an army by choice and consent, within the boundaries of community. A formal charter from the legislature made the Kentish Guards self-governing, making their own rules by the majority vote of the men on the company roll.

In 1807, though, HMS *Leopard* fired seven devastating broadsides into the USS *Chesapeake* off the coast of Virginia, and British sailors boarded the helpless American ship to capture deserters from the Royal Navy. Americans prepared for war. In a country with a tiny standing army, Congress authorized President Thomas Jefferson to prepare a force of 100,000 militiamen for possible federal service, and the War Department assigned quotas for a militia draft to every state. In Providence, Rhode Island's adjutant general divided the statewide draft into local quotas by company—including the Kentish Guards. Six men from their ranks were to be chosen to serve in an army that would be formed from the state militia if war came.

And there the matter ended, because the commander of the Kentish Guards was appalled by his orders. Col. David Pinniger appointed a committee of sergeants and privates to consider the company's response, and its members voted unanimously to refuse the order. Privates voted not to obey the governor, the commander in chief of the state's military forces. The company had been formed some time ago, the committee wrote in the report of its decision. Since then, "voluntary members, from time to time, have associated with them for the express purposes held forth by the Charter." What's more, they added, "they now are willing to do military duty in a body agreeable to their Charter,

whenever, their services may be required." A state military organization was prepared to do whatever duty it saw as being necessary, whenever it decided that the time had come.

Two kinds of language run throughout the committee's
report, linking the obligations of a contract to the obligations
of volunteers. The state and the company had an unbreakable
contractual agreement, in the form of a legislative charter that
assured the independence of the Kentish Guards from militia
regulations and the orders of militia officers—but the company
and its members only had the perpetually renewable consent of
its members to serve together, voluntarily associating together to
do things they agreed to do. *We don't take orders, but we're willing to
do military duty.* Pinniger simply forwarded the report of his committee with his own brief letter informing the governor that the
Kentish Guards would be unable to obey the state's order. "You
will find many reasons detailed in it, why the order of his Excel-
lency cannot be complied with," the colonel wrote. "It is unnecessary for me to add others." The Kentish Guards received an
order, and they just said no.

A court-martial was appointed, but no trial followed—since
no facts were disputed. As the transcript says, "there were no
witnesses on either side to be examined." The court proceeded
straight to closing arguments, offering the officers of the Kentish Guards a chance to argue for the propriety of their acknowledged refusal to obey an order. They made that argument plainly
and directly, insisting that the men of their company "are not
only exempted from serving in the militia or any other companies than their own, and consequently from being drafted and
detached for that purpose; but they are also exempted from the
control of the militia laws. They are governed by their charter,
and by their own by laws. Neither the militia law of Congress
nor of this state can have any operation upon them." Eight years
after Vermont tried a general for beating his wife, a company of a

state's military forces refused the premise that the state's military laws had any effect on their military organization. The jurisdiction of the armed forces reached everywhere and nowhere: to toasts at private dinners, but not to the duties of military companies in the face of a possible war.

A court made up mostly of officers from the militia—from the thing the Kentish Guards thought they weren't—was unsurprisingly hostile to those claims, and the officers of the company were all convicted, stripped of their ranks, and removed from their commands. But the state didn't take the next step implied by its court-martial: The Kentish Guards never sent a list of men for a militia draft, and they were never forced to. They couldn't refuse orders, and they did.

THE TOWN MEETING in the open air, the militia of association, the men greeting one another as neighbor, kinsman, and friend: Militiamen never just understood themselves to be subordinates of government officials. They were prepared to use violence in defense of their self-definition.

At the end of September in 1821, a Rhode Island infantry regiment gathered on a parade ground in Providence for its annual review. They had an important spectator, the commander of the brigade to which the regiment belonged. Everyone on the parade field knew how Brig. Gen. Joseph Hawes was supposed to behave, because brigadiers had been showing up to watch the regiment train for as long as anyone could remember. Col. Henry G. Mumford, a former commander of the regiment, had always seen his brigadier at his regimental reviews. As he would testify during the court-martial of his successor, the brigade commander had been a kind of ornamental figure, very grand and basically useless. Sometimes he took a temporary and ceremonial command of the regiment, "by consent of the colonel," and other times "I have known the privilege refused to the brigadier." Then the day would end, and the brigadier's staff officers would escort him off the field in a grand display of plumes and epaulettes. The thing nearly everyone knew was that the brigadier general standing on the regimental parade ground was not there to command anything. He was there for the show.

For reasons that he never fully explained, Joseph Hawes decided to change the script. He did a deceptively simple thing: He sent a staff officer to convey an order to Col. Leonard Blodget. After many years in which no one on the parade field labored under the belief that the brigadier had any authority in the matter of the annual regimental review, he gave the regimental commander an order that was intended to govern the immediate operation of the regiment. He did exactly the thing that everyone else knew he had no authority to do.

Blodget responded just as the local precedent would suggest: He brushed the order aside. Capt. E. R. Billings, the staff officer who had passed the brigadier's order to Blodget, would tell a court-martial how Blodget had responded to him: "The colonel replied that he doubted the general's authority to give the order,—that he (the colonel) commanded the regiment that day."

But the other dispute between the two officers had deeper origins, and led to a far wider act of resistance. Blodget's regiment regularly met for its annual review on the same field in Providence, then marched every year to a nearby bridge at the end of its training. By its established custom, the regiment was dismissed at the bridge at the end of the day, and the companies left for their different homes. They finished their shared training at a symbol of connection, a place where everyone could march home from a central spot.

The order Hawes issued on the parade field in 1821 took direct aim at the regiment's custom, and at the culture of mutuality at its foundation. He ordered Blodget to dismiss the regiment on the parade field, and to do it immediately. They would not march away together to the bridge that connected their communities; instead, they would just leave, all gestures of mutuality and shared practice abandoned. But it didn't happen. The men of the regiment refused to let their brigadier general attack the custom that defined their shared duty.

In Lexington, nearly fifty years before, the men of the town militia had gathered around their commander "to *consult* what might be done." The militia of the 1820s still expected that right of consultation, and many of their officers still expected to honor it. Here's Billings, again, telling the court-martial what happened after he rode back to Hawes and told him Blodget had refused to obey his order: "The general rode up to the head of the column, and asked the colonel whether he would obey his order or not. The colonel replied, that his officers and men were opposed to the order. The general then replied, No matter, sir; it is your duty to obey the commands of your superiour officer." Leonard Blodget could give an order only if the men he led would agree to follow it.

The whole regiment shared in this conception of authority. As Hawes and Blodget argued, someone on the field—the testimony in the court-martial never established who—began to shout a repeated command: "Forward." The men of the regiment began to move, marching away from Hawes and toward the bridge, showing by direct action that they wouldn't be dismissed from the field. They wouldn't take orders from their own brigadier general. The argument instantly ceased to be abstract, a debate over differing conceptions of authority: Leonard Blodget's regiment didn't like an order from a superior officer, so it walked away.

Hawes tried to stop it, one man against hundreds, shouting from horseback that the regimental commander was under arrest. The "arrest" of militia officers in the nineteenth century didn't mean they were marched off to jail; it meant that they were stripped of their authority, arrested from command. Hawes had beheaded the thing that wouldn't obey him.

But removing Blodget from command didn't settle the confrontation—it made it instantly worse. The brigadier ordered the commander of the regiment's first battalion to take Blodget's command and dismiss the men on the parade field. That lieutenant colonel responded by turning to the regiment and shouting the single word that was already echoing across the clearing, "*Forward.*" Company officers at the head of the column took up the same command, and Hawes tried to move his horse into their path to stop them. Another officer, Capt. Caleb Williams Jr., described what happened next: "The general then repeated the order, 'Halt these troops,' when the word 'forward' was repeated by a great many. The general then wheeled his horse, apparently, to retire from the head of the column; at this time witness saw three or four of the men strike his horse with their guns; and to do this, were obliged to reach forward. The words, 'fix bayonets' were exclaimed by a great many."

In the space of a few moments, the men of a peacetime Rhode Island militia regiment were willing to gesture at deadly force to resist what they considered an inappropriate and insulting order from their brigade commander. They would *fight*—literally, physically fight—their own chain of command. The men around Hawes understood the seriousness of the moment. As testimony in Blodget's court-martial delicately put it, the brigade staff officers "advised the general to retire" once men in the ranks began to fix bayonets. And he did, the staff officers still urging him off the field until he had actually left it. The whole regiment, acting in unison without a single voice to command it, forced its opponent to retreat under threat of attack.

But then Hawes had become beside the point even as he fled the confrontation he had initiated, because the regiment's two battalion commanders had decided to take their own measure against his order: They split apart, marching their battalions away in two different directions. It would no longer be possible to dismiss the regiment on the field, because the regiment could no longer be found. Lt. Col. Job Angell and Maj. Edward S. Williams had reached their own decision: They would do whatever it took to prevent the regiment from obeying Hawes, even if Blodget improperly decided to obey their brigade commander's order.

Williams, who was not brought before a court-martial, told Blodget's court that he and Angell had agreed to disobey—and warned Blodget that they would do it. "The idea I meant to convey was, that I was willing to march off the second battalion, let the consequence be what it would," he testified, openly describing a conspiracy against military authority. "This conversation with the colonel was about five minutes before the agreement with colonel Angell, which was, that we should march off the battalions different ways, in order to take responsibility upon ourselves, as I was fearful the colonel would comply with the order to dismiss."

A major was *fearful* that a colonel would obey a brigadier general, and made sure he couldn't. Battalion commanders worked together to find ways to prevent obedience up their chain of command, preserving social unity down their chain of command.

The record of Blodget's October court-martial reveals confusion and dismay on every page, as Blodget argued (among other things) against the right of his superior to give orders that violated local custom. Military command, the confused brigadier responded, "descends, and not ascends." There could obviously be no such thing as privates and captains and colonels telling a general officer what their custom would or would not permit them to do. "The powers of a major general or a brigadier-general, or any other officer enumerated in the laws of congress are uniform throughout the United States," Hawes argued, in a direct attack on the entire tradition of the militia of association and its aggressively local historical descendants. "A colonel of a regiment in Rhode-

Island has the same power and is subject to the same control as a colonel of a regiment in Maine or Georgia."

And then Hawes laid out the whole conflict of premises in just two sentences: "This honorable court are now called upon to determine not a mere local question applicable only to the second brigade or to the second regiment of the militia of Rhode Island, but a question equally applicable to all the brigades and regiments of the militia in the United States. This strikes at the root of local usage, for such a usage must be illegal and void if it derogates in any degree from the authority vested in each officer by the law military of the United States."

Hawes was right: His argument did strike at the root of local usage, at the nourishing and vital custom developed in neighborhoods and communities by decades of action and precedent. It wasn't possible to strike at that root without killing the tree that grew from it. But it also wasn't possible to reliably command the militia without striking at that localist root.

The post-Revolutionary American militia was everything and nothing, possessing unlimited jurisdiction and almost no authority at the same time. On the one hand, governors and generals insisted on their power to command, even reaching so far as to try to punish men for personally insulting them. A wife beater could be court-martialed; a bad neighbor could be tried as a military offender; a sentence spoken at a private dinner could be parsed by a military court. On the other hand, a regiment could just walk away if it didn't agree with its orders, or the person giving them. A state-chartered company, ordered to provide men for a military draft as part of the state militia apparatus, could pronounce itself to be free of the militia laws and independent of the militia.

The militia was an association that grew from community, and it was a government organization ruled from the top down. And it couldn't work as both. Gathering at courts-martial and courts of inquiry to examine the acts of disobedience that grew out of this great conflict of premises, men exposed these competing ideas—and they negotiated at length over the limits of each. The universal militia was worn down by their inability to resolve that irresolvable dilemma.

WHEN THE MODEL of universal white male militia service died, a cultural premise died with it. The shots fired at Lexington and Concord had brought thousands of farmers pouring down onto Boston from all over New England, men rushing to carry a shared duty in the common defense. Everyone would fight; every man would reach out to carry the burden and take on a portion of the danger. The colonel who commanded the militiamen at the Old North Bridge in Concord on the morning when American colonists first killed British regulars went into combat in the leather apron he'd been wearing in his workshop when he heard that troops were marching on the town's military stores. Americans began to build a society on the model of mutuality and voluntarism, of neighborliness and community: When your community is attacked, you run to join your neighbors in its defense.

But the decades that followed tore that premise apart in the relentless turmoil of competing ideas. Joseph Hawes knew that military authority "descends, and not ascends"; Leonard Blodget knew he couldn't give an order his men wouldn't agree to obey. Everyone believed in the importance of the militia; everyone knew that every farmer should be prepared to throw aside his plow and rush to the common defense. But they couldn't agree on all the rest of it: When was that farmer a soldier, and when wasn't he? Who could give him orders, and when? When could he be punished by military authority? What rights did he have to shape his own service by the limits of his consent?

Today, the military is a calling and a profession. A nation of 310 million people has 2 million people in a military that has increasingly little connection to the rest of the country. But imagine a different past. If the idea of the universal militia had survived the early republic, it would surely have expanded through the later changes in the American definition of citizenship and equality. The universal white male militia would have become more authentically universal, a duty of all adult citizens; today, if the armed forces of the United States reflected our historical fear of standing armies and our early conception of what the militia should do, we would all have body armor and a rifle in the closet. We might be a big Finland, with its 900,000 military reservists and 8,000 professional soldiers. The absolute failure of the federal militia laws of 1792 shapes the way we live now. We've delegated the common defense to professionals. Attacked, we don't run to join our neighbors in the common defense; we turn to the people who do that sort of thing for a living, and wait for them to go deal with it.

That change carries profound cultural implications. We're a different people because of it, relating to one another in different ways. And it happened gradually in countless small crises of definition as the men of the early republic tried to figure out what it meant for them to serve in the militia: Was authority entirely formal and structural, controlled by rank and manifested in orders from above, or did custom and community expectations control the limits of military power? They answered the question in so many different ways that they never actually answered it.

2

"A Blind Lottery"

Discipline and Justice in the Old Navy

In the early nineteenth century, federal law allowed the captain of a warship or the commodore of a fleet to discipline ordinary sailors by flogging, but set a clear limit on the severity of the physical punishment that could be inflicted without a court-martial. At most, through the quick and informal shipboard hearings called captain's mast, the commander of a navy vessel or squadron could sentence a sailor to just twelve lashes. But Commodore Edward Preble disliked formal trials, finding them an inconveniently complicated way to handle disciplinary problems. And so, when the ordinary seaman Thomas Ayscough, "a notorious lower-deck troublemaker," got drunk at sea and ran wild aboard the flagship *Constitution* in 1804, Preble held captain's mast on four different charges. At each different hearing, he ordered that Ayscough be flogged twelve times, the legal limit. And so the sailor wasn't flogged forty-eight times all at once, which would have been illegal; rather, he was flogged twelve times—four separate times in a row.

Culture and social custom always shape the application of the law, and the early American navy is no exception. But discipline in the antebellum navy was shaped by tradition and unwritten rules in radically different ways from those in the land forces.

The early navy was a deeply strange creature. Officers stayed in the service for decades, holding the small number of senior ranks in an officer corps of a few hundred men. Careers languished, and were expected to; it was entirely possible to be a lieutenant for twenty years, while elderly captains held tight to a rank they didn't actually put to use. "By 1854 there were captains who had not been to sea for thirty years," the historian James Valle writes, and two-thirds of the captains carried on the navy's rolls were officially on leave of absence. Officer status was also frequently a kind of family property, as sons followed fathers into the service—and families of naval officers intermarried. In any case, officers were understood to come from a particular social class, and to form a particular kind of status group. President Thomas Jefferson described the midshipmen of his own moment as a "corps of young gentlemen of the best characters and standing." The United States had, in effect, a kind of oceangoing aristocracy in its naval officer corps, men who held positions of honor through their connections and expected to die in their epaulets.

This small, inbred, and deeply entrenched officer class ruled at sea over a rotating gang of mostly low-status men, as ordinary sailors signed on to serve—sometimes in the navy, sometimes on a merchant ship, going back and forth between the two—for only a few years at a time. A warship took on its crew, went to sea, and spent three years or so on a foreign station, sometimes replacing men in overseas ports as sailors casually deserted. Then the ship and its officers came back and started over with a new crew, recruited in port for another tour.

Landless men were drawn to the docks, men of little social substance or economic status; the historian Marcus Rediker has famously described eighteenth-century merchant sailors as a "maritime proletariat." In a nation that didn't allow black men to serve in its land forces, the navy also routinely took on black crewmen. Neither did the navy turn aside immigrants or foreigners, while serving a nation that harbored considerable nativist sentiment. "Crews turned over at the rate of almost 60 percent per year," Valle writes, "and as late as 1888, less than half the men were native born." A small and stable corps of high-status and highly self-regarding officers held the practically unchecked power to discipline a large and shifting group of poorly regarded men, swept up from the wharves and sent to places far out of sight and direct supervision.

The resulting atmosphere "was more appropriate to a penal institution" than a military organization. Hard and regular punishment was merely the custom of eighteenth- and nineteenth-century navies, the way the gentlemen of the officer class managed the rabble of the enlisted class. In the Rhode Island militia, Col. Leonard Blodget didn't believe he could give an order his men wouldn't agree to obey; nothing remotely like that thought would ever have occurred to an officer of the early American navy, who most certainly didn't command his neighbors. The only *community* that influenced the characteristics of naval discipline and justice was the community of officers. A captain faced no peers on his own ship.

And so Edward Preble had come close enough to complying with naval regulations. The commodore wanted to inflict punishment, and didn't want to be limited in his ability to do that, so he very loosely faked obedience to a set of rules he preferred to ignore. It was a naked enough gesture that he could have been caught, but no one much wanted to catch him. No one stopped Preble, Valle concludes, "because his victims were not sympathetic characters and because Congress and the Navy Department were willing in those early days to give commodores on distant stations a fairly free hand." There was the law, and there was the status of the men it affected; the two realities, one official and one social, often pointed in different directions. But the law was still there, and so was the navy. Preble wasn't the king of his own little nation, however much an isolated leader may have felt like it from time to time; he was a very senior member of a hierarchy, but not the top of it. He balanced the things he learned in a long career, going just as far as he could—tossing aside the restrictions on his own power, but lightly.

Sort of making rules and sort of ignoring them, the early navy "came to rely perhaps a bit too heavily on informal procedures not subject to review." Navy officers did what they believed they had to do, isolated on moving islands and commanding men they generally regarded with distaste. A few officers had to control a few hundred enlisted men, alone and crowded together for long weeks or months—the brig *Somers*, the scene of a conflict described below, was 100 feet long and 25 feet across at its widest point—in the middle of the ocean. "Like pears closely packed," the erstwhile sailor Herman Melville would write, "the crowded crew usually decay through close contact, and every plague spot is contagious." A few defiant men could instantly broadcast their recalcitrance through the entire space of a warship; let one man disobey, and a hundred men instantly see that disobedience is tolerated.

Under those conditions, severity usually made some kind of sense, whatever a set of laws and rules might try to say. And so *close enough* became the prevailing standard of naval justice. Valle, who has written the only detailed general study of early navy courts-martial, concludes that there were "stunning irregularities in verdicts, sentences, and acquittals." Navy justice became so haphazard that it looked like a "blind lottery," outcomes depending on whim and chance more than law. "In this regard," Valle writes, "it was hardly a legal system at all, but more like a caricature of a system."

Early naval justice was haphazard because the early navy was haphazard, a neglected creature with an insular culture. At the end of the Revolution, the same new republic that intended to make do with a vanishingly small standing army decided it didn't need a navy at all, and disbanded the one it had built to fight for its independence—along with the small corps of Continental Marines who had served within it. Ten years passed like that. "In 1793," writes the naval historian Christopher McKee, "the United States had no part of a navy—neither warships, nor commanders, nor dockyard." Congress began to reverse that course in 1794: it authorized the construction of six ships, but waited until 1798 to create a Navy Department that could be in charge of them.

Creating a department to oversee the navy, Congress also created "a corps of marines, which shall consist of one major, four captains, sixteen first lieutenants, twelve second lieutenants, forty-eight sergeants, forty-eight corporals, thirty-two drums and fifes, and seven hundred and twenty privates." Marines became a kind of auxiliary police force on navy ships as well as the navy's infantry, assisting the master-at-arms and standing watch over prisoners. The United States slowly and incrementally began to return to the sea with armed force, and gradually developed a way to govern its oceangoing service.

Rules trickled into place—then kept trickling in, with no clear sense of system or order. In 1798, President John Adams issued the first regulations for the federal navy. The next year, Congress passed a set of Articles for the Government of the Navy of the United States, the analog to the Articles of War that governed the army—and the first since the obsolete code that governed the Continental Navy. The next year, a new set of articles replaced the naval laws, and a new set of regulations followed. By 1815, Valle writes, naval regulations had grown to 194 articles—contained in the "Black Book" that captains took to sea—that were widely understood to be inadequate.

A mishmash of sources and ideas, the regulations "included numerous British codes originally copied by Adams, acts of the long-defunct Continental Congress, and additions inserted by the legislative and executive branches after 1798." Marines were subject to navy laws while at sea with the navy, and to army laws while on shore in a land campaign with the army. It was a random pile of regulations, generated and managed in an atmosphere of inattention.

Reform didn't fix the problem—it made it worse. In 1818, the Navy Department created a new set of regulations, the Blue Book, that was "technically illegal" in the absence of supporting law. So the Blue Book went out to commanders "with a general order annulling large parts of it because they set aside acts of Congress which had never been repealed." Fourteen years later, a board of senior officers issued a new set of regulations, the Red Book, which the navy partially adopted in an atmosphere of contention among officers. The Black Book and the Blue Book remained in use, with portions of the Blue Book excluded from use, and the Red Book providing a supplementary set of rules. The navy, Valle concludes, was left with "a confused and almost unworkable tangle of contradictory documents that were its rules and regulations." In the early 1840s, the Navy Department tried again, creating a new set of regulations patched together from nearly eight hundred articles. Sloppiness and excess marched hand in hand.

And so commanders could order an ordinary sailor flogged twelve times, but do it several times in a row. The absence of clear and well-ordered rules—or, rather, the presence of a metastasizing jumble of poorly designed rules—meant that actual regulation at sea was the product of individual personalities and the caprice of commanders. Captains and commodores—the latter also being captains in rank, but assigned to the command of a fleet in a small navy that had no admirals—did more or less what they felt like doing. So did junior officers, casually ordering petty officers to inflict regular beatings with a "ratline"—the end of an ordinary rope—as an on-the-spot corrective. That punishment, McKee writes, "was one that the law in no way recognized," except for the language in the Articles for the Government of the Navy that vaguely allowed for discipline "according to the laws and customs in such cases at sea."

Individual commanders made individual shipboard regulations. In 1821, the future Commodore Robert Stockton staged a burial for the disciplinary practice of flogging, "throwing a cat-o'-nine-tails overboard and informing his crew that he would never use flogging to discipline them." Inventing his own rules, Stockton could disregard them whenever he felt like it; in 1847, facing widespread insubordination off the coast of California, "the commodore discreetly looked the other way while the ship's officers flogged the men back into good order with exceptional severity." Fixed by whim, rules floated with the tide of expediency. "The whole body of this discipline is emphatically a system of cruel cogs and wheels," Melville wrote, and "unmanning to think of." The novelist spent years at sea as a common sailor, where every ship nurtured "a sinister vein of bitterness." A warship at sea was an island of casual and arbitrary brutality. It wasn't a secret or an error; it was the essence of the thing itself, the way the navy was understood to work.

BUT THE CULTURE of the officer corps also restrained captains who had to think about the larger audience of their peers in the whole navy. A commander who needed to resort to constant physical punishment and disciplinary proceedings to manage his crew revealed his weakness; he announced to other officers that he was holding control with white knuckles. The captain of a ship at sea, wrote Commodore David Porter, "dare not unbend." His carriage and demeanor were a foundation of his authority; men obeyed him in part because of the fear of discipline, but also because he announced with his body and his voice that he was to be obeyed. A captain who only took perpetual recourse to the irons and the lash obviously lacked the *other* foundation of his power over other men. "Discipline is to be effected by a particular deportment much easier than by great severity," Commodore Thomas Truxtun wrote to a captain in 1800. The presence of one implied the absence of the other: An officer who relied too much on great severity necessarily lacked a correct deportment. "The amount of flogging on board an American man-of-war is, in many cases, in exact proportion to the professional and intellectual incapacity of her officers to command," Melville concluded. The navy had, in many instances, "put a scourge into the hand of a fool." A martinet was unmanly, weak, and unable to lead. He was not properly a navy officer.

More fatal still to an officer was poor seamanship, an announcement that a leader lacked ability in the most basic component of his job; a ship that ran aground or flirted with destruction was a ship with a crisis of authority. The commander of a warship had to know how to drive the thing.

As in so many things, Melville showed this dynamic at work in his semifictional *White-Jacket*. Rounding the deadly Cape Horn in a vicious storm, the officer on the deck of the frigate *Neversink* is Mad Jack, its second lieutenant; the first lieutenant, a useless popinjay with a taste for perfumed handkerchiefs, is nowhere to be found. "Every eye was upon him," Melville writes, "as if we had chosen him from among us all, to decide this battle with the elements, by single combat with the spirit of the Cape." The lieutenant turns into the wind, "running the ship into its teeth," a brutal confrontation with the storm that allows him to retain some small control over the ship. The character of the ship's commander is implied by his name: Captain Claret. Stumbling out of his cabin with flushed cheeks, the captain orders the helmsman to turn away from the storm, putting the wind at the ship's back. The order, Melville writes, "was an unwise one in the extreme," a choice that "makes you a slave to the blast" and threatens to sink the ship. But Mad Jack refuses the order, "husky with excitement" screaming defiance at the commander of the ship: "Damn you!" he shouts, "hard *down*, hard *down* I say, and be damned to you!" The crew obeys the second lieutenant—and ignores the order from the captain.

"In time of peril," Melville concludes, "like the needle to the load-stone, obedience, irrespective of rank, generally flies to him who is best fitted to command." Captain Claret slinks back to his cabin, and the matter is forgotten. Damned and nakedly disobeyed on his own quarterdeck, the captain of a ship concedes authority to the more competent seaman. Power is derived from rank—except when it's derived from competence, and rank is driven aside.

Poor officers revealed themselves in their failures of command and their habits of discipline, two intertwined problems that tended to grow worse over time. At the beginning of January 1800, two navy frigates left Newport together, sailing for the East Indies. One, the *Essex*, was commanded by Preble; the other, the *Congress*, was commanded by Capt. James Sever, an "avid and vocal Federalist" in a navy built by Federalist administrations. In an event described by the historian George Daughan, both ships ran into a long and horrible storm, lashed for days by high winds. The *Essex* survived in good condition and sailed on for the Cape of Good Hope; hit by the same storm, the *Congress* was demasted, and "limped into Norfolk, Virginia for repairs." Sever's subordinates filed a complaint alleging that their captain's failures of seamanship had damaged the ship, but a court of inquiry officially cleared him—and left him with a terrible reputation.

Known for the bad leadership of a damaged ship, Sever feuded with subordinates and lashed out against men he was supposed to lead. In 1801, McKee writes, the captain was wrapping up his ship's work in the earlier Quasi-War with France by pur-

suing "a series of acrimonious courts martial with subordinates
. . . on charges sufficiently minor that more skillful commanders of men would certainly have found other means of dealing
with them." The trials were held in the Navy Yard, "practically on
the front steps of the Navy Office," putting Sever's lack of command authority and self-control on vivid display—at precisely the
moment that the navy was looking for ways to reduce its list of
officers. He was quickly dismissed from the service on the recommendation of the navy's efficiency board, his naval career ended.

The captain of a navy warship, David Porter wrote, was the
"petty despot" of a personal fiefdom, asserting an iron authority as a "solitary being in the midst of the ocean." But he was
only a solitary being in a physical and immediate sense. Officers
were watched by other officers, on their own ships and in the
whole navy. They were discovered and judged, their character
permanently revealed by choices made in the heat of a few difficult moments. And too much punishment was one of the clearest
tells. In practice, then, naval officers were barely restrained or
guided by formal systems of law; in the context of their official
lives, they could get away with a great deal. But other gentlemen
were watching what they did with their power—and they always
knew they were being watched.

Before he was thrown out of the navy, Sever had reported a
plot among his crew to commit mutiny. He asked his fleet commander to convene courts-martial to try the plotters, and two
supposed ringleaders were sentenced to death. Truxtun was
the commodore who got Sever's report; it was the irritant that
provoked his written rebuke about particular deportment and
great severity. He reduced the death sentences to flogging and
dismissal, and reported the results to the secretary of the navy
with a withering condemnation—not of the plotters, but of the
man they had plotted against. James Sever, Truxtun wrote, was
"not regularly bred to the sea." The commodore moved the crew

of the *Congress* to a different ship, and left Sever alone in the command of an empty frigate. Too obviously afflicted with personal weakness and an absence of seamanship, one of the navy's petty despots had discovered the limits of his personal despotism—not because of the law, but because of his opinion among other men. The official rules were a mess, but there was another system of generally clear and effective rules that ran beneath them.

FOR ORDINARY SAILORS, the slow workings of an informal system premised on the social reputation of officers was a decent protection—broadly, and over a long period of time. In immediate circumstances, though, it meant close to nothing. In practical terms, a warship at sea could still be an island of casual and arbitrary brutality, but an officer could destroy his career over the course of a decade if he really overdid it.

The arbitrary use of power at sea in the early navy is hard to exaggerate. In the spring of 1846, Valle writes, a series of courts-martial for crewmen of the sloop-of-war *Portsmouth* had been conducted with an appalling disregard for procedural rules. The courts had arrived at verdicts and sentences without allowing the accused to present defense statements. So the ship's first lieutenant, John Missroon, ordered an ordinary seaman known for his literary talents to write fake court-martial transcripts with detailed statements from the defendants. The sailor, Joseph Downey, did produce a set of defense statements—but it was a set of defense statements that satirized the courts-martial, in "impudent and hilarious burlesques of the proceedings." He responded to a request to participate in the corruption of naval justice by mocking the corruption of naval justice.

The full strangeness of the early navy is captured in the response of Missroon and his captain, Commander John Montgomery. Having been foiled and mocked in their efforts to stage manage unfair courts-martial by an act of fraud, they took the very course that would make the least sense if they had been afraid of being caught: they asked the commander of the Pacific Squadron, Commodore John Sloat, to convene a court-martial and try Downey for disobedience. Montgomery's letter to the commodore was carefully vague about the sailor's supposed offenses, and Sloat declined the request; there was, he replied, no evident reason why Downey should be charged with anything. So the captain and his first lieutenant brought their shipboard satirist before a captain's mast, with Missroon himself presenting the charges to Montgomery—who found Downey guilty of mutiny and other offenses, and sentenced him to be lashed. Nothing in the naval law allowed the dire crime of mutiny to be tried by anything but a formal court-martial, but they did it anyway.

Their strange and cruel performance caused the officers no harm. Missroon went on to be a commodore himself, and Montgomery—as the Civil War expanded the rank structure of the navy—retired as a rear admiral. It wasn't necessarily an impediment to an officer's career that he fraudulently sought to falsify court-martial records and subjected only the *occasional* sailor to illegal punishment. Downey's flogging, Valle concludes, is an example of the way navy officers used the charge of mutiny "to cover a multitude of lesser offenses which in their eyes threatened their status and image rather than the actual safety of their ships." At sea, the law was a malleable instrument.

The malleability of navy justice allowed officers to avoid punishment as much as it allowed them to capriciously inflict it. Particularly in cases involving shipboard sexual acts, Valle writes, the navy mostly chose to avert its eyes. The service meted out nearly 6,000 floggings in captain's mast proceedings during 1846. Reporting to Congress on those floggings the following year, navy officials listed the charges with varying levels of precision; in a total of three instances, sailors were plainly punished for sodomy, but many other cases trailed away into careful vagueness: "improper conduct too base to mention," or "filthy and unnatural practices," among others.

The men appointed to courts-martial in sexual offenses often preferred to look away from the acts they were supposed to be examining. The officers appointed to try marine private George Crutch for sodomy in 1805 began to hear a detailed description of the way that he'd been caught in the act—so they closed the testimony, pronounced the marine not guilty, and adjourned. Similarly, a court of inquiry found clear evidence that Lt. Edward Burns frequently called his ship's boys to his cabin to "frig" him—to stroke his penis. One of the boys, John Julian, told the court that Burns "asked me almost every night to do it." Presented with the clear and detailed findings of the court, Commodore Daniel Patterson declared the lieutenant wholly innocent of the charges—and promptly transferred him out of the squadron.

Many complaints of sexual misconduct never made it that far. "More than once," Melville wrote, "complaints were made at the mast in the *Neversink*, from which the deck officer would turn away with loathing, refuse to hear them, and command the complainant out of his sight." Warships were "wooden-walled Gomorrahs"; it was best to "forever abstain from seeking to draw aside this veil." Discipline had to end where the offended gaze ended. You could punish men for depravity, but only if you first chose to look at it. Few did.

THE MOST INFAMOUS INCIDENT in early navy history brings together all of the major themes of antebellum naval justice. At sea, the captain of a ship was forced to make a choice that balanced an imminent physical threat against the likelihood of institutional embarrassment and harm to his career in a deeply politicized officer corps. Making his decision, the captain inflicted punishment of great severity that he had no authority at all to inflict; returning to port, he was cleared by the formal system of navy justice but damned by the social verdict of his peers.

In 1842, the brig *Somers* sailed to the coast of Africa and back across the Atlantic to the West Indies. In a nation that didn't have a naval academy, the trip was meant to give a group of apprentice midshipmen a chance to learn seamanship and the duties of officers. Less than two weeks before the ship's return to its homeport, though, a member of the crew told the captain about a mutiny being organized by men who wanted to turn the vessel into a pirate ship. Most absurdly, the leader of the plot was supposed to be one of the midshipmen, a young man named Philip Spencer—who happened to be the son of a cabinet official, Secretary of War John Spencer. The most politically connected person on the ship, the young man with the clearest social status and the most obvious path to a bright future, was supposed to be plotting to steal a warship and take up piracy. Commander Alexander Mackenzie laughed off the warnings.

But Spencer had another background: He was a persistent failure as a midshipman, and a burgeoning disaster to a respectable family. He had good reasons to run away from the navy. The *Somers* was his third ship, the place he had bounced to after the wreck of his other assignments. In his first tour as an apprentice officer, his long display of entitlement, indiscipline, and habitual drunkenness had ended with an attack on a superior officer. As the legal historian Buckner Melton has noted, Spencer had committed a hanging offense. But he got away with it, as the ship's first lieutenant warned Passed Midshipman William Craney not to report the act of violence—"in light of Spencer's connections."

Then Spencer attacked him again, from behind and without provocation or warning. This time Craney did send a formal report up the chain of command, where it was quietly laid aside. Frequently drunk, never attentive to duty, openly contemptuous of authority, and repeatedly violent in attacks on a superior, Spencer was discreetly transferred to another ship, the frigate *John Adams*. The outcome of that decision isn't a surprise: He got drunk and deserted. Threatened with a court-martial, the son of the secretary of war offered to resign quietly instead— and the offer was accepted with the navy's gratitude. Arriving home, though, Spencer asked for another chance; he took his appeal directly to the secretary of the navy, his father's colleague in the administration of president John Tyler. And so the persistently reckless and self-indulgent Philip Spencer showed up for his third tour of duty as a midshipman, a posting to the *Somers*. He arrived with a series of lessons in mind: The navy was afraid to punish him.

On board the ship, the rumors about Spencer kept making their way to Mackenzie. They arrived in what was becoming the usual context for the midshipman, who was well on his way to failure again. Spencer "took his duties too lightly," sometimes so lightly that it endangered the ship. Once, as he supervised the lookouts on the forecastle, they fell asleep; Mackenzie noticed before he did. "A sleeping lookout is a dangerous thing," Melton writes. "Without him the ship can be blind, both to the elements and the enemy." Mackenzie began to rebuke Spencer loudly and often, and the midshipman retreated into a sullen anger—that he didn't bother to hide from crewmen, who were supposed to regard him as a part of their chain of command. "God damn him," a group of sailors heard him muttering about Mackenzie. "I should like to catch him on that roundhouse some of these dark nights and plunge him overboard; it will be a pleasure to me." He was growing a long chain of witnesses who had heard him fantasizing out loud about his desire to attack the captain of the ship.

The rumors and warnings grew more insistent; a crewman reported that Spencer had told purser's steward James Wales about a fully developed plan to kill the officers and take the ship. The midshipman had a simple question for Wales: "Dare you kill a person?" The commander took the news "cooly." He was trapped: He could ignore the warning and risk losing his ship, or heed it and arrest the son of one of the most powerful men in the country. Whatever action he took, Melton concludes, the captain of the *Somers* "was courting professional suicide." There was no good ending.

But there was ultimately no way to ignore the possibility that a midshipman was walking around on a ship asking crewmen if they were prepared to kill their officers. Mackenzie decided to put the question to Spencer directly, surely confident that the son of a cabinet official couldn't really be plotting a mutiny. He called all of his officers to the quarterdeck, effectively surrounding himself with an armed guard, and finally just said the thing they had all been whispering about: "I learn, Mr. Spencer, that you aspire to the command of the *Somers*." He got a remarkable answer: The midshipman plainly admitted that he'd talked to crewmen about taking the ship, but said that he'd only been kidding. Had he told Wales he had a plan to kill all the officers? "I may have told him so, sir, but it was in joke." No one took it as one. Mackenzie ordered Spencer confined in double irons, chained to the deck by his hands and feet—and the officers prepared for Spencer's supporters to make their move. The sun was setting; the attack would come in the dark.

But who would attack them? As the officers had heard rumors about Spencer and his plot, one story kept coming up: He had a list of names, members of the ship's crew who had committed to a mutiny. A lieutenant and a midshipman tore through Spencer's locker and found two pieces of paper wrapped inside another piece of paper, in a case inside a drawer inside a case. Spencer had tried to conceal its meaning, badly—the three columns were labeled in ancient Greek. But nineteenth-century gentlemen read ancient Greek, and another midshipman only needed a moment to decipher that it divided the ship's crew into categories: "certain," "doubtful to join in," and "unknown." Only four names were listed in the column of certain mutineers, with Spencer's at the top. They had the whole plot, in writing—evidence for the court-martial that would be convened when they got home.

But the *Somers* was 100 feet long, and there were eighteen names in the column of men who had neither refused nor committed. With Spencer chained to the deck, twenty-one men were of at least uncertain loyalty, and in a space that could be covered in seconds by men willing to murder their officers. And then the sun was gone, and it was dark.

That night, officers questioned the crew, focusing on men whose names were in the wrong two columns on Spencer's list. The responses weren't reassuring. Men who had been seen whispering with the midshipman denied having spoken to him at all. In the dark, Melton writes, "most of the officers felt that something was wrong," a sense that came mostly from an intuition shaped by finding the list. As Melton notes, a conspiracy to commit mutiny was punishable by death whether or not it was brought to fruition; a sailor who admitted to discussion on the topic would have been turning himself in to be hanged. But men behaved strangely, regardless of whether anyone would admit to plotting against the captain. Several members of the crew were persistently sullen and slow to follow orders. And then the officers began to see things in what looked like ordinary behavior. A man rubbed his hands on his face—was it meant as a signal? The morning came without an attack, but the bad feelings lingered.

Then a mast collapsed. It wasn't an accident, and everyone knew as it happened why it was happening: A sailor, Elisha Small, had fastened a brace far too tightly, ignoring shouted orders to stop. Moments later, "the topgallant mast, the royal yards and booms, and the attached rigging and sails pulled loose from the topmast completely." It was the day after Spencer's arrest, and the officers knew what it meant: The plotters were sabotaging the ship, slowing it down while they were still out at sea. They made two more arrests; one, of course, was Small.

That night, a midshipman saw still more members of the crew "skulking around, some of them talking in low tones." He drew a pistol and broke up the group—sending them aft, toward Mackenzie and Lt. Guert Gansevoort, who saw the stampede as an attack. "God, I believe they are coming!" the lieutenant shouted. The two officers prepared to fight for their lives. The midshipman appeared as they raised their pistols to fire, shouting the information they had been missing: "I am sending the men aft!" They lowered their pistols.

"It was a very near thing," Melton writes, and a sign of a miserably decaying situation. Some men were sent aft, so they went aft, so their officers almost shot them as mutineers. The real and the imagined were smashing together, in the confined and isolated space of a ship at sea. The officers "were a haunted, hunted group," abandoning sleep and settling into a constant watch. A steward stole some brandy, and Mackenzie guessed it was for Spencer: another plotter, revealed. The steward was flogged, in the company of an apprentice sailor who had stolen a hat, the officers putting on a display of discipline for a crew that was shaking loose of their control. That night, a boom came loose—and swung wildly across the part of the deck where the officers gathered. A gunner's mate found weapons hidden in the ship's launch; he removed them, then found them there again later that same night, and removed them again. Then he saw a sailor searching through the launch, not long after he had taken the weapons the second time. Other sailors failed to report for duty, petulant and shirking. Mackenzie ordered more arrests.

The *Somers* was still a week away from port—any port—and the Articles of War required that mutineers be tried by a court-martial before they could be punished. But a ship's captain couldn't convene a court-martial, an authority vested only in the president, the secretary of the navy, and commanders of fleets and squadrons. According to the law, Melton writes, "Mackenzie had already done all he was able to do with regard to Midshipman Spencer, and nearly as much with regard to the others." He still faced a possible mutiny, was exhausted and far from port, and led a small group of officers who had barely slept for four full days. And the law offered nothing that could help him save his ship.

So he went beyond the law. The captain of the *Somers* first did an extraordinary thing under any dire military circumstances, and a still more extraordinary thing given the culture of naval command in the nineteenth century: He handed Lieutenant Gansevoort a note asking all of his subordinate officers for their "united counsel as to the best course to be now pursued." The captain of a warship was supposed to be the absolute and final authority on his own vessel, but this absolute authority was asking for advice.

Asked to do an extraordinary thing, the ship's other officers did a still more extraordinary thing. At first, they went to their wardroom to discuss the captain's note. But then, still secluded in the wardroom, they began to send out for sailors they wished to question—for witnesses, in other words, to be interrogated. Invited to offer an opinion, the officers of the *Somers* locked themselves in a room, convened as a court, and began taking testimony, without orders and in a way not authorized by any law or regulation. A court-martial appeared spontaneously, ordering itself into being.

At least they kept notes. And the consistent theme of those notes was that the witnesses testifying to the ad-hoc court thought the ship would be safer if the ringleaders were dead. Missing from those notes, though, is firm evidence that the ringleaders had anything to actually lead. "A mutiny seemed to be hovering around, just out of reach," Melton concludes. The exhausted members of the made-up court had largely assumed the fact of the plot, and moved to a debate over their verdict. When they finally delivered that verdict, it came in two parts. First, they were doomed. The ship wouldn't make port. Without a doubt, it would be taken over first, unless something happened to crush the plot. And that led to the second part. The self-convening court pronounced the penalty of death on three men: Spencer, Small, and Samuel Cromwell. But only the captain of the ship could confirm that choice and give the necessary order.

Standing on the quarterdeck, looking out at the sea in every direction, Mackenzie had to make his decision alone. He had nowhere left to turn for help: He was far from any coast, and the threat to his ship seemed perfectly clear. The navy had a well-established tradition of ignoring incidents that could embarrass the service or result in political conflict; Spencer himself had repeatedly benefited from just that institutional habit. And no court-martial had actually been conducted, no lawful process that could give real authority to something as serious as a death sentence. Mackenzie could have pushed away the decision. He could have kept the plotters in irons, taken refuge in the legal limits on his power, and pushed on for a port. But he didn't. The captain of the *Somers* responded like a man hearing the very thing he expected to hear. He didn't hesitate: The plotters would be hanged—right away.

But even this decision, premised as it was on the need to end the danger to the ship, threatened to make the danger worse. If much of the crew was ready to kill their officers, throwing ropes over the yardarm could only be a signal that it was now or never. The attempt to execute the ringleaders might be exactly the thing that would trigger the mutiny. Mackenzie immediately summoned all of the ship's petty officers onto the deck, not knowing how many were loyal, to prepare for the executions. The smaller group of commissioned officers and midshipmen armed themselves, and spread out across the deck. The captain told them exactly what he expected from them. "If a rescue attempt took place, he commanded, the officers were to shoot the prisoners and rescuers both."

And then they brought the condemned men forward. Standing on deck waiting to be hanged, Spencer admitted to the plot. "I do not know what would have become of me had I succeeded," he said. Then the three men were lifted off the deck, strangling slowly before the audience of the entire crew. It was December 1, 1842.

The captain left the bodies of the three men hanging from the yardarm for an hour. And the crew went quietly back to their stations.

The *Somers* reached New York two weeks later, and Mackenzie reported his extrajudicial executions. His own court-martial began in January, and instantly became a national sensation, a life-and-death scandal that touched the family of a senior government official. The nation was still more than a century away from having a secretary of defense, a single officer of government who oversaw the entire military, so Secretary of War John Spencer had no authority over the branch of government where his son had met his death. But Spencer insisted on being present for cabinet discussions of Mackenzie's fate, a decision that led to a fistfight with Secretary of the Navy Abel Upshur. John Tyler stepped in to separate them, the president of the United States breaking up a brawl between senior government officials in the White House.

As Mackenzie heard the verdict in his trial, naval courts-martial had a well-established custom for the acquittal of officers. Courts declaring an officer to be not guilty of military charges would add a statement that wasn't required by law, declaring the accused to have been "honorably acquitted." It was the extra verdict, the decision derived from the other system of judgment: This officer isn't guilty under law, and retains his honor as a gentleman. The captain of the *Somers* faced four charges, standing accused of murder, oppression, cruelty, and conduct unbecoming an officer. The members of the court heard testimony and argument that suggested two points, both much debated afterward: that Mackenzie had faced real danger, and that he had lost control of himself and his ship, going further than the law or the traditions of command could justify. On each charge and specification pursued to the end of the trial, the court read the same verdict: "Not proved." And then, tersely, they declared that they had acquitted Mackenzie on all of the charges that he faced.

No one failed to notice the statement they left out.

COMMANDER MACKENZIE made his decision in a moment when the navy's disciplinary traditions were under relentless political pressure. After decades of intermittently cruel and capricious naval discipline, ordinary sailors had received an important gift: They had become slaves. Stripped and flogged with the cat-o'-nine-tails, or locked in irons, navy crewmen became a symbol of the nation's larger antebellum debate; the sailor under the lash became a symbol for the slave under the lash, one swept up into the campaign against the other. Newspapers began campaigning against naval brutality in the 1830s, precisely as the American abolitionist movement was born. Narratives, and activists, overlapped: Abolitionists demanded that the navy stop brutalizing its sailors.

Just as *Uncle Tom's Cabin* had shaped the debate over slavery, books shaped the debate over flogging in the navy. The Cambridge lawyer Richard Henry Dana, a Boston Brahmin who had signed on for a long tour as an ordinary seaman aboard a merchant ship between his undergraduate years at Harvard and his years at Harvard Law School, made the connection between slavery and sea service explicit in his 1840 memoir, *Two Years Before the Mast*. "You've got a driver over you!" Dana's captain shouts at his crew as he flogs a sailor. "Yes, a slavedriver—a negro driver! I'll see who'll tell me he isn't a negro slave." In a growing rhetorical assault, ships became plantations, places where a despot and his henchmen terrorized the powerless men they ruled with absolute power. Slaves and sailors weren't the only victims in the narrative. While the escaped slave Frederick Douglass described the degradation of slave owners by the sadistic milieu of slavery, a series of sea memoirs described officers turned into monsters by their unchecked power. To be flogged was to be demeaned and brutalized; to flog was to be coarsened as a man and destroyed as a moral being.

Ten years after Dana's important book, Melville's *White-Jacket* depicted the sadism of flogging in the navy. Melville typified the ordinary sailor who moved back and forth between commercial and military service at sea, having sailed on whalers, trading ships, and the navy frigate *United States*. For a writer who had watched the flogging of his fellow sailors many times, taking in their agony and their helplessness, the practice was "unrepublican": It wasn't a thing that happened to the sturdy freemen of a properly structured society. "Or will you say," Melville wrote, "that an American-born citizen, whose grandsire may have ennobled him by pouring out his blood at Bunker Hill—will you say that, by entering the service of his country as a common seaman, and standing ready to fight her foes, he thereby loses his manhood at the very time he most asserts it? Will you say that, by so doing, he degrades himself to the liability of the scourge, but if he tarries ashore in time of danger, he is safe from that indignity?"

Only a disordered republic could acquiesce to the kind of undisciplined authority that allowed men to whip other men bloody—to unman fellow citizens who had shown the courage to fight for their country. And so flogging wasn't a failure of the navy; it was a national disease, and "would to God that every man who upholds this thing were scourged at the gangway till he recanted." For Melville, the suffering of the individual men who were flogged was an important point, but not the only problem. The deeper point was what flogging said about America.

White-Jacket was politics. Activists delivered copies of the novel to every member of Congress, and the year of its publication became the year that a ban on navy flogging was signed into law. The historian Myra Glenn has written at length about the many overlapping campaigns against physical punishment in the antebellum United States. People who argued against the violence of slavery and the flogging of sailors also fought to end the physical chastisement of wives by husbands and the abuse of students by teachers. Debate over physical punishment was debate over the nature of humanity itself: Do human beings respond to moral persuasion and good examples, or do they have to be coerced into obedience? Can a person be good without being threatened and punished? Flogging, in this argument, "allegedly blocked a seaman's moral elevation." A man directed by brutal outside force was an animal, an ox driven ahead of the plow, "bereft of all self-respect and moral dignity." Freemen self-governed on the strength of rational choice; beasts were beaten.

The senator who introduced the ban on naval flogging— repeatedly, as amendments to a navy appropriations bill—was "a staunch and controversial antislavery advocate" from New England. The men who joined Sen. John Parker Hale in opposition to the physical punishment of sailors were a who's who of Free Soilers, Salmon Chase among them. Hale and his allies were linked, Glenn writes, by an ideology "which viewed an individual's freedom from external constraints either in economics or politics as the *sine qua non* of economic growth, upward mobility, and republican liberty." Coercion was atavism; brutality was a journey into the degraded past, social regression made physically manifest. An officer ordering the flogging of a sailor was attacking progress itself.

Running alongside the debate over the expansion of slavery in a nation growing to its west, the congressional deliberation over navy discipline became sectional. Anti-flogging petitions poured in from northern states, and especially from New England. "During the first six months of 1850," Glenn writes, "the Senate received approximately 117 petitions from the citizens of Massachusetts alone demanding the abolition of the naval lash." Southern congressmen denounced anti-flogging sentiment as yet another radical "ism" from a section drenched in the absurd fantasy of abolitionism; the North Carolina representative Abraham Watkins Venable complained about the "hyperphilanthropy" of men who misunderstood human nature.

In the end, the vote to end flogging split along the same lines as the debate: "Twenty-four of the twenty-six senators who voted to abolish corporal punishment in the navy came from northern states," with the remaining two votes in the Senate coming from border-state senators.

But a nation that turned against flogging in law and policy still harbored considerable sentiment in favor of degrading physical discipline, and not just in the Southern states that had defended corporal punishment. If iron chains and the cat-o'-nine-tails were inappropriate for use against the rational and dignified freemen of a republic, another question had to be answered: What about men who weren't believed to be rational, dignified, inherently free, or reliably committed to republican principle? Richard Henry Dana warned against the sadism of officers at sea, but he also declared that they needed strong authority to deal with a serious problem: Their crews were heavily populated by "ignorant foreigners," men who mostly understood the language of force. Six years after he published that pair of conflicting warnings, Americans went to war with an army built quickly from an influx of recent immigrants. The great disciplinary failures of the war with Mexico were neither sudden nor accidental—and they anticipated another problem the American military would soon have as it struggled to incorporate another new group of soldiers.

3

"A Lawful Going Home"

Conflict and Coercion in the Jacksonian Military

BECAUSE AMERICAN MILITIAMEN BELIEVED THE TERMS OF THEIR service were controlled by custom and their own conception of the duty they owed, 200 Tennessee soldiers fighting Creek Indians in Andrew Jackson's federal army during the War of 1812 decided they had done their time. They'd served three months—by earlier law and persistent custom, the longest period the militia could be held to active service. So they petitioned Jackson for release, but he said no. Ordered to stay for six full months, the men drew rations for the road and started walking. The militia, they knew, couldn't be made to serve beyond the limits of its consent. So they just went home.

Or at least they tried to, because some were chased down and marched back to camp. Others made it all the way home before hearing that their departure was contested, and they returned voluntarily to argue for their right to leave. Courts-martial followed for all, but only the six men identified as ringleaders found themselves in front of the firing squad—over a choice they believed they had every right to make.

We've drained the meaning from this piece of our past. Most recent histories of the War of 1812, and of the Creek War that took place within that conflict, dispose of the punishment of

Jackson's deserters in a paragraph or less; meanwhile, the long political echo of the event is dismissed as mere partisan sniping, a cheap bit of campaign mudslinging.

But nineteenth-century writers were more likely to treat the event as the thing it really was: a political calamity that was debated for decades. In a narrative of Jackson's life written in the 1850s, the English-born biographer James Parton called the executions "an unexampled slaughter of American citizens." Today's footnote was yesterday's long and urgent debate. The mutiny of Jackson's Tennessee militiamen happened over the course of two days in September, 1814, led to executions in February of 1815, was still being examined by voters and congressional committees at the end of the 1820s, and continued to be the subject of debate as the Civil War began.

The men who left Jackson's army didn't skulk. They announced their departure, usually after having discussed it for days with their commanders, two of whom also faced later trials for countenancing mutiny. John Harris, a private and a Baptist minister who had enlisted to protect his sixteen-year-old son at war, readied for his departure from the army by preparing a roster of his fellow deserters, so they could be sure to draw sufficient rations for the trip home. He was a conspirator in a capital crime who kept a list of the plotters. When the time came to leave, he turned in his musket to his company commander and waited for a receipt.

Deserters at a moment when everyone knew the Articles of War said that desertion could result in death by firing squad, these men marched away together in daylight. They didn't think they were deserting; they thought they were leaving in good faith at the end of their service, even if the general commanding their army didn't agree. Antebellum soldiers felt confident that they could just disagree with their commanders, and act on it.

The subsequent courts-martial started on December 5, and lasted for twelve days. In a federal army that had troops from other states, Jackson appointed only men from Tennessee to try Tennessee militiamen on capital charges. Like would judge like; men would be tried and sentenced by their own. For mere followers, trial was quick and simple. One hundred and ninety-seven men were "tried in batches." They were sentenced to the thing they had tried to evade, ordered back to duty for the remainder of their six-month terms of service. At the end of those terms, most of the deserters had half their heads shaved, and they were drummed out of camp in shame—normal punishments in the nineteenth-century army.

In context, none of that was especially dire punishment. The point of drumming a man out of camp is the message that he's unmanly and not fit to stand in the company of soldiers—but it's unlikely that men took this message to heart when they were drummed out by the dozens, in the company of their friends and neighbors. Meanwhile, ten of the youngest deserters were convicted, sentenced to that same shaming ritual, and then pardoned by Jackson for their youth. Shamefully egged on by men of greater maturity and status, how could they have known better?

For officers, though, and for soldiers identified as ringleaders, courts-martial slowed down and tried one man at a time. Over and over again, witnesses testified to the entirely open debate that had taken place in camp. Men had simply walked around asking one another if it was appropriate to leave after three months, and they didn't hesitate to raise the question with their officers—casually, conversationally, as though striking up a discussion on a street corner to pass the time. Capt. John Strother had discussed the possibility of departure with many of his privates and sergeants, witnesses said, and he initially had no idea what to tell them. So he borrowed a copy of the Articles of War, looked over the orders they had all received, and gradually came to a decision that they couldn't leave.

Hearing that many of his men had rejected orders to stay in

camp, a captain wasn't sure what to say about it, so he went and *researched* their argument that they had a right to walk away. A proposal to desert was something to be looked into and discussed with soldiers.

When Strother finally decided that his men couldn't properly leave his company, he didn't tell them as a commander; he told them as a gentleman, disapproving of their conduct on purely personal terms. "Have you no breeding?" he asked a group of potential mutineers. What Strother didn't ever do was act like a military officer, organizing armed force to put down a rebellion in the ranks. He had eventually gotten around to telling his colonel about a spirit of insubordination growing among his troops, but with no apparent urgency. As Parton would later summarize it, Strother had suggested to his men that they would be wrong to walk away from the army, but "he had done this in the familiar, unauthoritative manner which generally characterized the intercourse between officers and men in a western army at that day." That's exactly right: Off the battlefield, the officers of the antebellum militia, and especially the company officers, were more likely to give their men advice than orders: *This desertion thing sounds like a really bad idea, guys.*

But the custom of consensual service was contested, and social habit didn't save Strother from the judgment of his fellow officers. The court found him guilty of conspiring in a mutiny, and sentenced him to dismissal. Another officer, Lt. James McCauley, "opposed the departure of the troops languidly." He had his sword broken over his back before he was drummed out of camp. The symbol of his status as an officer was destroyed against the anvil of his body, a vivid physical display of personal shame. Formally or not, officers were expected to be manful and vigorous. Their soldiers weren't supposed to just walk away from them, a powerful symbol of their inability to command other men.

Finally, six ringleaders were tried, convicted, and sentenced to death, their sentences personally approved by Jackson. Again, they had attempted to explain to their courts-martial that they hadn't done anything especially wrong. Pvt. James Webb "stated, in his defense, that he had served faithfully three months, and conceived, from the best information he could get, that his term of service had expired; that he was told, by both non-commissioned officers and privates, that it was nothing but right to go home." They seem to have been genuinely surprised that the argument didn't work, and for good reason. Soldiers were having different conversations entirely, a discussion about the tradition of custom and consent in the militia smashing head-on into the harsh disciplinary logic the federal army applied to common soldiers. Militiamen signaled that they were yeoman farmers under arms, freemen assembled consensually in the common defense; courts-martial answered that they were privates in the army.

Marched in front of firing squads, though, most of the ringleaders put on the performance that men expected of men. Soldiers lined up six coffins in a field outside Mobile, Alabama, where the army was camped. A crowd of civilians gathered around the 1,500 soldiers who stood in formation to watch their fellow militiamen be shot. A colonel encouraged the condemned to die manfully, and five rose to that hard task. One, Henry Lewis, loudly announced to the crowd that he had served with honor, and fought with courage; loudly conceding his point, the colonel in charge took care to be heard by their shared audience. Then the men were forced to kneel on their own coffins, and six firing squads did their job. Or they almost did: Five men fell dead, but Lewis, the most respected of the condemned soldiers, was left without a wound that could quickly kill him. He fell off his coffin, then crawled back onto it. The commander of the firing squads approached him, and Lewis demanded that the colonel take note of his courage: "I am not killed, but I am sadly cut and mangled. Did I not behave well?"

Colonel Russell, whose first name doesn't appear in the records of the execution, replied "with faltering voice," offering the clearest social verdict he could give: "Yes, Lewis; like a man." For a nineteenth-century military audience, this was the highest theatre, a spectacular demonstration of manhood: Shot four times, a soldier climbed back up to the place he'd been officially posted, and resumed a spirited defense of his personal character.

He won the argument. Facing death with manly firmness, a soldier had atoned for his crimes. The colonel called out urgently for surgeons, and ordered them to save the life of a brave soldier. But their best efforts would fail. Lewis died in agony four days later, condemned as a deserter and honored as a man of undeniable courage, killed and saved and lost again. Lewis overturned the sentence of his court-martial with the strength of his character, and the commander of the firing squad tried to prevent the outcome he had just tried to cause. When Henry Lewis died, his death was mourned by the men who shot him.

John Harris, the sixth of the convicted ringleaders, would do less well in the nineteenth-century memory. More than a decade later, a congressional committee would reference his name with an aside: "John Harris, to whose name such remarkable notoriety has been attached . . ." Harris died crying—in Parton's description, as in so many others, "a weak, heavy-laden man . . . unable to control his emotions." Though his son stood with the rest of their regiment to watch his father's execution, Harris was unmourned, and his killing undertaken without protest. He and Lewis had done the same thing to merit death under the Articles of War, but had done wholly different things in the eyes of other men at the most important moment. Whatever meaning the legal process ascribed to their appearance in front of the firing squad, it meant something else altogether to the men who stood and watched them. Courage redeemed a brave man, whatever verdict had been given in court, and weakness socially damned a man who was already condemned by law. It was still possible to be a soldier after the guilty verdict and the condemnation to death. A man could die correctly—and should.

Jackson would not be allowed to forget that he had approved the execution of militiamen for the mere act of going home when they felt like they were done. As he ran for president in 1828, his Whig opposition lashed at him with a series of damning images. The coffin handbills, as they're now called, illustrated Jackson's crimes with the images of six caskets, arranged in a row on the page as they had been arranged in a row at the execution site. "Some Account of the Bloody Deeds of Gen. Jackson," a broadside promised in a headline above the six coffins. But the pamphleteers were wrong about the shared assumptions that prevailed among their fellow Americans. The tradition of the militia of association was not the foundation of a universal assumption; it had always been contested. Americans were split over the meaning of the executions, and the coffin handbills didn't draw enough blood to matter. Jackson was elected to the presidency.

Thirty years later, one of Jackson's many biographers expressed his own irate verdict with an argument that had been mostly founded on military orders and federal law. But the biographer James Parton also insisted on considering the lives of militiamen and the tradition that should have governed their service. "For three months a farmer may be absent from his farm without losing the entire product of a year, not so if he is six months away," Parton wrote. "Law, custom, convenience, necessity, all combined to root it in the western mind that three months was the term for the service of militia in the field." Militiamen got a vote in their duties; as Leonard Blodget had insisted, commanders couldn't give orders their men wouldn't agree to obey. The executions, Parton wrote, were a "hideous mistake."

In the end, Jackson's biographer concluded, "the conclusion

seems irresistible, that the men were correct in their 'simple notion,' and that their departure from camp was not desertion, but a lawful going home after they had done their part as citizen soldiers." That view is an important example of a significant American tradition, but it was also far from being universal. A congressional committee examining the same events concluded that the execution of the six militiamen had been an example of "the most perfect justice."

The execution of ordinary men serving in the militia could be *the most perfect justice* and a *hideous mistake*, necessary and monstrous in the reading of the very same events. This kind of dueling certitude is the signature of Jacksonian military politics: Complicated and ultimately irreconcilable views, stated with unyielding passion. Soldiers absolutely had a duty to perform the full service required of them by their commanders, and absolutely had the right to withdraw their consent regarding continued service. Under and through all of this debate about law and custom, a single value rang through the noise of disagreement: Whatever actions were right and wrong, whatever the place of law and the place of custom, manly strength always merited respect. A man of courage on the wrong side of the argument was, finally, a man, dying before the firing squad with the redemption of honor. He had the esteem of the men who shot him.

THE AGE OF Andrew Jackson was an era of military democratization, as the country gave up on mandatory militia service and transitioned to volunteer forces made up of men who generally chose to serve—and gradually also to a profusion of private military organizations that were officially illegal, but tolerated in practice. The boundary between private, extralegal forces and the government-run military could be highly notional, as when Jackson defeated British infantry in the Battle of New Orleans by freeing captured pirates from the local jails and assigning them to artillery batteries. Men at war had chosen to fight—sometimes officially, sometimes for a private army, and sometimes for some hybrid of both. It was an age of *We're going to have a war, if anyone wants to jump in.*

But the Jacksonian era was an age of paradox, because it was also a period of growing military coercion. It was more free and less free, more indulgent of ordinary men and more punitive for ordinary men. It was, in short, like Andrew Jackson, a complicated and mercurial mix of competing impulses.

For a few decades, Jackson was America; perpetually in motion, plotting and dreaming, endlessly determined to advance and conquer. His countrymen were enthralled. "At one time in the history of the United States," his biographer Robert Remini wrote, "General Andrew Jackson of Tennessee was honored above all living men." The choice of personal title is telling: He was *General Jackson* even after his presidency, forever a warrior and the embodiment of martial spirit. Jackson fought personal enemies in duels and national enemies on the battlefield, sometimes doing one while still bearing wounds from the other. He was force itself, bristling with complicated ambitions. The political scientist Michael Paul Rogin describes Jackson's "ubiquitous rage," a permanently agitated state of mind that always needed to fight something and defeat it. The spirit of the age and the character of its favored leader were deeply aligned. It was an age of brawls.

The fighting culture of the Jacksonian era developed a robust theatre of manhood, with a set of expected performances that defined the relationships between soldiers and men. And so the performance of challenge and defiance appeared constantly in the courtrooms of the antebellum military, in extremes of posturing that could descend into low comedy.

Near the end of 1847, the explorer and army officer John C.

Fremont was brought before a court-martial at Fort Monroe, Virginia, accused of disobedience and mutiny in California shortly after the war with Mexico. His lawyer was the senator and parallel force of nature Thomas Hart Benton, who had once shot Andrew Jackson in a duel—one of many for both men—before becoming his proud ally in the Senate. With the trial dragging on into 1848, Fremont's superior officer in California, Brig. Gen. Stephen Kearny, appeared at Fort Monroe as a witness—and promptly clashed with Fremont's lawyer over the topic of facial expressions. Benton, the brigadier told the court, sat in front of him while he testified, "making mouths and grimaces at me, which I considered were intended to offend, to insult, and to overawe me."

And then Benton replied, not refuting the claim at all. Kearny had looked at his client with insulting facial expressions, the senator explained, so he had decided to act. "When General Kearny fixed his eyes on Colonel Fremont, I determined if he should attempt again to look down a prisoner, I would look at him. I did this day; and the look of today was the consequence of the looks in this court before. I did today look at General Kearny when he looked at Colonel Fremont, and I looked at him till his eyes fell— till they fell upon the floor." Senator Benton unmanned General Kearny with a staring contest, a little action on the side during courtroom testimony.

Newspapers across the country printed news of the exchange— reporting Benton's statement as, "I looked him down"—along with "a card to the public" provided by Kearny: a written denial that he had been "pierced" by Benton's eyes. *The Farmer's Cabinet*, a newspaper in Amherst, New Hampshire, offered its own verdict on the exchange, comparing the senator and the general to infants. "Surely our great men are fast writing themselves asses," the newspaper concluded. The endless conflict and posturing of the era made asses out of more than a few great men, and on more than a few occasions. The Jackson biographer Robert Remini decided that there was "something petty" about all of his duels. "None of Jackson's quarrels did him credit; all diminished him," Remini wrote.

But Jackson—and Jacksonian America—also sheltered a corresponding habit of dignity, and a quiet admiration for men who rose to a deadly challenge. For a warrior who wasn't known to relent, Jackson could be strangely merciful to enemies who had earned his respect. In March of 1814, the general was hunting for the mixed-ancestry Creek leader William Weatherford, the leader of a devastating attack on an Alabama fortress that had killed hundreds of militiamen and civilians. He demanded that other Creek leaders bring Weatherford to him "tied as a prisoner" so he could be punished for murder. A few years later, Jackson's troops would catch the Creek leaders Josiah Francis and Homathlemico, and Jackson would summarily order the immediate execution of both men.

Weatherford wasn't captured: He calmly walked into Jackson's headquarters, alone, and surrendered in person, almost certainly expecting to die. Jackson had no idea what to do with the moment. "I had directed that you should be brought to me confined," he said. "Had you appeared in this way, I should have known how to have treated you." Weatherford is supposed to have replied with the quiet acknowledgment that he was entirely in Jackson's power. "Do with me as you please," he said. Jackson just sent the Creek leader home, a warrior honoring a warrior—and expecting that he would help to secure the surrender of other Creeks who remained at war. A simple personal exchange ended the possibility of official retribution, as a man of courage recognized another man of courage.

Above all, Jackson, and Jacksonian America, valued a set of socially derived principles that were often elevated above the terms of any mere law. In a contest involving enemies and the national interest, the important qualities were manhood, firmness, and determination; formal compliance with official rules wasn't really the point. In 1818, President James Monroe sent Jackson to the border of Spanish Florida at the head of an army that was supposed to control Creek and Seminole raids into the United States. Jackson got to the border and kept on going, taking Pensacola and deposing the Spanish governor. He was sure he had made the right choice, whatever his actual orders may have been. The spirit of that decision—taking what was understood to be the firm and manly course rather than the strictly lawful one—animated the military discipline of the era.

Democratic and aggressive, valuing action and conquest above order, Jacksonian military culture would give birth to the private filibuster armies that spent the years between the war with Mexico and the Civil War trying to conquer more foreign terrain for the United States. In a wave of mostly hapless efforts, private organizers recruited men to invade large portions of the Caribbean, Central America, and Mexico. Privately invading other countries could be hard on a man's life expectancy. Most famously, William Walker repeatedly led privately recruited filibuster armies into Mexico and Nicaragua, but died in front of a Honduran firing squad in 1860; before that, the Venezuelan-born Narciso López died leading a private American army into Cuba in 1851, grimly executed by iron garrote.

While filibusters had to worry about foreign justice in the countries they invaded, they had less to fear from American authorities—particularly of the military variety. Filibustering was illegal, a violation of federal neutrality laws, and military officials were regularly ordered to take action against private armies. They regularly managed not to. In 1850, for example, a group of men washed up on the coast of Florida after a failed invasion of Cuba. They were "pleasantly surprised by the hospitality of an army captain" who showed up soon after with some of his troops. "The officer drank with them, sympathized with their cause, informed them that he expected orders for their arrest, and intimated that they should depart so that he would not have to commit such a 'repugnant' act," writes the historian Robert May. So they left for Tampa—where a more senior army officer immediately recognized them as illegal filibusters, and offered them rations.

These were not men who were principally interested in legal procedure.

MILITARY JUSTICE doesn't always extend only to military personnel. As General Jackson practiced the task of military command, the conflict between military necessity and the boundaries of the law also appeared in the military regulation of civilians in wartime. Even as the six Tennessee militiamen under his command were awaiting execution in Mobile, Jackson was 140 miles away in New Orleans, readying to meet a British invasion. On December 15, 1814, worried that the city was full of British spies and sympathizers, the general issued a public warning that he was preparing to "separate our enemies from our friends." The former, he added, would be "dealt with accordingly." Preparing to declare martial law, he turned to a pair of local lawyers who were serving on his staff, and the two men split over their legal opinion: One said such a thing would be "unknown to the Constitution or laws of the U.S.," while the other declared that a military officer acting as "guardian of the Public safety" had the discretion to act as he needed. The law was a pair of competing guesses.

The next day, Jackson issued his declaration. Curfew would be 9:00 p.m., and violators would be arrested by soldiers. No one could come or go across city boundaries without reporting their movements to military authorities. As historian Matthew Warshauer writes, "New Orleans was officially an armed camp and

General Jackson the only authority." Even after Jackson's forces crushed a British attack and saved the city from invasion on January 8, citizens remained subject to military justice.

Jackson's military justice would work on principles of necessity, not on the expectations of a legal system. "From the beginning of February to early March," Warshauer writes, "the military incarcerated well over thirty men without stating crimes or violations." Jackson's army listed the captives on its morning guard reports, describing them simply as "Citizens Without Charges." Citizens, not charged with anything, indefinitely imprisoned by the military. Louisianans celebrated Jackson and condemned him, saved from a British invasion and then subjected to military occupation by their own government. Governor William Claiborne wrote to the general to demand the end of martial law. Jackson threatened to arrest him, and the legislature too.

As Jackson had tried to defend the city, his officers had prodded its men to join his ranks. When the many French citizens still living there refused to do the duty of Americans, Jackson released them from the imposition of military service—and then "promptly banished them from New Orleans with orders not to return until the restoration of peace." If they wouldn't fight, they couldn't stay. Every man in New Orleans was to regard himself as a kind of soldier, regardless of whether he was currently in uniform. Jackson had thoroughly militarized his "armed camp," managing the whole city as a garrison. He had no authority to do so, and he did so.

New Orleans got tired of its role. On March 3, nearly two months after Jackson's devastating defeat of a British invasion force, a newspaper in the city published an open letter signed by "A Citizen of Louisiana of French origin." The unnamed writer suggested the very thing Jackson wasn't ready to concede, arguing that "the moment of moderation has arrived." With the enemy turned back, "it is high time the laws should resume their empire . . . [C]itizens accused of any crime should be rendered to their natural judges, and cease to be brought before special or military tribunals."

Jackson did the opposite. Urged to restore civil law and the conditions of peace, the general tracked down the unnamed author and ordered soldiers to arrest him. He also anticipated the local response, ordering his troops to arrest anyone who attempted to serve a writ of habeas corpus to free the author from military custody. Jackson was not deterred by the real identity of "A Citizen of Louisiana of French origin," who happened to be a state senator named Louis Louaillier. Then a local lawyer obtained the very writ that Jackson had anticipated, and the general ordered soldiers to arrest the person who had issued it: Dominick Augustan Hall, the federal district judge in the city. Jackson accused the judge of "exciting mutiny within my camp" by challenging his authority to detain citizens.

Finding himself on a roll, the general also ordered soldiers to arrest anyone who incited sedition by publicly expressing support for Louaillier, which they promptly began to do. The state senator and the federal judge "languished in the same jail cell" while the warrior Andrew Jackson waged his military campaign against civilian interference. A government lawyer petitioned a state judge for a new writ of habeas corpus to free Louaillier and Hall; Jackson ordered them arrested too, then later changed his mind while the lawyer sat in army custody.

While Jackson raged, his own army seems to have been far more circumspect about its power and place; if the general wouldn't stay within the limits of his authority, then his military tribunals would. This prevailing caution became clear when the general ordered a court-martial to assemble and try Louaillier on a laundry list of charges that have not, two hundred years later, lost their power to amaze. Most extraordinary among the charges was the seventh: "unsoldierly conduct."

Louaillier wasn't a soldier; in fact, he wasn't even subject to militia duty, being exempted as a member of the legislature. Jackson had casually turned every man in New Orleans into a military subordinate, an operation that took place entirely in his mind. It had become *unsoldierly* for civilians to disagree with the man who regarded himself as their commander, and they were to be tried before military courts. Jackson also ordered the court-martial to try the senator for libel, a charge not to be found in the Articles of War. Louaillier's court-martial quickly abandoned six of the charges, agreeing that it had no jurisdiction—but still insisting that it would try Louaillier over the transparently silly accusation that he was a spy caught inside American lines. He was quickly acquitted.

But Jackson wouldn't give it up. Seething, he disapproved the "sentence" of the court-martial—the very thing it hadn't handed down. "Martial law, being established, applies, as the Commanding General believes, to all persons who remain within the sphere of its operation, and claims exclusive jurisdiction of all offences which aim at the disorganization of the army over which it extends," he wrote. "To a certain extent, it is believed to make every man a soldier to defend the spot where chance or choice has placed him; and to make him *liable* for any misconduct calculated to weaken its defence."

He was just saying it plainly: Andrew Jackson believed that he could make every man a soldier by the power of his own unilateral declaration. If a general declares martial law, then the whole population is composed of his subordinates. But he was stuck with the limits imposed on him by his own officers. Realizing he wouldn't be able to get a court-martial to convict Hall, Jackson banished the federal judge from New Orleans.

In the middle of March, Jackson finally got word on the southern coast of a peace that had been concluded more than a month before. He revoked martial law the moment he learned he was no longer at war, and released his prisoners. Jackson granted himself absolute power in wartime, but also acknowledged the moment when his own premise evaporated.

And then he submitted to the civilian authority he had attacked. Free to enter New Orleans without the threat of military detention, the federal judge Dominick Hall returned to the bench and summoned Jackson to his courtroom. The general strolled through the doors "in the plain garb of a common citizen . . . to the cheers of a large crowd," refused to answer the judge's questions, and made a show of paying a $1,000 fine from his personal funds, declining contributions from grateful locals. It was a finely crafted performance, mixing equal parts proud defiance and elaborate submission; he even assured the judge of his intention to "shield and protect this court, or perish in the effort," just as he had shielded the city.

Thirty years later, though—old, broke, and still seething over a punishment imposed on him because he had protected the city—he asked the federal government for a refund of that grandly settled fine, with interest. Congress voted to give it to him: $2,732.90.

Jackson created a precedent, but other men played their part. President James Madison quietly stepped away from a serious examination of the events in New Orleans. Did Jackson take justified and appropriate action? Warshauer, the historian who has given the closest attention to the general's application of martial law, concludes that "Madison never answered the question. Still reeling from his own unpopularity in connection with the war, the president had the alternative of chastising a newly crowned national hero and in so doing upholding the supremacy of the civil law or letting the entire episode rest. The choice was clear."

A general who wins his battles can get away with things; and once he does, so can others. Warshauer argues that Jackson's unchecked use of military power over civilians "presaged the future of a doctrine of emergency powers . . . Madison's failure to act opened a gaping hole in the future protection of civil liberties."

Jackson did learn a lesson from New Orleans, discovering that he could act on his own inflated conception of his authority without consequence if he was conspicuously serving the larger national purpose. Later, leading his unauthorized invasion of Spanish Florida in 1818, the general arrested two British citizens who were supposedly "stirring up the Creek Indians to war against the United States," supplying Indians and escaped slaves fighting alongside them with "the means of war," and spying for the Creeks and Seminoles. Civilians and foreign nationals, Robert Ambrister and Alexander Arbuthnot—the latter a seventy-year-old Scottish trader—were tried by a supposed court-martial by an army that had crossed an international border to wage war without orders. The court sentenced Arbuthnot to be hanged, and Ambrister to be shot; then, reconsidering, the members voted a second time and instead sentenced Ambrister to be flogged and confined at hard labor. Jackson ignored the court's revised sentence; both men were executed.

Look at the pattern of Jackson's decisions regarding enemies in his power: Josiah Francis and Homathlemico summarily executed without even a pretense of legal process; William Weatherford quietly released on the strength of personal honor; Ambrister and Arbuthnot tried, convicted, and executed by military authority, the actual verdict of a court-martial ignored by a general who embraced the appearance of legal process but not the limits of the court's final decision. These weren't choices that reflected a consistent philosophy of justice or martial jurisdiction. He wasn't worried about the scope and sources of his authority; he was worried about victory. New Orleans became his camp, and in his mind its citizens became his soldiers. They would serve the cause of victory or be punished. Go back, for a moment: Imagine what a man like this was thinking when some of his actual soldiers decided to desert from his command.

We can only guess at Jackson's thoughts, but we know from his actions what he invariably valued and wanted. For a man who expected to give every part of himself only to the single cause of victory against the nation's enemies—or, in other words, to prevent the conquest of his own country—Jackson's manic application of authority seems likely to have come from something other than a hunger for power. He was the soldier who would always fight when the need arose, throwing aside every other consideration. Jackson went into combat while he was recovering from serious illness, swaying exhausted on horseback; he led troops while still suffering horribly from wounds sustained in a duel. Other men didn't. They talked about the limits of their service, the contractual and customary end of their military obligation, and the legal protections afforded by their status as civilians. The habitual and eternal warrior looked at men who had no natural instinct to join a fight, and he was appalled. The best guess available to us on the evidence is that Jackson's lashing out against militiamen leaving his army, or men in New Orleans declining to fight, is that the general was expressing an outraged sense of mutuality rather than a pure craving for power. The natural warrior, facing enemies, looked around to see who would stand with him; some didn't. Not quite fifty years later, William Tecumseh Sherman would make similarly outrageous claims about the reach of his military authority, on similar grounds. The born soldier doesn't understand men who aren't soldiers at all.

In any event, officials in a position to restrain General Jackson tended to get out of his way when he acted on his sense of outrage. Secretary of War John Calhoun, who would later become Jackson's vice president, wanted to punish the general for killing British citizens in Florida with nothing more than a dubious gesture at legal process, but Secretary of State John Quincy Adams successfully argued that the executions were lawful as "retributive justice." Adams had one other good reason to argue against public censure for Jackson: The general's unauthorized invasion had plainly revealed Spain's weakness in Florida, and the American secretary of state was about to negotiate the treaty that would make the peninsula part of the United States. Jackson exceeded his orders, refused to recognize limits to his authority, convened courts-martial to try capital cases they had no business considering—and conquered rich new territory for his country. President James Monroe waited a few months before mildly rebuking him in a private letter.

Andrew Jackson was will and force, an embodied desire for the destruction of enemies and the victory of the American cause. He got away with things. With urgency and flagrancy, often and loudly, he rushed past the limits of the law and his official power. And Americans—many of them, at least—loved him for it. He fought and won.

THE JACKSONIAN SPIRIT survived Andrew Jackson. Antebellum America was desperate for conquest and expansion, in a sustained burst of national energy that relentlessly aimed to make the country bigger and more powerful. Military law remained a loosely structured adjunct to the project of victory—and a way of achieving retribution in the face of cowardice and betrayal.

The improvisational and paradoxical military justice of the Jacksonian era reached its apotheosis in a war that began a year after Jackson's death. Army officers fighting a war with Mexico applied different kinds of discipline to different kinds of soldiers, and made up the law as they went along, inventing military commissions to bring Mexican citizens and their own troops to justice. The American war with Mexico was an endlessly creative act that contained elements of cruel and shoddy behavior. It was Jacksonian: brilliant and brutal, glorious and ghastly.

On the morning of September 13, 1847, thirty men stood on army-built gallows with nooses around their necks. But no one was in a hurry to hang them. The condemned men faced Chapultepec Castle, watching the sun rise over a redoubt held by Mexican soldiers. As the men waited to die, American artillery opened up on the Mexican troops, preparing for an infantry assault. Irish American soldiers would watch as the army they had deserted defeated the army they had joined. The officer in charge of their execution, Col. William Selby Harney, explained his plan to them: When the American flag was raised over the conquered Mexican citadel, the mule teams on the other end of the ropes would raise the men into the air. They would die watching the victory of the army they had betrayed.

The road to a mass execution on a hillside in Mexico began on the other side of the Atlantic Ocean. The United States would make war on Mexico with a much-too-small professional army— and well after the collapse of the universal militia obligation for white men. But a country that desperately needed new soldiers for a war that began in 1846 had the good fortune to have a deep well of men in desperate circumstances—because the Irish Potato Famine began in 1845.

The Irish recruits who poured into the army in 1846 were already accustomed to the realities of antebellum American nativism. The country had been rocked by anti-Catholic riots even before the famine produced new waves of Irish immigrants; in Boston, Protestant mobs had burned a convent in 1834, and Philadelphia had seen mob attacks on Irishmen ten years later. So the recent immigrants who enlisted for war with Mexico weren't surprised to encounter nativists in the army. They were very much surprised, though, by the intensity of the anti-Irish sentiment they faced from their officers—a social sentiment that was expressed through official discipline.

To be sure, the small corps of regular army officers in the 1840s started with the assumption that all enlisted men required harsh and relentless chastisement. Many forms of physical punishment for privates and sergeants didn't require a court-martial, or legal process of any kind. Men in the ranks could be reduced to submission by the direct and immediate application of naked force. Disobedient or inept soldiers were bucked and gagged for hours, or forced to ride a wooden horse until it wore away the skin of their legs and left their pants soaked in blood. Men who couldn't control their drinking could be branded, the letters "HD" burned into their foreheads to signal the presence of a habitual drunk, though branding required a court-martial. Even for native-born soldiers, the regular army wasn't a gentle institution.

But recent Irish immigrants found that the army's harsh discipline could be their unrelenting and brutal discipline. A traveler writing about his encounter with American troops in camp "stared at officers hanging Irishmen by their thumbs from tree limbs for sloppy salutes." Native-born officers ranted anti-Catholic sentiment at their immigrant troops; members of courts-martial "punctuated verdicts with diatribes against offenders' nationalities and Catholicism."

The Irish American journalist Peter Stevens has closely studied the treatment of new immigrants in the ranks of the American army during the war with Mexico, comparing cases of military justice across lines of identity. Sgt. James Bannon and Pvt. George Miller, for example, were tried by the same court-martial. Both were "accused of verbally threatening officers, but not striking them." Miller was born in the United States; he was sentenced to fifty lashes. Bannon, an Irish immigrant, "was stood in front of a firing squad." The army had one kind of justice, but many of its officers had two.

Discipline is meant to preserve order in armies, but excessive and nakedly biased discipline did the opposite. Exhausted by their brutal routine, Irish immigrants in the army began not just to desert in large numbers as the army camped on the border, but also to cross into Mexico. They fled their new country as they fled their new army. Particularly since some were experienced soldiers who had served in the British Army before immigrating to the United States, men crossing into Mexico found a warm reception on the other side of the border. Some even found military commissions, becoming officers in the force fighting against the army they had served as privates.

As Mexican soldiers, deserters would kill some of the officers who had brutally disciplined them. Most famously, John Riley had been trained as an artilleryman while serving as a British soldier, and would eventually rise to the rank of lieutenant colonel in the Mexican Army. As the leader of the all-Irish St. Patrick's Battalion on August 20, 1847, Riley commanded artillery at the Battle of Churubusco, fighting to keep American forces from entering Mexico City. Americans storming the Mexican positions that day began to notice that "an unusually high number of officers had been hit and realized that Riley's men were singling out the Yankee disciplinarians whom they hated so bitterly." But the battle turned. Brilliantly organized flying batteries of American artillery ripped apart Riley's position, putting his cannons out of service, and the American deserter prepared his men for a last stand behind the stone walls of a nearby monastery.

The fight over the monastery was fierce and horrible, hand-to-hand combat in narrow corridors and barricaded doorways. But native Mexican troops discovered that they weren't able to surrender: Every one of the several times they tried to raise a white flag, men from the St. Patrick's Battalion ripped it down.

Deserters who had gone over to the enemy, they knew they weren't likely to survive capture. And so men fought desperately, with "bayonets, fists, and feet," but they ultimately couldn't stop the enraged American soldiers pouring into the redoubt they had chosen for their last stand. Finally, the men on the Mexican side couldn't fight anymore, wounded and exhausted, and the Americans started taking prisoners.

Riley was among the wounded, Stevens writes, with eighty-four of his men. "It was with much difficulty that the American soldiers could be prevented from bayoneting these miscreants on the spot," a witness would recall. Instead, the survivors from Riley's unit were tied together and forced to march into captivity, wounds notwithstanding. Other Irish American deserters were caught elsewhere in Mexico as the army rolled up the majority of its deserters who had gone to the other side and lived to be caught.

Together, the deserters all faced courts-martial that had the power to take their lives. Some of the accused bothered to defend themselves, trying a variety of unsuccessful arguments. Some claimed to have been drunk when they deserted, then coerced into joining the other side. One, a private named Lachlin McLachlin, claimed that he'd been forced to desert to save his life, after an officer threatened to kill him. Brushing aside the claim, a court-martial sentenced him to be hanged. Seventy Irish American deserters were sentenced to death, though not all were executed.

Character still mattered, even for a deserter who fought for the other side, and Sgt. Abraham Fitzpatrick elicited testimony in his own trial that proved his quality as a soldier—right up until the moment he snuck away and changed sides. Capt. James Longstreet, Fitzpatrick's company commander, paid him a high compliment from the witness stand: "I have not known a better noncommissioned officer." And so the sergeant was condemned to death, but with honor. He would be shot by a firing squad, a soldier's death, rather than being hanged in disgrace. For soldiers, and under the circumstances, this was mercy. Fitzpatrick could die like Henry Lewis, condemned for his failures and redeemed by his courage at the moment of death.

There would also be mercy before the killing began, in a mix of legal process and the application of cultural values. In some instances, the legal process was straightforward. At Tacubaya, a court-martial tried forty-three deserters, and sentenced forty-one to death. "Only Edward Ellis, a dragoon who had somehow neglected to sign an enlistment paper and was not technically in the army, and Lewis Pieper, insane, a 'perfect simpleton,' were spared," Stevens writes.

Reviewing convictions, Winfield Scott—who was leading combat troops in Mexico while serving as general in chief of the entire US Army— overturned a surprising number of death sentences. Like Jackson in 1815, Scott spared underage soldiers, two teenagers from the ranks who were captured at the ages of fifteen and sixteen. Another twelve men escaped death in favor of flogging and branding, "the letter D high up on the cheek-bone," Scott having accepted their arguments that they were coerced into fighting for Mexico. And one man was pardoned altogether, released despite being a deserter who had fired artillery at American troops at Churubusco; whatever Edward McHeran had done, his son had served with honor in the same company his father had fled. A soldier's courage could redeem his family.

Finally, six deserters who had joined Mexican forces were released from the army despite having been sentenced to death. They had crossed the river into Mexico in early April 1846, shortly before the war began—so they were peacetime deserters, not legally subject to execution. Scott reduced their sentences to flogging and branding. Among the men who had crossed into Mexico before the war began: John Riley, the commander of the

St. Patrick's Battalion, who had commanded the artillery that tore apart American soldiers. Many of Scott's officers demanded that Riley be executed anyway, without regard to the law. The general responded to the flood of protest from his own army with the firm reply that he would not commit "judicial murder." They were released later in the year, heads shaved and cheeks branded with the letter "D" for desertion, drummed out of the army in shame; in later years, American tourists occasionally recognized Riley by the letter burned into his face.

For thirty other men, Colonel Harney did his duty in front of Chapultepec Castle, leaving them hanging where they died. "I was ordered to have them hanged," Harney told the men of the execution detail, "and have no orders to *unhang* them."

AMERICAN FORCES in Mexico didn't just use military courts against soldiers who violated the Articles of War. In a series of general orders, Scott granted himself the power to make laws. The general placed Mexican civilians, foreign nationals, and his own troops under a wholly new system of martial justice, forbidding a long list of offenses that ran from murder and rape to "the interruption of religious ceremonies." His "General Order 20," issued in February of 1847, made those crimes the potential subject of trial by military tribunal "whether committed by Mexicans or other civilians in Mexico against individuals of the US military forces, or by such individuals against other such individuals or against Mexicans or civilians." Everyone in Mexico could be tried by American military courts for any offense that involved American troops as victims or offenders, though crimes committed by Mexicans against Mexicans remained subject only to the jurisdiction of Mexican courts.

Scott's tribunals weren't courts-martial, and could try American soldiers on charges not contained in the Articles of War.

Since they didn't just do what courts-martial did, he called them something else—and the name is still with us. "The origin of today's military commissions can be traced directly to Major General Winfield Scott, who created the 'military commission' in 1847 during the Mexican-American War," writes the lawyer Haridimos Thravalos, a close observer of contemporary efforts to try suspected terrorists in front of tribunals run by the armed forces.

Scott also created another kind of tribunal, the council of war, to try Mexican insurgents launching guerilla attacks on American troops. But actually applying occupier's law could be difficult in practice.

In Puebla, for example, US Army officers noticed a "tall, well-dressed blond man" talking with the German-born immigrant soldiers in their own ranks. They didn't know what to make of his presence until they began to catch those same soldiers with pamphlets—written in German—that urged them to desert "with their horses and weapons." Arrested by soldiers in June of 1847, the watchmaker Martin Tritschler turned out to be a naturalized Mexican citizen, and a commissioned officer in Puebla's local armed forces. He was an enemy, waging a war of subversion against the American military. He was brought before Scott's council of war, quickly found guilty on two charges of spying and fomenting desertion, and sentenced to death by firing squad—strangely, since spies were supposed to be hanged.

Commanding the American forces in Puebla, though, Scott quickly found that he had a serious problem: Tritschler was widely admired among the 80,000 residents of the city, who had to be held back at bayonet point from overrunning his trial. Scott commanded an occupying force of a few thousand soldiers, surrounded by tens of thousands of enraged locals. The American commander carefully discovered signs that Tritschler was legally insane—and so not subject to execution. Released from custody and sent home, Tritschler miraculously managed to display no signs of mental illness, and Puebla remained pacified. "Scott's pragmatic handling of the Tritschler affair helped cement a better relationship with Puebla's bishop and his clergy, whose antipathy toward Santa Anna Scott had quickly detected," Stevens writes. He was waging "lawfare"—tailoring legal outcomes to tactical and strategic needs.

That lawfare agenda was also practically difficult for another reason: Scott was exposing American soldiers to legal jeopardy in a system of courts that he had simply invented. He did so wholly without support or guidance from either Congress or his superiors in the executive branch, who debated the need for law and order in occupied portions of Mexico but carefully declined to do anything in response to Scott's many requests for instructions. As the lawyer Erika Myers has written, "Congress did nothing—slowly." Meanwhile, Scott's memorandum to the War Department on legal issues was "silently returned, as too explosive for safe handling."

So Scott had a decision to make, far from home in a foreign country as the agent of a government that declined to provide answers to basic questions about the course he should take. But Andrew Jackson had arrived at his own clear answers in less murky circumstances than these; the nineteenth-century American military had a well-established tradition, or at least a little-contested habit, of successfully winging it. Scott took confident action on his own authority, and a "traditional view of the law of war" in which "the powers of a military commander over enemies—including citizens of a hostile nation as well as anyone engaged in hostilities—were absolute." His legal position was less clear with regard to American soldiers tried by military courts for civilian crimes, but Myers concludes that the experiment worked: "By helping to change the culture of the army and decreasing offenses against civilians, Scott's commissions destroyed the guerrilla's most effective recruiting tool, helping him avoid an insurgency that could have been fatal to his campaign."

The law, even in a dubious form invented by a general in a moment of need, could have salutary military effects. In Mexico, Winfield Scott took a firm and resolute course rather than a strictly legal one. He created a system of courts generally staffed by combat-arms officers who had no legal training, and tried to make it more or less procedurally fair. And he was able to make that ad-hoc simulation of a legal system work because it followed a reasonably coherent American military tradition in which justice mostly came from a commonsense application of values rather than statutes and official regulations.

For several decades, American military law was mostly not law. It was a set of fair guesses and reasonable assumptions, carried out on the run by men whose full attention was directed toward victory and conquest. Imperfectly, unevenly, improperly, it mostly worked toward its intended purposes. But one problem broke the unspoken and haphazard consensus about the operation of justice in the armed forces: Officers and organizations struggled to apply reasonable rules to men who didn't fit into the prevailing social consensus. Military punishment was sort of reasonable, except when it wasn't. But no one was especially interested in the details.

PART TWO

AUTHORITY AND EXPANSION

*The Civil War
to the Philippine War*

*I*n the last four decades of the nineteenth century, the scale of the American experiment changed. The Civil War changed it, as a start, and then the change continued as a growing nation consolidated control across a continent and stretched its power across the oceans.

The change in the country reflected the change in the scope of its wars. In 1777, George Washington had led 12,000 men into winter quarters at Valley Forge. In 1846, as soldiers crossed into Mexico, the entire US Army had all of 7,365 soldiers; over time, total American forces in that country grew to a peak of almost 30,000. And in three days at Gettysburg in 1863, Union and Confederate armies together took between 45,000 and 51,000 casualties. Those numbers are just guesses, since there were too many dead and wounded for anyone to count precisely. Americans hadn't imagined a war like this before they found themselves fighting it.

The massive scale of the Civil War was one of several reasons the Southern writer Robert Penn Warren described it as the "secret school" for the world wars of the twentieth century. "Between 1861 and 1865," Warren wrote, "America learned how to mobilize, equip, and deploy enormous military forces—and learned the will and confidence to do so." Warren was one of the many writers who have identified the Civil War as the pivot in the decades-long shift from Small America to Big America, from a nation of family farms toward the world of corporate industry. A sprawling set of "island communities," in the description coined by historian Robert

*Wiebe, gave way to a connected national order organized by bureaucratic management. Another historian, Alan Trachtenberg, described—as the title of his book puts it—*The Incorporation of America; *it opens with the surrender at Appomattox.*

Warren used an important word in his description of the war: "learned." The Civil War was an extraordinary period of concentrated experimentation and discovery. Rising institutional power shoved against its restraints; both the North and South learned to use the law as a political instrument. More precisely, both sides in the war learned to use gestures that looked like law, containing internal opposition with dubious arrests and trials. Governments weaponized legal forms. But the lessons men learned in these four sharp years were lessons of scope, not of type. They took from, and intensified, the half-formed American traditions of military legal authority that soldiers had begun to develop in earlier conflicts: Abraham Lincoln did what Andrew Jackson and Winfield Scott had done, but he led a larger effort and did more of it. War still allowed men to learn power.

Learning their way through war, Americans used the language of law to explain to themselves what they were doing. Two years into the conflict, Lincoln issued General Order No. 100, "Instructions for the Government of Armies of the United States in the Field"—better known today as the Lieber Code. Written by the Columbia professor Francis Lieber, the code embodies the awkwardness of its moment. It's an extraordinary artifact of the journey to an unexpected and horrifying destination—a guide to the rational management of organized violence.

Reading the Lieber Code is like watching a man try to run in two directions at the same time. In clear, short sentences, the code tries to place the conduct of war within reasonable boundaries—and plainly acknowledges the need for the large-scale application of brutality. Article 16 declares, "Military necessity does not admit of cruelty"; the very next article concludes that war "is not carried on by arms alone. It is lawful to starve the hostile belligerent, armed or unarmed, so that it leads to the speedier subjection of the enemy." Pain and hunger and death—for enemy soldiers and enemy civilians alike—are just expected consequences of war, so get on with it.

"Commanders, whenever admissible, inform the enemy of their intention to bombard a place, so that the noncombatants, and especially the women and children, may be removed before the bombardment commences," Article 19 reads. "But it is no infraction of the common law of war to omit thus to inform the enemy. Surprise may be a necessity." As legal historian John Fabian Witt has written, the idea of military necessity offered an exception to most of the limits the nation had decided to impose on its military; it offered "both a broad limit on war's violence and a robust license to destroy." You shouldn't fire artillery at women and children—unless you have to, in which case you should go ahead. "The more vigorously wars are pursued, the better it is for humanity. Sharp wars are brief," Article 29 declares. The unrelenting application of destructive force would bring a quick and sure end to a war, and the end of a war is a vital kindness. War is awful, so fight it hard.

That immense application of institutional force was half of a larger story, a long narrative of community custom and insistent personal choice. Within giant organizations, many soldiers still believed they could define the terms of their service, leaving when they decided their duty had expired and refusing assigned duty or discipline when they thought it went too far. And so the Civil War was a great collision between North and South, but an equally great collision between competing conceptions of authority, consent, and law. In battlefields from Pennsylvania to California to the Philippines, the demands of expansion were sorted out in military courtrooms.

4

"I Won't Be Quiet"

Force and Consent in the Civil War

WHEN WAR BEGAN IN 1861, BERNARD MCMAHON WAS A MINER IN California. But he was a soldier at heart, a veteran of the Mexican War, and he rushed to participate. In San Francisco, he organized a company of volunteers and mustered it into federal service. But then he realized he'd made a mistake: He was too far away, commanding soldiers on the wrong coast to be in the heart of the fight. So he resigned his commission and started traveling east, a warrior looking for his war. He found a regiment that would have him, the 71st Pennsylvania, and gladly joined it. By the Battle of Fredericksburg in December of 1862 he was a company commander, directly leading men into combat. But in the words of historian Lorien Foote, the other officers of his regiment "never let him forget that he was a stranger in a unit recruited mostly from Philadelphia." Strangers who went to war together treated one another as strangers; locally recruited companies and regiments became less cohesive as outsiders moved into their ranks in a war that kept going and growing. Honored with responsibility as an officer but ostracized as a gentleman, McMahon began to hear other men running him down. He fought well enough, they said, but he's too scared to ever do it again.

The worst offender in this whispering campaign was an officer in another Pennsylvania regiment, Capt. Andrew McManus, who had friends in the 71st. McMahon heard that McManus had called him a coward in the presence of other officers, and sent him a private letter demanding that he stop; McManus wrote back, casually dismissive, brushing aside a serious challenge. Two nights later, McManus sought out the target of his personal attacks, and deliberately took a seat just outside his tent. In the company of other officers, he began to loudly denounce McMahon's supposed weakness and laziness. Some officers laughed; others walked away in disgust at the unwarranted attack on a good officer's name. McMahon listened for a while, but then he couldn't listen to any more. He walked out of his tent, holding a pistol, and stood right over the other captain. He asked if McManus had been insulting him, already knowing the answer. Without standing up, McManus replied to McMahon's question: "I have, you are a coward and a loafer." McMahon didn't hesitate. He raised the pistol and fired.

ELIZABETH SAMET, who teaches literature to future army officers at the US Military Academy, describes an early American ethic of "willing obedience," the idea Leonard Blodget had embraced in Rhode Island in 1821 when he refused to give an order his men wouldn't agree to obey. The American sense of military duty wasn't supposed to reflect the mindless submission of conscripts; rather, it was supposed to be the informed consent of the *liber*, the free man, obeying his officers so they could accomplish their shared purpose.

But Samet also opens a book titled *Willing Obedience* with a story about its opposite, tracing a more confident turn toward martial coercion. She describes an early moment in the Civil War, an exchange between William Tecumseh Sherman— who was still a colonel—and a captain from a volunteer regiment whose ninety-day term of duty had expired. The captain announced that he was leaving, and wished Sherman well. Like the Tennessee militiamen who served in Andrew Jackson's army in 1814, he didn't sneak away; he walked up to his commander and said goodbye. The captain knew without a doubt that he had the right to evaluate the terms of his own service and decide when he could leave the army and go home.

Like Jackson before him, Sherman knew no such thing. He reached for the pistol in his coat. "You are a soldier," he said, "and must submit to orders until you are properly discharged. If you attempt to leave without orders, it will be mutiny, and I will shoot you like a dog." When President Abraham Lincoln visited the camp the next day, the captain presented his grievance: The colonel had threatened to shoot him. Lincoln leaned down to respond "in a loud stage-whisper," telling the captain that he guessed Sherman really meant it. "The chastened captain speedily retreated amid general laughter," Samet writes.

The argument Leonard Blodget had pursued with Joseph Hawes was apparently over: Military authority descended. Armies churned out punishment, at widely varying levels of quality. Faced with the need for the regular application of discipline on a massive scale, Congress created a new tribunal with a July 1862 law: the field officer court, which replaced regimental courts-martial composed of three officers with a quick and simple trial conducted before a single officer. Military justice had to be delivered in bulk, with maximum efficiency, so soldiers could get back to serving the needs of the institution.

But that's far from being the whole story. Military justice grew radically in scope and power during the Civil War, but was still rooted in the deeply personal as much as it grew from military necessity. "A man's knowledge that others did not consider him a gentleman was the source of more than one court martial in the Union Army," Foote writes. Perceptions of manhood and the status of gentlemen reached into the Articles of War and influenced their meaning. This kind of social influence always guided military justice, and still does, but the Civil War created a particular need for men to judge one another by social criteria, as strangers crowded together in massive armies—in the later years of the war, gathering in the company of less-respected conscripts and paid substitutes. The Articles of War prescribed their behavior as soldiers, but they were men first, and social creatures; they filed charges and deliberated in court because of the way they personally understood appropriate behavior. The law went so far, and then it had to yield to other forces.

The rich example that Foote describes was centered on the practice and prohibition of the duel. In the nineteenth-century army, the laws against dueling were serious, far-reaching, and frequently ignored. The Articles of War forbade fighting a duel, sending challenges to duel, participating in a duel by delivering a challenge or acting as a second, allowing other soldiers to leave camp to duel, failing to arrest subordinates who intended to duel, and insulting another soldier for refusing to duel. Congress, which had experienced its own share of duels between gentlemen, covered all the angles. Every aspect of a duel and its necessary preparation were banned.

The War Department also published orders that defined dueling broadly, pushing aside the elaborate ritual of the gentlemanly code duello to make any kind of challenge to fight with weapons into the thing strictly prohibited by Article 25. "No particular phraseology, no set form" defined a duel. One soldier walks up to another soldier and shouts a challenge to go outside and fight with swords or pistols *right now*—no written challenge, no demand for satisfaction, no reference to honor, no choice of seconds, no proper choice of a time and place, and no need for the superior social status between contestants that makes a proper duel possible—and it's close enough to prosecute. Under the War

Department's definition of the term, *privates* could "duel." Whatever the regulations said, this is not at all how the gentlemen of the officer class understood that word.

We have a decent number of examples to study. During the Civil War, at least dozens of men in federal armies engaged in behavior "that included some element of the dueling ritual"; Foote found thirty-four in the surviving records of general courts-martial, a number that without a doubt "vastly underrepresents the actual number of affairs of honor that occurred in the Union Army." And the officers who composed those courts-martial knew about the War Department's definition of the duel. In many cases, the judge advocate took care during the trial to define the term under the law and regulations.

But they didn't care. The Northern military officers who constituted courts-martial—self-consciously *gentlemen*, and careful to perform that role for their peers and subordinates—pursued lines of questioning at trial that casually shrugged off War Department definitions of the duel. They asked witnesses about all of the things that weren't supposed to matter: Was there a written challenge? Which gentlemen were chosen as seconds? "In several cases," Foote writes, "courts substituted words within the specifications of a charge to make the distinction between men setting up a *duel* and men who wanted to *fight*." That's exactly the distinction the War Department no longer permitted, but formal orders couldn't eradicate deeply held social conceptions. A duel was what men knew it was, no matter what the law and the regulations might say.

Even when men did adopt the social rituals of the code duello, dueling was both officially forbidden and actually allowed. Men of the right character and class were permitted the practice, because at some level in the hierarchy they could find men who were willing to look past the law and see the social symbols that made a duel into a reasonably conducted affair of honor.

Capt. Charles Horton was a staff officer of good background in a regiment filled with Boston Brahmins, and treated the less-well-bred Capt. Charles Booth with careful disdain. When Booth wrote to a superior officer to say that Horton was neglecting his duty, another gentleman delivered a message on Horton's behalf demanding that Booth make the necessary retractions at once. Booth refused; the insult stood, communicated to other men and not publicly retracted. Horton, Foote writes, "had received a devastating blow to his honor from a man that was his social inferior."

He responded exactly as one did, striding into Booth's office with a horsewhip to chastise a lesser man who didn't merit the form of the written challenge passed between equals by their gentlemanly seconds. His action was perfectly theatrical, the precise performance of calculated ritual: He touched Booth lightly with the whip, three times, then turned to the other officers standing in the office. "Gentlemen," he told them, "you see me horsewhip this officer." The devastating blow to his personal honor had been returned in kind, public insult for public insult. Booth's honor had been challenged by the man whose honor he had demeaned.

The full act wasn't needed, because the choreographed ceremony fully conveyed the necessary message. Horton didn't need to actually horsewhip the other officer, taking flesh and drawing blood; he just needed to perform horsewhipping as a gesture. Then, in front of the audience of other officers, he told Booth where he would be waiting to receive his written communication. "Horton had initiated an affair of honor," Foote concludes. "He expected that Booth would have to challenge him to a duel," having just opened that cycle of challenge and response himself. It was precisely the thing that Article 25 forbade.

The really interesting moments in history happen when people are following different scripts, and this is one of them: Charles

Horton was a man of antebellum high society, reaching back into custom and the past to understand his life; Charles Booth was a man of the big institution, living by the regulations. Booth *filed charges*. He didn't behave like a gentleman—he followed the law.

Horton was tried by a court-martial that applied both the law and the social understanding of the code duello. Taken together, the two systems of judgment made his actions clearly forbidden: authentically an attempt to duel, which was not allowed. The court sentenced Horton to be stripped of his rank and thrown out of the army.

But he wasn't. President Abraham Lincoln soon received a petition signed by men of status and authority, and endorsed by Sen. John Sherman. Horton, they warned, was a "high-toned gentleman," and the army would suffer a real loss from his absence. A few days before his assassination, Lincoln agreed. The president ordered that Captain Horton, a high-toned gentleman who had violated the Articles of War in the clearest imaginable way— theatrically turning to other men and announcing to them that they'd witnessed the violation—be returned to duty.

There's the law, and there's what really happens. And the two are always struggling to meet.

A gentleman could even be forgiven for a blatant act of murder if his character was understood in just the right light—and if the man he killed was regarded poorly enough. This was just what happened to Capt. Bernard McMahon after he shot the seated and defenseless Capt. Andrew McManus. Again, a court-martial found the matter easy enough, and sentenced McMahon to be executed by a firing squad as the murderer of a fellow officer.

But the 71st Pennsylvania found itself at Gettysburg before the firing squad could do its job, and McMahon—who already knew he was a dead man—successfully begged his guards to let him fight. The regimental commander reported after the battle that the condemned captain had "acted the part of a soldier and a man," the things an officer needed to be to prove his worth. As in Horton's case, recommendations for commutation poured in from general officers and other prominent men. Gentlemen looked out for their own kind. Judge Advocate Gen. Joseph Holt finally got a case file that described a brave officer who killed a man after he bizarrely damned him as a coward. Under the circumstances, Holt concluded, "the deceased must be regarded as having wantonly and wickedly thrown his life away." With that recommendation in hand, Lincoln pardoned McMahon altogether. He hadn't committed *murder*; rather, he was a gentleman of substance and courage who had understandably shot a man of poor character in provocative circumstances. The men recommending that McMahon be forgiven—and the men who actually forgave him—were putting themselves in his shoes: What man wouldn't defend his honor and his manhood?

Manhood was at stake; violence was a redemption, not a failure. Holt's report assigned a particular meaning to McMahon's use of violence against a man who had leveled a cheap and unwarranted insult at a gentleman. "Had the accused borne longer than he did, without resentment, the brutal contumely and persecution to which he was subjected," the judge advocate general wrote, "he would have shown a want of spirit that would have totally unfitted him to confront the public enemy." A military officer who would let another officer insult him and lie about him would be a man without courage or honor—and if an army had officers like that, how could it prevail on the battlefield? An armed force needed officers who would kill its enemies, and McMahon had just proved his worth as a warrior. He had the courage and strength to kill an antagonist, and the country was at war.

In a similar and more famous killing, Brig. Gen. Jefferson C. Davis (who was not related to the Confederate president) shot and killed Brig. Gen. William Nelson in the summer of 1862 after the other man slapped him and called him a coward in front of an audience of other soldiers. Nelson was widely regarded as a tyrant and a megalomaniac, and his death was greeted joyfully; in the ranks, men openly celebrated the killing. Davis was returned to duty without charges.

Davis told friends that he had no choice in the matter, making an argument built on exactly the conception of manhood Holt had used to understand McMahon's act of violence. "I belong to the regular army and not to resent an insult of that kind would have been to make me shunned by all my brother officers. I must either call him to account or be as the dog that sleeps under my father's floor."

In a moment of rising institutional power and growing legal formalization, these were not conceptions of propriety that came from the Articles of War. Soldiers were both governed by military law and uninterested in its requirements. They would do what was right, and the law would have whatever role they had room to allow it. Charles Booth's decision was anything but inevitable.

SOCIAL VALUES steered military justice, but so did political considerations. Or, to put that a little differently, so did political theatre. In the chaos of a new war and a rapidly expanding military, soldiers faced a system of law that was hardly a system. They could be subject to arbitrary expressions of power, undertaken outside legal boundaries that no one had the time or the inclination to observe with care. Among the most infamous examples is the arrest and imprisonment of Brig. Gen. Charles Pomeroy Stone, a respected West Point graduate and Mexican War veteran who had the misfortune to command a senator.

Expressing a desire to fight, Sen. Edward Baker had turned down an offer of a general officer's commission from the Lincoln administration, insisting instead on organizing a regiment of volunteers and becoming its colonel. He seems to have been putting on a bit of a show; as historian Stephen Sears writes, Baker was "partial to appearing in the Senate in full uniform to declaim against secessionists and all their works." But he wasn't a tactically proficient field officer, despite his earlier service in the war with Mexico, and his performance in the role of a colonel would be fatal.

The Battle of Ball's Bluff, fought on October 21, 1861, was a relatively minor Union tactical defeat fairly early in the war, of little meaning except for the lopsidedness of the casualties. It began when a captain leading a nighttime scouting mission mistook trees for tents, and reported the presence of a lightly guarded Confederate camp across the Potomac in Virginia. Stone was four miles away while the battle began, having left Baker with orders that gave him broad discretion about what to do in the event of enemy contact. Blundering around with that latitude to act, Baker was among the dead, shot repeatedly while trying to rally the troops he'd led into a crossfire. "Baker's tactical dispositions were as rash as his decision to give battle," Sears concludes. But the loss wasn't serious enough to endanger the war effort; on the battlefield, it was just a significant local defeat.

And yet politicians managed to enlarge the scope of the small-scale disaster. On the floor of the House, Rep. Roscoe Conkling declared the battle "the most atrocious military murder ever committed in our history as a people." For members of the Senate, Baker's death meant that one of their own had fallen in battle. Their response could be described in different language with an equal chance at capturing their intent, but senators either set out to understand the cause of the loss or to find a place to hang the blame.

Stone was one possible target, having been Baker's division commander. Another was Maj. Gen. George McClellan, Stone's superior as the commander of the Army of the Potomac. Yet another possibility was to properly assign the blame for the defeat to Baker, but he was a US senator, freshly martyred on the battlefield. It wasn't going to be his fault—even if Stone's official report on the battle, soon published in newspapers, assigned it there, in a conclusion publicly supported by McClellan. Declining to accept that conclusion, Congress took up the matter of Ball's Bluff in the Joint Committee on the Conduct of the War, formed in early December of 1861, and called Stone as a witness.

He was a ready-made scapegoat. The commander of a division that had just lost a battle on the periphery of the nation's capital, Charles P. Stone also had other liabilities in the winter of 1861. First, he commanded troops in Maryland, a slave state that hadn't seceded. Politically and legally, he couldn't shelter escaped slaves, and he issued clear orders that all such fugitives caught within his lines be returned to their owners. Massachusetts volunteers under his command complained to their governor, understandably disgusted to be made complicit in the evils of slavery. Stone and Gov. John Andrew traded a round of increasingly bitter letters, leaving behind a paper trail in which the brigadier—in the willfully political reading of the exchange—acknowledged his service to slaveholders.

Second, his commander was a well-known Democrat, and Stone was suspected of Democratic leanings while serving a Republican administration. Newspapers began to hint that there was something more to the defeat at Ball's Bluff. Edward Baker's tactical blunderings began to turn into Charles Stone's act of treason: Maybe he *meant* to lose. After all, hadn't he returned slaves? Wasn't he obviously in thrall to the *slave power*?

The joint committee that questioned Stone also took testimony from dozens of other witnesses—in secret, and without giving Stone a chance to review any of it or offer a rebuttal. One of those witnesses, Col. George W. Tomkins, testified that his division commander had sometimes parleyed with Confederate officers under a flag of truce, and "allowed civilians to pass back and forth across the Potomac"—between seceded Virginia and formally loyal Maryland. Stone and the Confederate officers he met with under those flags of truce had exchanged letters for prisoners of war; in testimony before the joint committee, those not-unheard-of wartime exchanges between enemies became a conspiracy between a secessionist army officer and his Confederate associates, trading sealed correspondence in the service of their shared cause.

In January, the joint committee delivered its report, suggesting on tortured evidence that Baker had been betrayed into death by his disloyal commander. Secretary of War Edwin Stanton didn't hesitate: He ordered McClellan to arrest his subordinate as a traitor. McClellan resisted, and Stone was allowed to return to argue his case. It did no good. Stanton repeated his order, and McClellan—informed by his chief of intelligence, Allan Pinkerton, that witnesses had heard Confederate officers describe Stone as a gentleman and a "very fine man"—agreed to obey it.

The brigadier general sent to arrest his colleague in the middle of the night cringed with shame as he performed the act. "Stone," he said, "I have now the most disagreeable duty to perform that I ever had—it is to arrest you." Stone's response suggests the degree to which he had failed to understand the political game under way in the joint committee: "For what?" he asked. A detachment of eighteen infantrymen stood nearby, absurdly detailed to aid in the arrest of a dangerous public enemy.

No trial followed. Other army officers immediately and openly reacted to Stone's arrest with disgust and outrage, declaring him a victim of politics; no court-martial composed of his colleagues would have convicted him. Instead, the brigadier sat in solitary confinement, imprisoned in an island fortress for nearly two months. Finally transferred to imprisonment at another fort under less punitive conditions, Stone was held for another four and a half months, never notified of the charges against him. While he sat, newspapers howled for his punishment; the Philadelphia *North American and United States Gazette* wanted him to have "the death that a traitor in arms should have without delay." Not charged and not tried, a general officer was found guilty in print, and rhetorically sentenced to death on the strength of inferences and rumors that in no way resembled evidence.

Stone did have defenders, and they finally won his release. Ironically, the brigadier destroyed in part by the complaints of Massachusetts volunteers was a Massachusetts volunteer himself rather than a regular army officer, as a citizen-soldier who had rushed back into uniform at the first sign of conflict. But Stone nevertheless found vital support from a home state that was also a source of condemnation. "A month after his arrest," Sears writes, "a petition calling for justice and an immediate trial arrived at the White House from Massachusetts . . . signed by first families of the Commonwealth, the mayor and aldermen of Boston, major figures of business and the bar, the Harvard faculty, and hundreds of others." Finally, Sen. James McDougall dropped an amendment into a bill on military pay, inserting language requiring that military personnel "now under arrest" be informed of the charges against them within eight days, and brought before a court-martial within thirty. Signed into law by a president who had ignored complaints about Stone's lawless imprisonment, the measure forced the army to release its own falsely accused brigadier general.

Stone got both a measure of justice and no relief at all. He was allowed to return for another appearance before the Joint Committee on the Conduct of the War in 1863, where he was finally allowed to review the testimony others had given against him. He demolished it with clear and candid explanations of his actions, and the committee exonerated him. But his military career was over. Returned to active duty, Stone bounced through a few minor assignments for a while, denied appointments to positions of real responsibility and demoted from his assignment as a brigadier general of volunteers to colonel of the regular army. He finally resigned his commission in 1864.

Arrested but never charged or tried, Stone was exonerated as a commander and ruined as an officer. He was, Sears concludes, "guilty of nothing whatsoever," but still "destroyed by innuendo and the secret testimony of conspirators." He left the country and spent more than twenty years serving in the Egyptian military. A loyal soldier, a skilled leader, and a brave man, Stone had been driven out of the wartime army by fools.

Defeat on the battlefield would remain a political event, and courts-martial could be used to assign blame for military failure. Maj. Gen. Fitz John Porter was court-martialed and cashiered in January of 1863 over the Union defeat at Second Bull Run in August of 1862—a defeat better blamed on Maj. Gen. John Pope, Porter's superior, who had more friends in Washington. Porter spent the decades after the war trying to clear his name, in a long, slow wave of frustrating success: An investigative commission appointed by President Rutherford B. Hayes recommended in 1879 that the verdict in Porter's court-martial be set aside, but Porter wasn't pardoned until 1884. The politically charged military justice of the Civil War was still being debated and rectified two decades later.

BRIGADIER GENERAL STONE'S EXPERIENCE with the capriciousness of military authority was exceptional only for its scale. In a recent book that demonstrates the extraordinary value of deep research in disciplinary records, historian Jonathan White discovered a previously unnoticed reality of the most studied war in our history: The Lincoln administration and its generals used force and intimidation to shape the political views of men in the ranks. The worst of that imposition of political control through military discipline centered on the Emancipation Proclamation and the men in federal armies who disagreed with its purpose and power.

Like Stone, many Union soldiers found their military careers destroyed without anything resembling due process. A staff officer, Maj. John Key, was reported to his chain of command as having questioned the object of the war; Lincoln personally dismissed him from the army. The president's explanation made the matter distinctly personal, as he told Key that "no man shall bear a commission of mine, who is not in favor of gaining victories over the rebels." Key was in favor of precisely that, wanting to fight against secession despite his doubts about the emerging project of emancipation, and asked to go on fighting for the victories he was accused of opposing. But his dismissal was reported to the newspapers, creating an example to warn other men in uniform. Without having committed an act of disloyalty on the battlefield, he was publicly shamed as an officer who couldn't be trusted. His request for reinstatement was denied.

Other officers followed soon after. Maj. Charles Whiting was "overheard saying that the Republican emancipation policy would divide the North and unite the South and that Lincoln had violated the Constitution by freeing the slaves and suspending the writ of habeas corpus." His offense was an act of speech, not an act of disloyalty or a failure in the execution of his duties. But he was dishonorably discharged.

In other instances, officers took it upon themselves to question their subordinates regarding their political views, reporting critics and doubters to the War Department for dismissal. Still other officers were purged following complaints from soldiers and civilians. Col. John Warner of the 108th Illinois Volunteers was "summarily dismissed" after a letter from a neighbor in Peoria who revealed that his wife "expresses disloyal sentiments and alleges that her husband shares the same views." Yet again, no one claimed that Warner had behaved dishonorably in uniform, or demonstrated his disloyalty while leading soldiers at war; the allegation was hearsay about his wife, uninvestigated and accepted at face value.

To be sure, a few reckless soldiers did it to themselves. Two months after the Emancipation Proclamation went into effect, for a particularly vivid example offered by White's recent scholarship, an officer in the 42nd New York Volunteers poured out his heart in a private letter to a friend serving as a missionary in China. In an environment that made open criticism of the war effort dangerous, Lt. John Garland was sending his forbidden thoughts across an ocean, venting his anger in a safe direction. The proclamation was "unjust," he wrote, and the president had no authority to issue it. The Lincoln administration had proved that "their principles and their hearts are blacker than the 'nigger' they are fighting for." Garland had been transferred to the ambulance corps, and he celebrated the news as he relayed it to his friend in Shanghai; he would no longer fight Southerners, and could help their wounded on the battlefield, as he was already proud to have done. Sealing the self-revelation, Garland wrote that he had wept as he watched Union artillery shell Confederate positions.

The lieutenant understood the significance of his words. "Were it known that these were my sentiments," he wrote to his friend, "I would not only be summarily dismissed from the service, but probably boarded, at the expense of Uncle Sam, in Fort Lafayette, or some other sea-side prison, for the benefit of my health, until the war is over." Then he sealed the letter, added postage, and dropped it in the mail.

But Garland hadn't figured the postage correctly—he was short by fifty-four cents. Post-office employees spotted the mistake, and opened the envelope so they could find the identity of the sender and return the letter for proper postage. Reported to the army, Garland wasn't just dismissed: He was marched all the way out of West Virginia by armed guards.

In the middle of all this political tattling and summary purification of the army, some officers tried to establish something resembling due process to manage the removal of political dissenters from their ranks. In February 1863, still commanding the Army of the Tennessee, Maj. Gen. Ulysses Grant "established a board of examiners to remove disloyal officers." No law authorized or described a thing called a "board of examiners" that could be empowered to discharge officers from the American military on political grounds, but the board nevertheless went about its work. Assigned as its president, Col. Thomas Bennett of the 69th Indiana Volunteers wrote that "the army shall be purified." He performed his duties with enthusiasm.

"We will give the army a good *purge* and a healthy *puke* of all 'Copperheads,'" Bennett wrote to his state's adjutant general. "Resignations are 'played out' with such fellows; they are to be *kicked out*." Action didn't matter, and battlefield valor wasn't enough. The army expected ideological compliance, or a convincing simulation.

The rigidity of that expectation intensified in the months leading up to the presidential election of 1864—the first time in American history that soldiers were able to vote in large numbers while they were at war, as many states let them cast absentee ballots from the field. The Democratic candidate was the fired commander of the Army of the Potomac, Maj. Gen. George McClellan, running against the president who had relieved him of his command. McClellan ran on a personal pledge to keep fighting and win the war—but with a party platform demanding that "immediate efforts be made for a cessation of hostilities" as a prelude for negotiations with the South. For a long time, historians have treated Lincoln's reelection as a soldiers' referendum

on the conflict, a moment in which men at war rose up in democratic unison and chose to stay at war until they'd finished the job:
Peace Democrats wanted to quit, so the army turned Republican
and voted to fight. "War-weary rebel soldiers hoped fervently for
McClellan and peace," writes the important Civil War historian
James McPherson, but the Southern hunger for peace "provoked
opposite feelings among Union soldiers." They saw victory coming, and wanted to secure it. Absentee ballots cast in army camps
delivered a crushing majority for Lincoln, delivering 78 percent
of the vote from soldiers in the field.

But we've learned from Jonathan White's new scholarship that
the vote among Union soldiers tells a more complicated story.
First, soldiers were like everyone else: Their support for the war
wasn't a single sentiment, but a basket of mercurial views that
shifted with the course of events. "They wavered and ebbed,"
White writes. "Their feelings about the war improved in times of
success and dipped when things were going badly." And they were
guided by the same flawed sentiments that appeared in civilian
discourse on the war, as when the Michigan soldier Mack Ewing
wrote to his wife that "this war has become a niger war instead
of a union war." His wife wrote back and demanded that he vote
for Lincoln, and he quickly fell back into line. Families mattered;
men wrote home for advice about what they should do.

When soldiers couldn't find their enthusiasm for their commander in chief and the cause he led, though, Union armies
had a mechanism that allowed them to compel such enthusiasm. Nineteenth-century voting didn't take place by secret ballot. Instead, parties handed out their printed ballots, and voters
walked to the polling place with that ballot in hand—on display
for everyone they passed on their way there. Soldiers couldn't
vote against Lincoln without putting their choice on display, and
letters from soldiers show what happened next. Sergeants who
voted against the shared cause of the army were reduced to the

ranks, replaced by other men who had voted correctly. Privates who were too obviously anti-Lincoln in camp found themselves assigned to the front of later assaults on enemy positions.

And commanders found reasons to court-martial men whom they thought had voted (or tried to vote) for dishonorable peace while fighting a war. Pvt. Rufus Miller of the 75th Ohio Volunteers tried to take a Democratic ballot to the polling place in his camp, White writes, but couldn't find one. Then he went searching throughout the regiment, found a Democratic ballot, and returned to his company to vote—but had the ballot ripped out of his hand and torn to pieces by other soldiers. Insulted and manhandled, Miller said out loud that he'd rather vote for Jefferson Davis than for Lincoln. Pvt. Richard Lynch of the 12th Pennsylvania Cavalry said in public "that he was not in the Army as a soldier but as a Politician for McClellan." Lt. Edward Austin of the 50th New York Engineers told other soldiers he'd be "God damned" if he would vote for Lincoln, even to save the government. Like many others, they were tried by court-martial for their political declarations in the army. For soldiers in 1864, Republican political preference was an expectation that could be enforced with charges and a trial.

DESPITE ALL OF THE PRESSURES of the big army, the ethic of willing obedience survived its long trial by fire. It would still be in evidence at the end of the war, standing in opposition to newly developed institutional structures built on coercion.

Like Jackson's Tennessee militiamen in the earlier Creek War, many of the German immigrants who served as volunteer soldiers in the 7th New York believed that they could declare an end to their Civil War military obligation. In the very late moment of June 1865, finding themselves not yet released from the army despite the end of the fighting, soldiers began "making speeches in the barracks asking the men to stand together and refuse to do duty." The provost guard from another regiment made arrests, and broke up soldier meetings with their bayonets fixed, but the men being dispersed by force refused to abandon their argument. A private named Chasse, ordered by an officer to shut up, still asserted his claim openly and plainly: "I won't be quiet . . . My term of service has expired and I'm a free man."

In one kind of American military tradition, the officers of the 7th New York ended the near revolt quietly and patiently, exhorting rather than commanding. Like Blodget in Rhode Island, they declined to simply give orders. "The incident began with the action of the enlisted men," Lorien Foote writes, "and ended only with their consent." A captain suggested that his men "drill for a while" in a manly display of good order, and they agreed. Facing a possible mutiny, officers appealed to the pride of their subordinates, not to their fear of punishment. They asked men to consider how other men saw them, and invited them to publicly display their sense of discipline and duty as soldiers. Arrests by the provost guard made the atmosphere of disobedience worse; manly exhortation produced order. Asking was more immediately powerful than telling. Leading men who insistently believed that they had some degree of self-government in the ranks, shrewd officers could find that social discipline sometimes worked better than formal military discipline.

In the defeated South, soldiers also retained for themselves the right to decide when their war was over. After the critical surrender of the Army of Northern Virginia at Appomattox, Gen. Edmund Kirby Smith resolved to fight on with his own army in Texas, preserving the Confederate cause in an effort to secure a less painful defeat. So he addressed his soldiers, in writing, urging them to "stand by your colors." A strong army still in the field, he told his men, "will secure to our country terms, that a proud people can with honor accept." But the men he was addressing knew the war was over; as historian Mark Weitz writes, Smith's army "dissolved into the Texas countryside." He wrote them a final address, a letter to an army that wasn't there to receive it. They had, he told them, "voluntarily destroyed your organizations."

He was right. An army just went home, reflecting an authority that American soldiers had long believed themselves to possess.

And so the Civil War contains two stories about force and consent, each pushing against the other. Neither explains the entire war. It was two things at once, the coercive weight of a big army imperfectly reaching into the lives of men who sometimes declined to be coerced. Culture and manly self-presentation mattered: A man who chose to fight a war for cause and country couldn't be the same as a man who was forced, or who did it for money, and a man who fought with great courage couldn't be punished by the standards applied to a man who flinched from danger. These were not distinctions that could be found in the Articles of War, even as they affected their application. Formal rules, written in orders and enforced by authority, intertwined with social rules. It became difficult to see where one ended and the other began.

For better or worse, law didn't live on paper. It lived in the act of making it manifest; it took its actual form in the actions of the people who applied it. In giant bureaucracies of force, and in a long historical moment defined by power and coercion, social values and human choice insisted on their place in shaping events. In a nation turning toward a modern order structured by bureaucracy and coercion, the local and the personal persisted.

5

"AMENABLE TO MILITARY LAW"

Policing Civilians with Military Authority

LAW CREATES A SUPPOSED STRUCTURE, A SET OF RULES THAT imply a resulting system and a way to make it. Under the best of circumstances, that structure is more malleable than the rule of law suggests. In the chaos of a metastasizing war for existential stakes—the survival of a newly declared nation versus the preservation of an old and broken nation—the ambitions of law and the realities of the actual diverged all over American society during the Civil War. When governments put the tools of coercion to use, they often applied those tools in distinctly political and capricious ways. As Charles Pomeroy Stone discovered, the legal boundaries on government power could be thrown aside for someone who had become a target of the powerful. But the first target of this little-restrained military justice was the civilian population.

In the struggle between the North and South, soldiers began to arrest civilians before it was clear they were really at war. On April 12, 1861, only seven Southern states had seceded, and Lincoln hadn't called for volunteers to put down the rebellion by force. As the first shots of the war were fired at Fort Sumter that day, Brig. Gen. Braxton Bragg was far away, newly appointed to the nascent Confederate Army and placing artillery on the Gulf coast of Florida. Like the Southerners gathered around Charleston Harbor and Fort Sumter, Bragg was preparing to drive the US Army out of a coastal fortress: Fort Pickens, which sat on an island just off the coast of Pensacola, a stubborn outpost of the United States of America inside the new Confederacy. Thousands of volunteers poured into the area, anxious to help—an armed throng trying to become an army.

Newspaper correspondents flooded into Pensacola alongside the military volunteers, ready for a big story. No one knew what would happen next, but Fort Pickens was as likely a place for an armed confrontation as Fort Sumter. Witnesses thought they were gathering to watch the opening act of the new Confederate military. Among the newspaper reporters was the Irish immigrant Lawrence Mathews, an ardent secessionist who wrote for the *Pensacola Observer* and other newspapers. Mathews wanted war; he was a cheerleader, not a critic. "War is in everybody's mouth," he wrote in late March, cheerfully describing an event he hoped to see.

And then Mathews published a story saying that Bragg was about to take action to capture the fort, using the artillery he was already digging to put into place. It's not clear if Mathews's story reached the federal garrison, which might have just spotted or received word of the Confederate artillery being moved into position for a siege. But that same night, the US Navy landed reinforcements at Fort Pickens, and observers drew a connection: A story about a pending attack was followed by enemy preparations to meet that attack, so one caused the other. The next day, April 13, Mathews published another enthusiastic story. "Everything now indicates the solution to our difficulties by a resort to arms," he concluded. But it seemed that he had already thrown a wrench into the plans he was describing. The more he wrote about conquest, the better the fortress became defended.

Braxton Bragg was never in danger of being lauded for his

patience and kindness. During the Mexican War, his own troops had rolled bombs into his tent—twice—in failed attempts to kill a commander they regarded as a particularly dreadful martinet. At his own court-martial in 1844, the members of the court had found Bragg's demeanor so repellent that they announced their inclination to accept charges of disrespect to a superior officer despite the thinness of the evidence; defending his character, he had accidentally revealed it. And now he revealed his brittle character again, summoning Mathews to his headquarters on April 14 with the intention of arresting him. The situation was at least a little bit ambiguous. Bragg was preparing for a possible battle in a standoff that hadn't quite become a war, the US Army was still more of an antagonist than a plain enemy, and the fort could very well have been fortified for reasons that had nothing to do with Mathews and his stories.

But the general acted like the circumstances left no question. First he demanded that Mathews identify the source of the information he had reported about preparations for a siege. For someone who was digging positions for artillery batteries in front of an audience of citizens, the demand was just silly, and Mathews reasonably replied that it was "the general rumor for two days on the streets." Bragg accused him of writing the story to make it look like the information had come straight from his own headquarters, and then dropped his bomb on the journalist: "You are a traitor, sir."

For Mathews, whose eager reports uniformly cheered on the infinitely glorious Southern cause, the accusation of disloyalty came as an obvious shock. He responded in a rage: "General Bragg, whoever calls me traitor speaks falsely of me. I would shed my last drop of blood for the South." Among Southerners, these were fighting words: A man told another man that he had spoken falsely of him, the kind of charge that could lead to an affair of honor. He was giving Bragg the lie.

But Bragg wasn't thinking in those terms, evaluating speech as a gentleman speaking to a gentleman. Standing in his headquarters, in uniform, talking to someone he would surely have regarded as being beneath him on the social scale, he didn't take it personally—he took it militarily. "I place you under arrest, sir," he said. Most accounts of the exchange note that Mathews was a single father with a five-year-old son in Pensacola; Bragg ignored the child he was leaving momentarily fatherless, and sent Mathews under guard to the city that was still the Confederate capital, Montgomery. "Allow him no communications whatsoever," Bragg told the guards; the reporter would have no opportunity to arrange for a lawyer or settle his family affairs in the city. The event was quickly drained of all doubt and uncertainty: The *Charleston Mercury* reported that a "trifling fellow" suspected of being "a spy for the enemy" had been arrested.

This is exactly the kind of moment in which governments were still learning how to wage a war as they arrived on its threshold. No infrastructure existed to support military arrests, so Mathews was imprisoned on the top floor of Montgomery's best hotel. His military arrest wasn't followed by a military trial. Instead, he was briefly "tried" by the Confederate cabinet—who were mostly living alongside him in the same hotel—and quickly released, the accusations of treason and sedition refuted by his own published stories. But the message of his arrest would remain clear as war began in earnest: Civilians jeopardizing the Southern cause could be subject to military detention, however that sort of thing would turn out to work.

In the North, the early message was at least equally harsh, though the context was less ambiguous. The second wave of secession began a few days after Fort Sumter fell, as Lincoln called for military volunteers to force Southern states back into the federal union. On April 17, horrified by the federal recourse to armed coercion, Virginia seceded, with three other states following in the next two months. Border states teetered, and the threat to the federal government was clear: If the slave state of Maryland joined Virginia, then Washington, DC, would be cut off and indefensible, a federal island in a Confederate sea. The national capital would necessarily fall.

As a political standoff quickly became a military conflict, Northern states rushed volunteers to the District of Columbia. But those volunteers only had one remaining choice as they moved by land to DC: They had to pass through a state with a Southern identity and a desire to protect slavery. Mobs attacked Massachusetts and Pennsylvania troops passing through Baltimore. On April 19, soldiers of the 6th Massachusetts "marched through the city exchanging volleys with civilians who hid in upstairs windows." Four soldiers died, one beaten to death in the street. Maryland hadn't seceded, but its citizens didn't uniformly agree with that choice.

The desire to make local peace collided with the need to make national war. The governor of Maryland and the mayor of Baltimore both asked the federal government to stop moving troops through their jurisdictions, seeing the violence it caused and wanting to hold off the political controversy in a border state full of secessionists. But there was little choice. After April 17, the District of Columbia bordered on the Confederacy. It was right next to the enemy, and had to be defended. A series of meetings between city, state, and federal officials resulted in one concession, as Lincoln promised not to move troops through Baltimore. Soldiers already there would be withdrawn, and then regiments bound for DC would take a route through a less-populated part of the state.

Maryland officials decided to make that promise impossible to break. On April 22 and 23, as Pennsylvania troops left Baltimore, they were followed: Maryland militiamen from the Baltimore County Horse Guards traveled along the railway, burning

bridges and tearing up tracks. They were led by Lt. John Merryman, a prominent farmer who owned substantial land and a
handful of slaves. "Like the other members of his company, Merryman claimed that he was obeying orders intended to prevent
bloodshed in Maryland by keeping more federal troops from
passing through the state," writes historian Jonathan White. But
witnesses also heard him "utter sentiments against the government" and rant about Northerners who wanted to steal slaves
from the South. Whatever he said, he burned bridges with great
personal enthusiasm, forcing railroad employees to pile up kin-
dling at gunpoint and sometimes wielding the torch himself.

In one of the great ironies from these early moments of the
war, the Baltimore Horse Guards also spent their days rounding up the disloyal—using their own definition of loyalty. Rep-
resenting the armed force of a slave state that hadn't seceded,
Merryman and his subordinates arrested people who too openly
opposed secession. A corporal and a sergeant detained a Union-
ist carpenter in his home, pistols drawn, and took him to their
lieutenant; Merryman told him they wouldn't tolerate any more
talk of supporting federal troops. The moment, White writes,
"can be appreciated only in hindsight," with Merryman's own
arrest for disloyalty just days ahead of him.

Lincoln met the tide of secessionist sentiment and armed
interference with a clear assertion of power. On April 27, the
president drew a "military line" connecting Philadelphia and DC,
and gave his military commanders the authority to suspend the
writ of habeas corpus anywhere along that line. They could now
take civilians into custody, and they didn't have to worry that a
judge could make them stop. The federal government was going
to protect the movement of soldiers marching to defend the
capital. Commanders on the ground in Maryland began to use
military arrests as a political weapon, taking a secessionist state
legislator into military custody and contemplating further arrests

of state officials. Lincoln reacted with dismay, but his response was probably centered on practical considerations rather than principle—since the heavy-handed military arrests of state officials threatened to inflame secessionist sentiment in a critical border state. Feeling his way, Lincoln discouraged further military arrests without actually forbidding them. "Unless the *necessity* for these arbitrary arrests is *manifest* and *urgent*," he wrote, "I prefer they should cease." They didn't.

Quickly enough, soldiers making arrests in Maryland came to the militia lieutenant John Merryman, who had been busy making arrests himself. Historians assumed for almost a century and a half that Merryman's arrest was a direct result of his leadership in the effort to burn railroad bridges, but Jonathan White—the same historian who changed our understanding of the soldiers' vote in the 1864 presidential election—recently wrote another book that forces us to reconsider the case. Merryman was dragged from his bed by soldiers in the middle of the night, arrested at two a.m. on May 25, and imprisoned in a fortress, but the army taking him into custody hardly seemed to know why. "The military officers at Fort McHenry seemed ambivalent about what exactly their prisoner was charged with," White writes. "In truth, they had not been informed of why they were detaining him. . . . Nothing in these original 'charges' accused Merryman of burning railroad bridges or cutting telegraph wires, the accusations usually cited by historians." At ground level, ordinary soldiers who were busy taking citizens into military custody hardly knew why they had received orders to it.

Reviewing newspaper reports and war memoirs, White discovered the more likely cause of Merryman's arrest: His neighbors had reported him to the military. The lieutenant who had overseen the arrest of outspoken Unionists while he was out burning bridges was chosen for military confinement after other men in the area told army officers "that no more overbearing, intolerant, and bitter secessionist lives than John Merryman." A militia leader who arrested men for their acts of political speech was arrested by another military force for his own acts of political speech. Maryland militia units and federal army units were trying out a role as thought police, both sides arresting people for their view of the emerging war.

In the case of the federal government, there were no plans to end that role. Merryman petitioned for a writ of habeas corpus, and Supreme Court Justice Roger Taney, acting in his other role as a circuit court judge, granted it. But the executive branch and the courts were at odds: The great writ had been suspended locally on Lincoln's broad, permissive, and constitutionally dubious orders. An army officer appeared in the courtroom to explain that Maj. Gen. George Cadwalader would be ignoring the writ, and so wouldn't be delivering Merryman to the judge. Taney sent a US marshal to Fort McHenry to arrest Cadwalader for contempt; the soldiers declined to open the gate for him, and the marshal quietly rode back to tell the court.

Taney was a Southerner, a Democrat, and a defender of slavery, though he'd freed his own slaves. His reaction to the acts of a Republican administration was surely motivated by partisan sentiment and sectional politics. But the written opinion on the case that he read to a crowded courtroom wasn't wrong. Civil courts were open and functioning in Maryland, and the power to suspend habeas corpus is found in Article I of the Constitution—the article that describes the powers of Congress, not the authority of the president. Lincoln, and his generals, had reached beyond their legal authority. Taney warned that the powers conferred upon the judiciary by the Constitution had been "usurped by military power"; under the circumstances, he concluded, "the people of the United States are no longer living under a government of laws, but every citizen holds life, liberty and property at the will of the army officer in whose district he may happen to be found." That was certainly true for Merryman, who had been arrested by the military because soldiers heard he was a secessionist.

Among the people who quietly agreed with Taney was a federal judge named John Cadwalader—the brother of the general who had refused to honor Taney's writ for Merryman. John wrote a private letter to his brother, arguing that the writ had been appropriately issued under the law. But he also suggested a way out, giving the Lincoln administration a way to avoid a collision between military power and judicial authority: Declare Merryman a prisoner of war rather than a civilian in military custody, explicitly imprisoning him as a militia officer with secessionist sentiments and a record of direct action against military preparations. Everyone who could have taken that advice ignored it. Neither the administration nor the army wanted to avoid the collision that John Cadwalader was trying to avoid. They had caused that collision and moved through it, and the conclusion they had drawn was perfectly clear: The army could make whatever arrests it wished to make, and ignore any judge who bothered to complain. What could they do about it? "Lincoln, in effect, gutted *Ex parte Merryman* of any legal significance and determined that as long as the war lasted *Merryman* would have no practical effect," White concludes.

The military started arresting civilians. A court said they couldn't. They did it anyway. And the courts couldn't stop them.

The army had learned how far it could go.

IN THE CATACLYSM that followed, the military arrest of civilians became unremarkable. And Braxton Bragg's first target remained a favorite on both sides of the war—so much so that a book about William Tecumseh Sherman's relationship with the press is titled *Sherman's Other War*. Newspapers were frequently wrong, given to hysteria and overwrought speculation. But generals could find their coverage more infuriating when they were right. And then there was the third possibility, in which reasonably accurate information was inflated beyond its actual meaning. For Sherman, who had sat out part of the war with a well-publicized nervous breakdown, newspapers were especially infuriating; "General William T. Sherman Insane," a headline had read. He took journalism personally because it was personal.

Near the end of 1862, back on active duty and commanding the right wing of Ulysses S. Grant's army in Mississippi, Sherman prepared his part of the vital effort to capture Vicksburg. Laying plans to control the *other* enemy, he issued General Order No. 8, barring civilians from joining the force moving against the city's defenses through the Chickasaw Bayou. There was only one kind of civilian who wanted to do such a thing, and Sherman's purpose was perfectly clear. "Punishment was set at conscription," writes historian John Marszalek, and any reporter writing about the expedition from inside Sherman's divisions "would be arrested and treated as a spy." Sherman was issuing military orders to the press, in a mix of personal distaste and tactical security. "No news could reach the enemy if there was no one present to write it up and see that it was published," Marszalek writes. Neither could any detailed reports of leadership failures or tactical mishaps reach the Northern public.

Predictably, the press signaled its intention to ignore him; reporters kept showing up to cover a story the general didn't want covered. Sherman found out, and issued new orders conscripting them as ammunition bearers, ordering them to the front lines. They ignored him again. Declining to be excluded, reporters were present to watch Sherman fail in the swamps protecting the approach to Vicksburg, getting both an intimate look at pieces of a single battle and little insight into its context. The press that had declared Sherman crazy now declared him a disaster in combat, and a familiar word crept back into their coverage: His plan for the assault had been "insane." Among the most virulent critics was a correspondent for the *New York Herald*, Thomas Knox. "Insanity and inefficiency have brought their result," he wrote.

So Sherman—true to his word—had Knox court-martialed as a spy. Writing to his brother, Sen. John Sherman, he explained that he had decided to bring a journalist before a military court "to establish the fact that all civilians whatsoever who follow an army are amenable to Military Law." He was putting a civilian on trial in a military court to show that he could put civilians on trial in military court.

The charges against Knox required something like the kind of invention that Andrew Jackson had used to try a state senator for libel and disobedience before a court-martial. He was, among other things, put on trial for publishing "sundry and various false allegations and accusations against the Officers of the Army of the United States, to the great detriment of the interest of the National Government and comfort of our enemies." Sherman made himself America. To defame him was to aid the nation's enemies; not liking William Tecumseh Sherman was treason. Knox had also been "knowingly and willfully" disobedient of the general's orders, the charges declared, as if he had enlisted and had Sherman as a commander.

But Sherman also had a stronger foundation for his actions than Jackson had been given, built from national policy. One of the other charges brought against Knox had been a threat hanging over the press since the first year of the war, but had been a manageable problem for journalists until Sherman became the first commander to make it really unmanageable. For decades, the Articles of War had forbidden soldiers from passing information to whatever enemy they happened to be fighting: "Whosoever shall be convicted of holding correspondence with or giving intelligence to the enemy either directly or indirectly, shall suffer death or such other punishment as shall be ordered by the sentence of a court martial," Article 57 said.

And then, in the early wartime moment of August 21, 1861, Secretary of War Simon Cameron applied Article 57—a law regulating the behavior of soldiers—to the entire American population. Cameron's General Order No. 67 required that "all correspondence" regarding military operations and troop movements be given the "sanction of the general in command" of the appropriate military district before being sent—by mail, telegraph, or any other mode of communication. Ordinary people would also be arrested for communicating with the enemy when they wrote to family members in Confederate armies, but the order had a particular effect on the press. To publish detailed information about the war was to give intelligence to the other side, an act akin to spying. In effect, reporters could be tried as turncoat soldiers, held to account under the Articles of War for the operation of the free press. Picking up that premise, Sherman charged Knox with violating Article 57. The reporter had given the names of division commanders and "the strength of one division," publishing without the general's permission. He had, Sherman decided, passed information to the enemy.

Except for one problem: Sherman, the only prosecution witness at Knox's trial, couldn't say which information had reached which enemy force. He had made up the charge in a snit against a reporter who'd called him an idiot in print, and spent two ugly days on the witness stand sputtering that he just knew Southerners got Northern newspapers. It wasn't good enough for the court, though it was a moment and a setting in which they could easily have disregarded the supposed legal standard in a trial they had dubious authority to conduct. "The prosecution had to prove that Knox's article had actually been copied and that the enemy had actually seen it," Marszalek writes. "Suppositions about articles in general, even when corroborated, were irrelevant."

Like the 1815 court-martial that tried Louis Louaillier in New Orleans, the members of Knox's court-martial exercised greater restraint than the general who had convened them. Declining to treat the reporter as a spy or a disobedient soldier, they dismissed one charge, then found him not guilty on all but one of the remaining counts. In particular, they decided, he hadn't violated Article 57. On the final count, a charge that he had ignored Sherman's order excluding civilians from his army, the court found the facts proved—but concluded that it "attaches no criminality thereto." He did it, but it wasn't a crime. Sherman, his own subordinates decided, didn't have the authority to issue direct orders to people who weren't under his command; journalists could disregard his orders without becoming criminals.

Having found Knox guilty of nothing at all, though, the court then pronounced a sentence: The reporter would be arrested if he remained inside the army's lines. They cleared him of criminal wrongdoing, then banished him. For Sherman, it was a horrible loss and a magnificent victory. He got rid of Knox, and few newspapers dared to complain. He set a precedent in fact without having set one in law. The headlines about the Union Army's lunatic general began to fade away, aided by Sherman's later victories.

The general's series of reactions reveal the important subtext lurking under the conflict, as he first raged over the court-martial's failure—and there was no question that he saw it as a failure—to convict a journalist of military offenses. The freedom of the press to operate inside military lines, he wrote to Grant's headquarters, "will continue to defeat us to the end of time." But then Knox wrote to him, trying to fix their conflict and talk his way back onto the battlefield. Sherman wrote back, refusing absolutely to repair the breach:

"Come with sword or musket in your hand," he wrote, "prepared to share with us our fate, in sunshine and storm, in prosperity and adversity, in plenty and scarcity and I will welcome you as brother and associate."

Until then? "Never."

This is a story often told in the heat of war, a narrative of insiders against outsiders. Men were dying, joined together for a cause and suffering in its service. Journalists were just an audience, sitting outside the thing soldiers shared between them, shamefully observing "no slight difference between truth and falsehood" as they described the efforts better men made in the service of their purpose. A man who would take up arms would become one of them, a part of a shared effort and its great doses of pain and loss.

To Sherman—to soldiers—this was a choice too obvious to argue for: You just did it. To choose not to fight during a war was to shirk, to evade, to hide. Sherman was making his categories too neat, and journalists paid for the war in many ways. The *New York Times* reporter Sam Wilkeson wrote a front-page dispatch on the Battle of Gettysburg from his spot at the freshly dug grave of the artillery officer Lt. Bayard Wilkeson—his own son, just killed in that battle. Other journalists were held as prisoners of war, and still others were killed in combat. The *Chicago Tribune* reporter Irving Carson was decapitated by a cannonball at Shiloh, where Sherman had commanded a division.

As he worked to capture Vicksburg, though, the general wasn't in the mood to see that point. To at least some degree, William Tecumseh Sherman court-martialed the journalist Thomas Knox for failing the choice he expected of a man. Reporters weren't soldiers, and they had to be punished for that transgression. Like Andrew Jackson in an earlier war, Sherman expected mutuality and a manly acceptance of duty: *Of course* every man would rush to fight for his country. But not every man would, and the instinctual warrior had no way to understand the other choice. As a commander in the armed forces, the court-martial gave him a way to do something about it. The legal limits of military jurisdiction were, once again, not really the point.

THE MILITARY also used arrests and military courts to control domestic politics in the North, repressing internal criticism of the war. The ironies of that effort make for low-hanging fruit: The war being fought for a "new birth of freedom" produced some remarkably blunt suppression of fundamental political liberty. On January 14, 1863, the Ohio Democrat Clement Vallandigham was on his way out of the House of Representatives, his seat carefully gerrymandered to prevent his reelection. At the end of his last term in office, Vallandigham delivered a parting shot from the House floor—a stem-winder of a speech now known by the title "On the War and Its Conduct." The war was going poorly, with the disaster at Fredericksburg just a month in the past, and some of his final address to his colleagues focused on the apparent futility of national reunification by arms. "The Union," he said, "is not restored. . . . You have not conquered the South. You never will." In short, Lincoln's war was "a most bloody and costly failure."

But Vallandigham also focused on the domestic costs of a total war between Americans. The "iron domination of arbitrary power" had come down hard across the North, he charged. "Constitutional limitation was broken down; habeas corpus fell; liberty of the press, of speech, of the person, of the mails, of travel, of one's own house, and of religion; the right to bear arms, due process of law, judicial trial, trial by jury, trial at all; every badge and muniment of freedom in republican government or kingly government—all went down at a blow."

And then his congressional term was over, and he went home to Ohio—as the most prominent antiwar Democrat in the country, the nation's best-known Copperhead. Determined to run for governor, Vallandigham sustained his high public profile as a critic of the war with a speaking tour built around the themes of his final speech in the House. He went from crowd to crowd, damning the war as it was being fought.

A civilian, Vallandigham ran headlong into another order from an army general that treated the whole population as the subjects of military authority. On April 13, 1863, Maj. Gen. Ambrose Burnside, the commander of the Department of the Ohio, issued General Order No. 38: "The habit of declaring sympathies for the enemy will not be allowed in this Department. Persons committing such offenses will be at once arrested, with a view to being tried as above stated, or sent beyond our lines into the lines of their friends." They would, in other words, be exiled to the Confederacy. Military commanders had granted themselves the power to decide what political sentiments civilians would be allowed to express, and to throw their critics out of the country.

Vallandigham's subsequent trial by military commission reads like an Escher lithograph: A civilian, he was arrested by the military for publicly claiming that the military was arresting civilians over the things they said in public. The first witness called to testify against the former congressman was a military officer, Capt. H. R. Hill, who had been in the audience for one of his speeches. The captain had taken notes as Vallandigham spoke, and now read his notes on the speech to the court. "He said that 'it was the purpose or desire of the Administration to suppress or prevent such meetings as the one he was addressing,'" Hill testified. It was—the speech took place under military surveillance. Vallandigham's crime was to describe the very thing that was actually happening.

Disloyalty could be shown without saying a word; just as important as the content of the speech was the nature of the audience Vallandigham had addressed. "I saw hundreds of them wearing butternuts," Hill testified, describing the dully colored, homespun clothing that marked Southern sympathizers. The military could also take action against the political implications of the wrong kind of shirt; a Northern audience that chose to dress like Southerners was dangerous, and soldiers would control what kinds of speeches they would be allowed to hear.

Rising to object to the trial, Vallandigham told the members of the court a series of things they already knew: He had been arrested by soldiers, taken into custody without a warrant from a judge, and thrown into a military prison, despite the fact that he wasn't in the military. He was, he insisted, "entitled to be tried on an indictment or presentment of a Grand Jury," and "by an impartial jury of the State of Ohio." But the court had no interest in jurisdictional questions or constitutional limits on its authority. Vallandigham, an active candidate for public office, was sentenced "to be placed in close confinement in some fortress of the United States, to be designated by the commanding officer of this Department, there to be kept during the continuance of the war."

Publicly claiming that the right to free speech and trial by jury had been shoved aside by military power, Clement Vallandigham was sentenced to indefinite detention by the army after a trial conducted by military officers. The response to his premise proved his premise. The Supreme Court declined to take up his case, unable to find its authority to intervene against a military commander exercising his authority in a military district.

But the effort to police domestic politics during wartime was itself political, and required a balancing of intentions and effects. Seeing the problem of validating a critic's complaints, and being seen by the public to validate them, Lincoln reduced Vallandigham's sentence. The administration wouldn't continue to imprison the most prominent symbol of internal dissent. Vallandigham was marched to Confederate lines and handed over to the South, delivered like an unwanted parcel to the side he had supposedly taken in the war. It didn't stick: He worked his way up to Canada by ship, and went on running for governor from a spot just across Lake Erie.

Then the supposed danger neutralized itself. Vallandigham was wrong about the future while being right in many ways about the growth of government power in the present. He had forecast that the South would never be defeated by armed force, that Vicksburg would never fall, that the Mississippi River would never be reopened under Northern control, and a host of other predictions that seemed reasonable enough during the early months of 1863. A few months later, the Confederate invasion of Pennsylvania had been crushed at Gettysburg, Vicksburg had fallen to siege, and the tide of the war had turned. It didn't matter what Vallandigham said about the war anymore. To much of the Northern public, he had become ridiculous. His trial by a military court, an effort designed to prevent him from speaking in public, hadn't marginalized him as a political force; rather, the things he said in public had marginalized him as a political force. A well-fought war was more politically powerful than the military suppression of wartime criticism.

Still, the habits of martial law were hard to break, and continued beyond the end of the war in many ways. In April of 1865, soldiers pursued Lincoln's assassin, and arrested his fellow conspirators, under an investigation ordered and overseen by Secretary of War Edwin Stanton. By the end of June, when a military commission handed down death sentences to four conspirators, the war was effectively over; the last Confederate army in the field surrendered earlier that month. In the absence of war, and with civil courts open and functioning, the army nevertheless tried, convicted, and executed its prisoners.

Respect for the rule of law bent to the urgent wish for retribution. Presented with a writ of habeas corpus from a federal judge on the day before the scheduled hanging of the four condemned conspirators, President Andrew Johnson brushed it aside. "I hereby declare that the writ of habeas corpus is suspended in cases such as this," he wrote, on the basis of no legal authority but the fact that he felt like doing it. On the afternoon of July 7, the four were taken to the gallows by soldiers and hanged. The war was over, and civil courts were open for business, but the army continued to impose its own justice on civilians.

IN THE SOUTH, civilians were no less subject to the military regulation of their lives, though it wore a different mask. The great irony for people who framed the choice of war in the language of states' rights was that fighting their war required considerable centralization of power. Throwing off the authority of the US government, Southerners found themselves subject to the expansive wartime authority of the Confederate government. "War is the health of the state," twentieth-century journalist Randolph Bourne would correctly conclude, and it was as true for the Confederacy as it has been in other places.

In particular, the erosion of Southern armies from a growing wave of desertion would lead officials to impose a domestic passport system on public travel, forcing ordinary people to apply to the government to get on a train. As historian Mark Neely Jr. argues, white Southerners had an exact comparison ready to hand as authority figures imposed tight controls on their movements through the operation of travel passes. "The odious system exposed white Southerners to the erosion of liberty certain to remind them of the perils of slavery. In Southern society before the war, slaves and free African Americans needed passes to travel, and free white people did not," he writes. War symbolically made slaves; the wartime regulation of Southern society imposed controls on people who associated those controls with a status they despised.

No one has looked more closely at the Southern military regulation of civilians during the Civil War than Neely, who spent years in the archives looking for Southerners arrested by their own armies. He found 4,100—whom he could identify by name. There are surely many others whose lives have vanished from the surviving record.

Differences of appearance between the North and South can make the use of wartime military authority look different to us. In the South, the use of military commissions was gradually abandoned, for example, while officials in the North never developed any wartime reluctance to try civilians in front of army tribunals. But the Confederate government was euphemizing more than it was abandoning a hated practice, and a new official called a habeas corpus commissioner examined civilian prisoners of the military to decide who could be released from army captivity. Most tellingly, the office of the habeas corpus commissioner was created by a modest bit of subterfuge: The office was created by executive authority as a volunteer post, so the War Department could establish it without approaching the legislature for funding—"and thus having to explain to the legislators exactly what the department was doing to civilians." By the time the Confederate Congress authorized the office, in one of the provisions of the Habeas Corpus Act of October 13, 1862, Neely writes, "War Department officials had already been interrogating political prisoners for a year."

Southern prisoners were held by the military as the parallel of Northern Copperheads; the phrase Neely found over and over again in Confederate records of civilian prisoners detained by soldiers was "Union man." And their detention could be fatal, as it was for a Virginia resident named Samuel Simmers, who was held in a Richmond military prison in the summer of 1862. An investigation by the War Department cleared the prison commandant of culpability in the death, but vague records meant that no one could be sure why Simmers had been arrested by the military—or why he had died in its custody. In any case, the commander of the Eastern District Military Prison had more than 5,000 prisoners in his care, a mix of Northern POWs and Southern civilians, and "could hardly be censured for losing track of this one citizen." It was an argument that would be repeated: The commander of the facility was Capt. Henry Wirz, who would go on to run the POW prison at Andersonville—and to be executed over the conditions there.

The wartime South, like the wartime North, developed a nasty informer culture, a virus of petty tattling that could have dire consequences. Examining Confederate military detentions, Neely writes with quiet understatement that the supporting evidence was "rarely strong." And much of it seems to have come from backbiting and local feuds. Like John Merryman, the Virginia farmer John Gilliland was turned in by a neighbor, Mary Peters, who told a local justice of the peace that he had engaged in sedition: He said in a discussion that the South had no right to secede. Examining the matter from his office in Richmond, the Confederate habeas corpus commissioner concluded that the case was weak enough to simply be sent back to the Greenbrier County courts. By the time he reached that conclusion, though, that county "was not then under Confederate control"; Gilliland lingered in military prison, waiting for the sedition trial that his local court couldn't give him.

Other cases uncovered by Neely pile up into a litany of the picayune. Dr. Charles Thatcher, for example, was imprisoned by the Confederate military for making the seditious claims that Richmond would one day be surrounded by Union armies, and the Confederacy would eventually be militarily defeated. By that standard, Robert E. Lee probably committed sedition in his heart on a number of sleepless nights. Charles Thatcher was perceived to be disloyal because he knew how to count guns and men, in a tenuous new nation that wanted to survive.

THE DEATH OF the Southern cause ended the application of Confederate military justice, but it would take a full year after the end of the war to reestablish the ordinary functioning of civil justice in the North—though the case that ended peacetime military rule reached back into wartime.

Like Clement Vallandigham, the prominent Indiana lawyer Lambdin Milligan was an antiwar Democrat with political ambitions, though he never won any of the offices he sought. In October of 1864, Milligan was tried by a military commission in Indiana, accused of a plot that was either farcical and real or farcical and mostly concocted in an atmosphere of wartime hysteria. The official recorder of the army tribunal that tried Milligan would later publish the record of his trial with an introductory note calmly explaining that the transcript revealed "a more perfidious, and, perhaps, more gigantic conspiracy than is found in the annals of any nation"; more soberly, and more recently, historian Frank Klement examined the activities of antiwar secret societies and concluded that the stories of their danger to the nation was "embroidered with many rumors and much hearsay, some incidental, some contrived."

Whichever it was, Milligan was supposedly a major general in a secret army that was preparing to march as a fifth column inside the Old Northwest, rising in common cause with the Confederacy. By 1864, when Milligan was arrested, the combat-hardened Union armies would have made short work of such a thing, if it really existed. But the lawyer was still taken to represent a serious threat, and the military commission held at Indianapolis sentenced him to death for a laundry list of charges that included disloyalty and fomenting a rebellion. Asked by Milligan's supporters in the Indiana legal community to issue a writ of habeas corpus, the circuit court split, and the case went to the Supreme Court for a decision—slowly. Milligan's supporters presented their petition to the circuit court in May of 1865; the case was argued before the Supreme Court in March of 1866; and then the court announced the substance of its decision the next month, ordering Milligan's release, but didn't deliver its full opinion until December.

While Milligan waited for a decision, the federal government was busy using postwar military commissions to try former Confederate military officers, and Jefferson Davis sat in a military prison. But victors' justice began to go wrong in ways that made government officials question the value of army courts in settling the outcome of a war. Capt. Henry Wirz, the commander of the POW camp at Andersonville, Georgia, was convicted and hanged for the deaths of thousands of captive Union soldiers, but his military trial had the unintended rhetorical effect of turning those deaths into the product of mere personal evil rather than the effect of wartime policy. Other Confederate officials, including subordinate officials at Andersonville, escaped scrutiny, as did the federal government's decision in 1864 to put a stop to the prisoner exchanges that would have freed Union troops from captivity.

In other trials by military commission, Confederate officers and guerilla warriors were acquitted on war-crimes charges, or had charges dropped. And federal officials found themselves in conflict over the propriety of putting their defeated enemies on trial at all, particularly under the terms of surrender agreements that had released them to go home in peace. "Most of all," writes John Fabian Witt, "the commissions seemed not to be targeting the leaders of the Confederacy, but to be scapegoating its minor players." Military commissions were for a time available as a forum for examining secession and the Confederate conduct of the war, but that never meant that they worked well or produced anything resembling real justice.

And then the Supreme Court took away military commissions as a forum for government power, allowing Americans to stop asking political questions about their use. Overturning Milligan's military conviction, and preventing the army from executing him, the court made an important concession about the timing of their decision. "During the late wicked Rebellion," wrote Associate Justice David Davis, an Illinois politician who had been appointed to the court by Lincoln, "the temper of the times did not allow that calmness in deliberation and discussion so necessary to a correct conclusion of a purely judicial question." The justices simply couldn't have analyzed the law while shots were being fired, a justice announced; their capacity for that kind of judgment had been driven beneath the fury of the moment. The court made explicit its wartime deference to executive authority: *We couldn't even* think *about this stuff during the war.*

With the war over, though, the Supreme Court was ready to consider how the law should have operated. "No graver question was ever considered by this court," Davis wrote, and the conclusion of the majority was unambiguous and important:

> The Constitution of the United States is a law for rulers and people, equally in war and in peace, and covers with the shield of its protection all classes of men, at all times and under all circumstances. No doctrine involving more pernicious consequences was ever invented by the wit of man than that any of its provisions can be suspended during any of the great exigencies of government. Such a doctrine leads directly to anarchy or despotism, but the theory of necessity on which it is based is false, for the government, within the Constitution, has all the powers granted to it which are necessary to pre-

serve its existence, as has been happily proved by the result of the great effort to throw off its just authority.

This decision, and the clarity of the carefully delayed opinion, lives on in our own experience. You can criticize a president or a general during a war without worrying that you'll end up in front of a military commission like Clement Vallandigham—though it's also possible that future military detention may not be blocked as courts again discover that the temper of the times doesn't allow the necessary calmness in deliberation and discussion to stop it.

Then, too, even this moment of victory for the rule of law was marked by a significant note of ambiguity. While the court's decision was unanimous—Milligan should not have been tried by a military tribunal, and had to be released—its decision over the particulars split, 5 to 4. In a separate opinion, Chief Justice Salmon Chase argued that Milligan had been improperly tried by a military tribunal. But that conclusion, he warned, didn't mean that there weren't circumstances under which other civilians might properly be tried and sentenced by the same kind of panel. "We think that Congress had power, though not exercised, to authorize the military commission which was held in Indiana," Chase wrote.

Even as the Supreme Court freed a civilian who had been condemned to death by a military commission, then, a substantial number of its justices believed that there was nothing inherently or necessarily wrong with that exercise of military jurisdiction over people who never served in the armed forces. The door to military trials was closed, but almost half of the Supreme Court wasn't sure that it should always be kept that way.

As Witt points out, the argument about the use of military commissions to try civilians during the Civil War was no longer really an argument about the Civil War. It was an argument about Reconstruction and the ability to use military authority in the South after the war. The federal government had discovered a power it didn't want to give up, even as it proved difficult to put that power to reliable and effective use. With the Supreme Court's decision in *Ex Parte Milligan*, government officials lost the easy use of a broken tool that they had wanted to keep using anyway.

6

"ALL THAT SAVORED OF THE OVERSEER"

Black Soldiers in the Nineteenth Century

WHEN JOSEPH MILLER RAN FROM SLAVERY IN OCTOBER OF 1864, the Emancipation Proclamation didn't offer him freedom. Along with his wife and four children, Miller lived in Kentucky, a border state that hadn't seceded—and Lincoln's proclamation only applied to states in a condition of rebellion. Legally a fugitive, with few safe places to go, Miller enlisted in the 124th US Colored Infantry. Military service offered a set of things he needed to survive: food, shelter, clothing, and work that would protect him from reenslavement. And it saved his family alongside him, as they settled into a tent inside the limits of his camp. As Miller would later remind the army in a sworn statement, his wife and children had joined him by the "express permission" of the officer who had sworn him into the ranks. Hundreds of other escaped slaves joined them, while their husbands, sons, brothers, and fathers joined the wartime army.

In late November, though, Brig. Gen. Speed Fry ordered his subordinates to clear Camp Nelson of hangers-on. It was winter, and "bitter cold." Miller's seven-year-old son had been sick, and had barely begun to recover. "I was certain that it would Kill my sick child to take him out in the cold," Miller's statement reads. "I told the man in charge that it would be the death of my boy."

But the officer in charge of the eviction had clear orders, and he told the family to get into the cart that was waiting to carry them out of the camp. If they didn't climb on, Miller remembered the other man saying, "he would shoot the last one of them." They left.

At the end of the duty day, Miller walked out past the lines and went looking for his family. He found them six miles away, in a village, cold and hungry—with the body of the seven-year-old whose death he had correctly predicted. Miller walked back to camp to avoid being absent without leave. The next night, he walked back to the town. "I dug a grave myself and buried my own child," he said in his statement to the army. Then he left his family in the village again and walked back to camp.

Miller never saw his wife or his other three children again, but he eventually learned what had happened to them after he buried his son and returned to duty. Historians Richard Sears and Jim Downs have both described the experience of the Miller family: His wife, Isabella, and another son died together three weeks later, followed soon after by the death of his daughter, Maria. "Then a day after the New Year, Miller's only remaining child, Calvin, passed away," Downs writes.

Protests poured in from officers who were watching the families of soldiers suffer and die, and newspaper reports lashed out at an army that was sending women and children to their needless deaths. By the end of November, Fry's superiors ordered him to shelter the families of soldiers, and troops at Camp Nelson began to build structures to house them. But it was too late for Miller. He died on January 6, 1865, broken and sickened, "just a few days after the death of his youngest son." A whole family died over the course of a month, six people who went quickly from slavery to death. Joseph Miller died in uniform, a soldier.

The Civil War resulted in the emancipation of 4 million slaves, a celebrated outcome that nevertheless left necessary questions dangerously unanswered. As Downs argues in *Sick from Freedom*, our conception of the end of slavery in the United States has been plagued by "the misunderstanding that emancipation led directly to 'freedom.'" Neither the Emancipation Proclamation nor the later Thirteenth Amendment said what was supposed to happen *next*; the first, a wartime document, provided for the release of slaves from bondage, but "contained no provisions for how they would survive in the midst of war." Instead, in the rapid course of a very few years, freed slaves were dumped into an economy and an environment in which no place had been prepared for them. Four million people: no place to go.

One of the first places freed slaves went was the army—so the army was one of the first institutions to puzzle through the problem of where and how they would fit into the rewoven fabric of American life. Black men had served in small numbers during America's early conflicts, but weren't welcome in the army at the beginning of the Civil War. Military service was the honored duty of citizens; to be a soldier was to be fully a man, invested with membership in political society. Defining the armed body of the people in 1792, Congress had required the militia service of "each and every free able-bodied white male citizen," explicitly establishing who was supposed to carry the rights and burdens of the American order. White Americans—North and South alike—were not ready to widely extend that status to black men in 1861, though a few hundred were already serving in the navy as the war began.

By 1862, though, as the full scope of the Civil War was becoming horrifyingly clear, it became harder for political and military leaders to avoid noticing an available pool of military recruits. Halting efforts to recruit black soldiers began even before the practice was officially authorized, but Congress formalized the process with the Militia Act of July 1862. The president, the law read, "is hereby authorized to receive into the service of the

United States, for the purpose of constructing intrenchments, or performing camp service or any other labor, or any military or naval service for which they may be found competent, persons of African descent."

By the fall, the government was actively recruiting black soldiers, and their presence within the army had become policy—in the form of black regiments led by white officers. On January 1, 1863, Lincoln's Emancipation Proclamation declared the freedom of slaves held in states that remained in rebellion. "And I further declare and make known," the president added, "that such persons of suitable condition, will be received into the armed service of the United States to garrison forts, positions, stations, and other places, and to man vessels of all sorts in said service." Emancipation had military utility, taking a laboring population from the South and arming it against the Confederacy. By the end of the war, nearly 180,000 black men would serve in the army—many of them newly freed slaves—and another 18,000 would join the navy, where crews were integrated and sailors received equal pay.

In the army, though, equality of obligation didn't extend to equality of status. Standard pay for army privates was $13 a month, plus an additional allowance for clothing, and some black soldiers had enlisted at that rate. But the new law required that "persons of African descent, who under this law shall be employed, shall receive ten dollars per month and one ration, three dollars of which monthly pay may be in clothing." Seven dollars a month in cash: black soldiers would make just over half the monthly pay of white soldiers.

For men who had enlisted and trained for combat, it seemed like a sick joke—especially for those early recruits who now found their pay reduced. Many refused to draw their unequal pay, and the pain of that inequality extended to families that had lost breadwinners to the army with no source of support to replace their labor. "The men are not discouraged," wrote Sgt. Maj. James Trotter of the 55th Massachusetts, "though often sad when thinking of the necessities of a dear wife and little ones and other beloved ones at home whom they have no power to relieve." Volunteering to fight, men found that the choice had cost them their ability to support their own families.

While they were offered unequal pay, black soldiers served under white officers, and were subject to brutal physical discipline that could remind them of slavery. And the danger they faced was similarly unequal. On December 24, 1862, as federal officials recruited black soldiers, Confederate president Jefferson Davis issued his infamous General Order No. 111. The recruitment of slaves to fight against their masters, he wrote, represented an official policy "to excite servile war." The Confederacy declined to view black men in the uniform of the enemy as soldiers, subject to the usual protections of the laws of war; they would only be regarded as armed slaves, just as if they were engaged in a violent revolt on a plantation.

That choice would have dire consequences. Assigned to the status of slaves engaged in servile insurrection, black soldiers captured by Southern forces would be subject to death, or to reenslavement with brutal punishment. The supposed slave revolt formulated within the US Army could only be deterred "by the terms of just retribution." And so, General Order No. 111 decreed, "all negro slaves captured in arms"—meaning all black soldiers—would be "at once delivered over to the executive authorities of the respective States to which they belong to be dealt with according to the laws of said States." Davis was leaving the denouement unspoken, but state laws about slave revolts were unambiguously harsh.

The Confederate president's next measure extended the threat of retribution to "all commissioned officers of the United States when found serving in company with armed slaves in insurrection against the authorities of the different States of this Confederacy." The South would take no prisoners from African American regiments. Black soldiers captured on the battlefield would be enslaved or killed, and their officers would be executed—treated as a dangerous abolitionist rabble inciting slaves to rise against their masters, not as military officers fighting under the laws of war.

Confederate military leaders mostly didn't put that policy into action, in part because some refused to descend to that level of brutality. Very shortly before Davis issued his order, Gen. P.G.T. Beauregard sought guidance from the Confederate War Department regarding the captured black soldiers in his custody. Anticipating the policy of his president, Secretary of War James Seddon responded with orders for Beauregard to summarily execute his prisoners. Sensibly fearing Northern retribution, the general quietly declined to follow policy; his captives remained in custody, passed back and forth between state and military authorities "with the scantest fare and most miserable conditions," until the Union Army captured Charleston. "Neither the Confederacy nor the state had ever notified the Union authorities of their identity," the lawyer Howard Westwood wrote. "They had been non-persons."

But the fate of its captured soldiers wasn't a matter the US government was just going to leave to its enemy, and Lincoln restrained the Southern policy of retribution with one of his own. In his proclamation of July 30, 1863, the president declared that "for every soldier of the United States killed in violation of the laws of war, a rebel soldier shall be executed; and for every one enslaved by the enemy or sold into slavery, a rebel soldier shall be placed at hard labor on the public works." If Southerners killed and enslaved Northern prisoners, the North would kill and enslave Southern prisoners.

For some Confederate officers, the way around the legal and institutional debate over the status of black prisoners and their officers was to not take them as prisoners in the first place. In 1863, hearing that Confederate troops had captured "negroes in arms" at the Battle of Milliken's Bend in Louisiana, Lt. Gen. Edmund Kirby Smith urged a subordinate to offer "no quarter to armed negroes and their officers. In this way we may be relieved from a disagreeable dilemma." Historians have debated whether Union soldiers were killed while in Confederate custody after Milliken's Bend, but there's little question that black soldiers and their white officers were killed in the immediate aftermath of several battles. In the most notorious incident of its kind, Confederate troops led by Gen. Nathan Bedford Forrest killed black soldiers as they threw down their arms at Fort Pillow in Tennessee on April 12, 1864.

As officials on both sides traded threats and demands over the treatment of black soldiers, the subjects of those exchanges understood the seriousness of their circumstances. And they understood the threat they faced while also knowing that their own army was paying them half wages. They were simultaneously threatened and insulted, freed from slavery and moved into a new position of danger and subordination.

But black soldiers acted in response. Empowered by their service and their sacrifice, the soldiers of African American regiments didn't tolerate the real personal loss and symbolic insult of lower pay. Some just went on strike, stacking arms and refusing to fight again until their complaints were answered.

And so the military legal system became a forum for the discussion of a larger kind of justice. The question of equal pay became a matter for courts-martial, which had to decide if a refusal to serve under unjust conditions was forgivable protest or simply the dire and harshly punishable act of mutiny. The debate within the army also had a larger meaning, as a nation freed African Americans from slavery—and then promptly imposed a new inequality on their lives. Military courts were called to answer much more serious questions than the kind discussed in the Articles of War.

Personal choices steer a system within the limits of its formal rules, or even beyond them; people in conflict look to the law and government regulations, but they also look to their own values. The debate within the army over black protest would also have the effect of pulling white officers in different directions. In the army, as in the larger society, the status and place of African Americans would be the product of an uncountable number of decisions made in moments of conflict. Black soldiers had to decide how much inequality they would tolerate; white officers had to decide how much injustice they would impose. The records of those decisions show us just how seriously soldiers took them.

ON THE MORNING of November 19, 1863, Lt. Col. Augustus Bennett was the commander of the 3rd South Carolina Colored Infantry, soon to be reorganized as part of the 21st US Colored Infantry. As he would testify at the trial of Sgt. William Walker two months later, the regiment was camped at Hilton Head when he discovered that the men under his command were "in a state of mutiny." Walking out of his tent, he saw his troops setting aside the tools of their trade, making a public declaration of their decision to stop doing the work of soldiers. "I noticed the accused, with others of his company and regiment stack his arms," Bennett testified. His regiment was disarming itself, his men divesting themselves of their identity as soldiers.

The colonel asked his men what they were doing; he "received no reply, and again repeated the question, when the accused answered by saying, that they 'would not do duty any longer for seven dollars per month.' I then told the men the consequences of a mutiny, and what they might expect." They could, he warned them, be "shot down," killed by the provost guard to stop an active revolt in the ranks. "While saying this," Bennett went on, "I heard the accused tell the men not to retake their arms." In his confrontation with a field-grade officer, many levels his senior in authority, Walker was undeterred by the explicit threat of immediate death. He would not fight for $7 a month, regardless of the circumstances; he simply expected equal pay. It would cost him his life.

In a hard irony, Walker was executed by the army that had freed him from slavery, and after he had volunteered to serve in its ranks. Emancipated by military invasion in late 1861 on the Sea Islands of South Carolina—one of the very early Southern places invaded and held by Union troops, and the first place slavery died a forced death in substantial numbers—the future sergeant had signed on as a civilian pilot on a navy gunboat, the USS *Wissahickon*.

Soon after, army officers on the Sea Islands began to recruit black regiments; then they began to conscript them. Not that it mattered: The navy had given Walker a pass to go ashore and visit family, and the document identified him as a valued gunboat pilot who was to be exempted from the military draft. But when recruiters found him, he volunteered for the army anyway—and he did so, he told his court-martial, "on the promise solemnly made by some who are now officers in my regiment, that I should receive the same pay and allowances as were given to all soldiers in the U.S. Army." As bad as the lie about his pay had been, Walker added, black soldiers serving under white officers had also been subject to treatment that was "tyrannical in the extreme, and totally beneath the standard of gentlemanly conduct which we were taught to believe as pertaining to officers wearing the uniform of a government that had declared a 'freedom to all' as one of the cardinal points of its policy."

And finally, he argued, no one had ever bothered to tell him the rules that governed his new life; the regiment had been "allowed to stumble along, taking verbal instructions as to the different parts of our duty, and taking a knowledge of the services required of us as best we might." He was being tried under Articles of War that he had never heard or seen, a soldier subject to hidden law.

It didn't matter. Demanding equal pay for equal service, Sgt. William Walker was "shot to death with musketry" on a date that varies in the different records that describe the event: Maybe February 29, or maybe March 1, 1864. Eleven men in the first firing squad managed to hit him a total of one time with their coordinated volley, flinching from the task. A second firing squad finished the job.

Even as they had ordered and carried out Walker's arrest, though, the officers of the 3rd South Carolina Colored Infantry had conceded the justice of the complaint that had led their men to stack arms. A letter to the War Department signed by Bennett and "each of the regiment's officers who was present" protested the injustice of giving unequal pay to men who had been recruited with a promise that they would be treated like soldiers of the US Army. The letter is dated November 19, 1863—the day of the mutiny and its resulting arrests. Walker was tried, condemned, and killed in a regiment that knew his complaint was founded in fact and fairness.

Military law and military justice diverged, and officers knew it. Black soldiers punished for mutiny were behaving in exactly the way that men expected other men to behave. In disputes among white army officers in the Civil War, Bernard McMahon and Jefferson C. Davis killed other officers who abused and insulted them, and were forgiven for the act. This is what soldiers did: A man stands up for himself, and doesn't allow other men to abuse him. And so, as black soldiers refused to tolerate unjust treatment, it became harder over time for some white officers to punish them. They began to see black subordinates as fully *men*, unflinchingly signaling their manhood—behaving in ways that demanded respect.

To be sure, military law remained firmly, harshly in place, and officers believed that mutiny had to be punished. But Christian Samito, a lawyer and legal historian who has closely studied the trials of black soldiers during the Civil War, argues that white officers serving on courts-martial "wrestled with providing fair judicial process to black defendants while maintaining necessary discipline." In particular, officers became reluctant to sentence men to death for protesting unequal treatment. As Samito writes, "In many cases, authorities consciously tried to avoid imposition of the death penalty, even when the Articles of War called for it." Soldiers appealed to the conscience of their army, speaking firmly in the language of manhood—and the army, or at least its soldiers, began to notice.

Insistently fighting inequality, black soldiers found some degree of procedural fairness in the very forum that existed to punish them for it. Men were often tried fairly for protesting unfairness. "Black soldiers enjoyed rights and opportunities denied them in civilian life because as soldiers they were entitled to uniform application of the Articles of War and other statutes concerning military discipline and trial," Samito writes. "Rather than devise a separate scheme to address military discipline within the United States Colored Troops, in this regard the federal government treated blacks on par with white soldiers."

In a remarkably ironic way, given the nature of the charges black soldiers faced over their refusal to serve for unequal pay, some limited form of African American equality began in court—and specifically in army courts. Black and white soldiers were paid by different standards, but tried under the same law.

They were even tried in some instances—by courts composed entirely of white officers—with what may have been a higher-than-required degree of mercy. On April 19, 1864, black

soldiers of the 55th Massachusetts Infantry fought with white officers while they traveled on a steamboat. One of the mutineers,
Pvt. Sampson Goliah, tried to strike a captain, untied himself
after being arrested, and disarmed the officer of the guard—
cocking the shocked lieutenant's pistol and apparently preparing
to fire it. At his court-martial, where Goliah was on trial for his
life, two officers testified that the regiment had been plagued by
deep discontent. In the words of the regimental commander, Col.
Alfred Hartwell, the widespread dissatisfaction of the men under
his command had arisen because "the Regiment had not been
paid at all, nor offered pay according to terms of Enlistment."

Summarizing the case at the end of testimony, the judge advocate assigned to the trial offered the court a half a dozen ways
to avoid sentencing Goliah to death. Mutinous acts had clearly
occurred, but "do they mean mutiny in the highest degree?" he
asked. And then he all but told the court not to take the private's life: "It is the duty of the Judge Advocate, further, to call the
attention of the court to other and extraordinary circumstances,
which by no means excuse, yet mitigate the offence. Col. Hartwell testifies there had been previously a prevalent discontent in
the regiment 'because the men had never even been offered pay
according to the terms of their enlistment.' It is for the court to
see that the dignity of the law is maintained as well as the rights
of the prisoner secured."

White army officers were offering testimony and argument
in the defense of a black soldier charged with mutiny—precisely
as they brought charges against that soldier, and argued for his
conviction. Military leaders were seeking a balance between
order and justice, knowing that they were speaking about men
who had been genuinely and shamefully wronged. The army
simultaneously sought to punish and to hold back punishment,
searching for a reasoned response in an untenable situation.
And it worked: Goliah, who had taken the extraordinarily seri-

ous step of disarming a superior officer and preparing to use his weapon against him, escaped from his trial with his life. He was sentenced to confinement at hard labor for the duration of his enlistment, and then a dishonorable discharge. By the wartime standards of the nineteenth-century military, this is extraordinary mercy.

The officers of Goliah's court-martial weren't bleeding hearts; ten days later, they tried another private from the same regiment, Pvt. Wallace Baker, on similar charges, and sentenced him to death. The atmosphere in the regiment was getting worse, and Baker—described by another private in court as being "*not* a sensible man"—had struck Lt. Thomas Ellsworth with close to a dozen "very severe blows." Justice had to be balanced with order; discipline could be restrained, but it had to be discipline. The severity of Baker's sentence reflected the seriousness of his actions and the severity of the Articles of War, not the fairness of his trial. Samito notes that the private, "a black soldier accused of committing grave crimes, received due process . . . and questioned both a white officer and fellow African Americans—a level of procedural fairness surprisingly typical of general courts-martial of black soldiers."

A great question faced the entire nation, and the army was trying to answer it.

The grievance over pay rose through the military and into national politics. In letters, petitions, and the records of courts-martial that described mutinies over unequal pay, African American demands for justice were heard outside the army. In June 1864, Congress passed an act to grant equal pay to black soldiers—and to do so retroactively, to the beginning of the year. A series of later legislative and executive actions promised back pay to black soldiers going back to the moment of their enlistment. But the promise was kept slowly and inconsistently, and the protests, petitions, and mutinies continued—and so did the trials, seeking balance and feeling for a way forward.

Anger between black soldiers and white officers didn't center only on pay, and tensions continued after that matter of inequality was officially—if not actually—resolved. At the center of that conflict was the use of physical punishments that officers had long inflicted on soldiers in the US Army, such as bucking and gagging or riding the wooden horse. Like Irish immigrants serving in the Mexican War, black men in the ranks of the Civil War found a limit to the brutality they would tolerate.

But the discord between black troops and white officers over discipline was also reflected in disagreement among the officers themselves. Many thought that severity would produce order, particularly among men used to the harshness of slavery. But others, especially those who were called to service in black regiments by their deep and longstanding abolitionist sentiment, sharply disagreed.

In his later book, *Army Life in a Black Regiment,* the Civil War colonel Thomas Wentworth Higginson—who had commanded the 1st South Carolina Volunteers, the first African American army unit formally mustered into federal service—argued for a radically different approach. "The more strongly we marked the difference between the slave and the soldier," Higginson wrote, "the better for the regiment. One half of military duty lies in obedience, the other half in self-respect. . . . So, in dealing out punishments, we had carefully to avoid all that was brutal and arbitrary, all that savored of the overseer. . . . A system of light punishments, rigidly administered according to the prescribed military forms, had more weight with them than any amount of angry severity."

But angry severity was the more likely response of army officers, especially when soldiers crossed—or were believed to have crossed—the sexual boundary between black men and white women. In February of 1864, at Camp Shaw in Florida, three men from the 55th Massachusetts were accused of raping a white woman on a road near the camp. Arrested at midnight, they were tried and hanged before the sun set the next day. "An audience of black soldiers sobbed aloud as the dying men dangled before them on hastily assembled gallows," writes lawyer and historian John Fannin; an officer watching the execution shouted at the sobbing men that it had "served them right."

Still, some of that severity was restrained by military courts. Fannin found several examples in his research on a mutiny of black soldiers stationed in Jacksonville. Lt. Col. Augustus Benedict—a different officer from the Col. Augustus Bennett discussed above—was a particularly sadistic officer who ordered black soldiers staked to the ground as punishment, helpless as their bodies were swarmed with biting insects through whole days under a brutal sun. "The army refused to accept his resignation, court-martialed him instead, and discharged him from the army," Fannin writes. More nakedly, Lt. Henry Cady said loudly and often that his black subordinates were unfit to serve as noncommissioned officers. "The damned nigger did not belong to the human race," he said of one sergeant, ranting in front of his entire company, "and the form of his head showed it to be a fact." Cady was also court-martialed and thrown out of the army.

Military justice pointed in many directions at once, trying to settle sudden questions with much deeper meaning. What were the rights of African Americans? What should a freed slave expect from the country that had freed him? The answers varied between places and moments, and between different officers and courts. Severity and mercy, and even both blended together, reflected the urgency and the confusion of a fundamental debate. Thomas Wentworth Higginson and Henry Cady were equally American.

WITH THE END of the Civil War, the citizen-soldiers who composed the federal government's massive armies were ready to go home, and quickly. But Reconstruction lasted another twelve years. Southern states were occupied with varying severity by federal troops, and governed by Republicans—against the persistent wishes of white Southern "redemptionists," who sought a return to a secure white supremacy and Democratic power. Needing soldiers and militiamen, both the federal government and Republican-run Southern states turned, again, to a population that had been displaced from its social and economic position without having secured a clear place in the resulting order. Black soldiers would help to garrison the conquered South.

Military occupation by African Americans galled nineteenth-century white Southerners for the same reasons that Jefferson Davis had complained about servile insurrection: Defeated, they saw their former slaves empowered as the armed force of the enemy that had defeated them. Fifty years later, the insult still burned. D. W. Griffith's 1915 silent film *The Birth of a Nation*, a landmark in the history of early cinema, depicted the savage freed slave, Gus, in an army uniform, wearing the insignia of a captain. "Gus, the renegade, a product of the vicious doctrines spread by the carpetbaggers," read the title card that introduced him to the audience: Tell a black man he's a soldier and an officer, and he becomes helplessly deranged, shoved into a status his mind can't manage.

Soon enough, Gus is chasing a young white virgin through the woods, a hunched-over animal in the uniform of a military officer. "You see, I'm a Captain now," he tells her, leering, "and I want to marry." She leaps to her death from a cliff as he closes in, escaping degradation in favor of the "opal gates of death." Another twenty years after that, Margaret Mitchell's *Gone with the Wind* sent agents of the US Army's Freedmen's Bureau into the streets of the defeated South "to say niggers had a right to—to—

white women." With that information delivered to her (by a gentleman of the ruined planter class who can barely bring himself to say it), Scarlett O'Hara has a revelation about the real meaning behind the military occupation of the South.

"Now she knew what Reconstruction meant," Mitchell wrote, "knew as well as if the house were ringed about by naked savages, squatting in breech clouts. . . . The negroes were on top and behind them were the Yankee bayonets. She could be killed, she could be raped and, very probably, nothing would ever be done about it. And anyone who avenged her would be hanged by the Yankees, hanged without benefit of trial by judge and jury. Yankee officers who knew nothing of law and cared less for the circumstances of the crime could go through the motions of holding a trial and put a rope around a Southerner's neck." This was a story the conquered South told itself for many decades: Reconstruction was government-sponsored rape, and a military authority founded on armed black power was its instrument.

The immediate answer for the defeated South was to fight the settlement of the war in a defiant peace organized by violence. In 1866, the former Confederate general Nathan Bedford Forrest founded the first Ku Klux Klan; in 1867, as Congress wrested control of Reconstruction policy from the more lenient President Andrew Johnson and imposed a severe military control on the former Confederacy, the Klan became a principal instrument of opposition. Armed Klansmen burned schools for emancipated children, and attacked Freedmen's Bureau officials. After the ratification of the 15th Amendment in 1870, they worked to suppress the black vote—a reliable base of Republican power.

The federal government responded with military force, undertaken through the language of law and justice. A series of federal laws passed in 1870 and 1871 authorized the use of troops in anti-Klan law enforcement, and allowed military commanders to declare martial law in Southern counties. The first Ku Klux

Klan was broken as an organization, though the broader armed power of Southern redemption continued to grow.

It was rule by military justice, but not entirely. The efforts of soldiers to enforce federal law and protect the postwar political order was mostly part of a hybrid system in which the army made arrests, but usually delivered its prisoners to civil courts for jury trials. The Supreme Court's decision in *Ex Parte Milligan* largely prevented the use of postwar military commissions against Southern insurgents; civil courts were open, so the military couldn't try civilians. The exceptions were relatively few, and legally troubled.

In twelve years and eleven states, legal historians have identified "at least 200 commission trials involving Reconstruction issues," and possibly closer to 1,400. "They are hard to disentangle from the regular courts-martial in the files of the judge advocate general," wrote the late legal scholar Detlev Vagts, "and many of them had little or nothing to do with Reconstruction, dealing with such offenses as selling liquor to army enlisted personnel and stealing government property." Military law enforcement in the defeated South was often about maintaining good order in the army and policing the civilian presence around army garrisons, alongside an often ineffective effort against racial brutality and retribution.

With limited risk of legal consequences, white redemptionists used astonishing levels of violence to bring on the end of Reconstruction. In the newly named Grant Parish, Louisiana, in April of 1873, black militiamen and elected officials were attacked and massacred by white paramilitaries; black men surrendering from their positions in the burning Colfax courthouse were lined up and shot in the street, leaving an estimated 150 dead. Federal troops arrived with New Orleans police (who were under Republican control), and together they started making arrests—but the subsequent trials took place in federal court, not before military commissions. Some convictions resulted, but even those were overturned when the Supreme Court ruled in 1875 that the federal Enforcement Act of 1870 was unconstitutional. Black militiamen and the US Army supposedly protected freedmen, and the political project of Reconstruction, but were well on the way to powerlessness against white Southern resistance.

During a period of supposed "bayonet rule" by hated Yankees, no consequences would follow massacres of armed black men. Military rule was not yet formally lifted in the South, a denouement that awaited the Compromise of 1877, but it was already unmistakably broken.

FOR BLACK MEN in the South, the military remained a refuge. After 1869, black soldiers in the US Army were consolidated into four regiments: the 9th and 10th Cavalry, and the 24th and 25th Infantry. Emancipation had led mostly to poverty and economic dependence for freedmen and their children, as they were confined—until the Great Migration northward in the twentieth century—to a region that reserved a place for them at the bottom of the agricultural and domestic labor pool. So the army was an escape and a secure livelihood, a way to decline desperate lives as tenant farmers trapped in debt peonage.

With fewer opportunities outside the ranks, black soldiers were less likely to abandon the army. Desertion rates reflected the attachment men felt to an institution that gave them a chance at stability and dignity outside a repressive civilian order. In a history of the 9th Cavalry, historian Charles Kenner compared the number of men who defected from black and white cavalry regiments with similarly tough frontier assignments in 1877: a total of six men deserted from the entire 9th Cavalry Regiment, compared to 184 and 224 desertions that same year in the all-white 4th and 5th Cavalry.

Again, the remarkable fact of military justice is that it delivered something close to equal rights for African Americans at a time when the larger society did anything but. The court-martial records that Kenner describes could be from any frontier army unit. One man stole some tobacco; one tried to sneak away with the pot during a poker game; one stole a spur. For stealing from other soldiers, black cavalrymen were usually discharged from the army—an unsurprising punishment that reflects the long-standing military opinion of the barracks thief. But the outcome of courts-martial for black soldiers between the Civil War and the end of the nineteenth century also tells much the same story as for white soldiers in one other way: good soldiers could get away with more bad behavior. Courage and prowess as a warrior gave any soldier leeway that weaker men didn't get.

In many instances, black soldiers were protected from unfair punishments or procedural defects by the white officers who convened their courts-martial. "Reviewing authorities often disallowed or mitigated sentences," Kenner writes. In 1881, Pvt. Edward McBain was accused of stealing a sack of potatoes, convicted, and sentenced to a short imprisonment with a heavy fine. His commander disapproved the verdict and returned McBain to duty—on the ground that "no legal evidence" proved his guilt. Kenner suggests that the court-martial knew the private's guilt hadn't been proved, even as it returned a guilty verdict, since thieves were thrown out of the army and McBain only received a sentence that allowed him to stay in uniform. Spotting that mismatch between accusation and outcome, the convening authority prevented a miscarriage of justice, and overturned an unfair conviction. Black soldiers served in segregated regiments commanded by white officers, but could sometimes be protected from severe injustice within the limits of that segregated system.

As black soldiers served under the command of white officers, the army opened a new opportunity to change that persistent imbalance: it admitted black cadets to the United States

Military Academy. The first two African Americans to matriculate at West Point arrived in 1870, nominated by Northerners serving as Southern congressmen—Reconstruction "carpetbaggers," agents of Republican rule. As historian John Marszalek has written, twenty-three black cadets arrived at West Point in the 1870s and 1880s. Only three graduated and took commissions. All found a cold reception that went well beyond the usual ostracism and hazing inflicted on social outliers in the corps of cadets.

One found himself on trial, a national symbol of the bitter racial conflict at West Point. The cadet Johnson Whittaker was found tied to his bed in his dormitory room on the morning of April 6, 1880, apparently beaten and tortured by his fellow cadets. But the army surgeon and duty officers who raced to Whittaker's room quickly decided that he was faking unconsciousness, with minor wounds that seemed to be self-inflicted and a threatening note—"You will be fixed. Better keep awake."—that may have been written in his own hand and on his own paper. West Point superintendent John Schofield convened a court of inquiry that drew a national audience and a parade of emissaries from Washington, DC; after that court concluded that Whittaker had faked the attack, Republican president and Civil War veteran Rutherford B. Hayes ordered his trial by court-martial. Whittaker was convicted on two charges involving dishonesty over the attack and to the court of inquiry, and sentenced harshly: a year in prison at hard labor and a dishonorable discharge from the academy and the army.

Because Whittaker's court-martial had been ordered by the president of the United States, its outcome had to be approved at the same level. On its way to the White House, the record of the trial passed through the hands of the army's top legal officer—where it ran into a wall. Judge Advocate General D. G. Swaim (who would soon face his own court-martial for alleged fraud) was a combat veteran of the Civil War, a lawyer for more than two decades, and a former abolitionist who had been among the founders of the Free Soil Party in Ohio. He responded to the court-martial of Johnson Whittaker with sustained fury and lawyerly precision, tearing apart the charges and the process by which they had been considered.

Swaim started at the top, attacking the authority of the president to convene a court-martial for relatively modest charges that should have been the responsibility of the commander on the scene. The whole trial, he wrote, was "void." The proceedings couldn't be considered as the work of a lawfully constituted tribunal. Then he attacked Schofield, who had "seemed to justify racial ostracism" at the academy. Then, having insisted that the whole proceeding was legally invalid and couldn't be considered, he waded into the evidence anyway, finding it of doubtful value to support the charges. "Citing exact page numbers of the transcript to document his detailed points," Marszalek writes, "Swaim probed the government case and found it wanting on all counts." Then he attacked the legality of decisions made by the court in its handling of evidence, which he believed had cost Whittaker his right to a fair trial, the doubtful legality of the whole event notwithstanding.

In short, the army's chief legal officer attacked every aspect of a high-profile court-martial from start to finish, at length, and in a report that was quickly leaked to the press. Attacked and ostracized by army cadets, and damned by both a court of inquiry and a court-martial, Whittaker found protection at the highest levels of the army.

A long and uncomfortable silence ensued. Hayes was gone from office, his successor James Garfield assassinated soon after his inauguration. Finally, on March 22, 1882, President Chester Arthur disapproved the verdict and sentence in Whittaker's court-martial, narrowly concluding that the court had improperly admitted some of the evidence. "Whittaker was, after almost two years, acquitted on a technicality," Marszalek concludes. He was free, released from a prison sentence and a dishonorable discharge.

But justice and injustice tangled together in inextricable threads. The very same day his guilty verdict was overturned, Whittaker was thrown out of West Point—for failing to pass the exams he had missed while standing trial.

IN THE FINAL DECADE of the nineteenth century, African Americans found their status and security slipping even lower in American society. Southern states began to formalize racial segregation in every aspect of public life, passing the Jim Crow laws that still shape our historical image of white supremacy.

After the promise of emancipation and the failed project of Reconstruction, the world of the "white only" drinking fountain and the "colored" movie-theater balcony wasn't inevitable or immediate; they arrived in force only during the 1890s, with laws like the 1892 Louisiana statute that required separate railroad compartments for black and white passengers. The New Orleans activist Homer Plessy would famously challenge that law by taking a seat in the car for white passengers, leading to his arrest—and ultimately to the Supreme Court decision in 1896 that proclaimed the constitutional standard allowing the "separate but equal" facilities that were rarely near being genuinely equal. Black Americans were being pushed behind a "thickening wall of racial separation," as historian Garna Christian writes, trapped by an emerging set of explicit racial barriers that endlessly screamed their status at them in the course of everyday life.

The same walls thickened in the American military. In between the passage of the Louisiana railroad segregation law and the court's decision in *Plessy v. Ferguson*, the US Navy rejected an important piece of its tradition. Black men had always served in the navy, even when they were barred from the army and not regarded as part of the militia. But Jim Crow showed up at sea as de jure segregation spread in the rest of American society. In 1893, new navy policy restricted black sailors to service as stewards and messmen—to cooking, cleaning, and serving, in a segregated class of shipboard helpers.

In the army, black soldiers serving on one frontier or another moved from place to dismal place, sometimes garrisoned in remote camps to limit their contact with white civilians. But they also earned a grudging respect in combat, charging up San Juan Hill alongside—many accounts say *ahead of*—Teddy Roosevelt's Rough Riders in 1898. After that war, all four African American regiments were sent to fight in the Philippines, playing a significant role in the counterinsurgency that followed the American acquisition of the islands from Spain. Several hundred stayed, marrying Filipino women and finding a lasting escape from Jim Crow.

Those who returned to the United States often found themselves back in the South, wearing a uniform that signaled status and authority in a place where black men were rarely allowed either. In a study of racial conflict between black soldiers and white civilians in Texas, Garna Christian has uncovered a steady parade of legal and physical assaults that took place all over the state—and elsewhere, as soldiers traveled across the South to get there.

Legal cruelty grew alongside racial segregation. In the face of an increasingly secure white supremacy, black soldiers began to lose even the limited equality of a military-justice system that applied the law with some level of fairness.

As one century ended and another began, Jim Crow standards settled into army justice. At the end of July in 1906, three companies from the first battalion of the 25th Infantry arrived at Fort Brown, "the southernmost continental military post." The town of Brownsville sat directly adjacent, both places just across the river from Matamoros. It was a hardship posting, or at least an unpleasant one; the wife of an army officer assigned to the camp had once described it drolly as "the birthplace of the flea." And black soldiers weren't especially welcome. "As other black units had found at San Antonio, Laredo, Rio Grande City, and elsewhere, elements of the town population resented their presence and freely expressed their feelings," Christian writes.

Then came payday and its weekend. The first evening, August 11, "passed peacefully," but the peace was deceptive; the next evening, a Sunday, white men in the town began to circulate a story about a uniformed black man attacking a white woman and throwing her to the ground. Late on the night of August 12, someone—maybe several people—began to fire shots near the wall separating the town from the fort, killing a white bartender named Frank Natus and nearly severing the arm of a police lieutenant who had rushed to the sound of gunfire on a horse. Locals insisted they had seen black soldiers in the streets, firing from the shadows but revealing themselves by their briefly glimpsed uniforms and the distinctive sound of Springfield rifles. A grand jury convened, discovered that the available witnesses couldn't identify any of the attackers, and declined to deliver indictments. "Ensuing investigations raised grave questions over what the witnesses actually saw or heard in a brief moment of panic on a dark night," Christian writes.

But whatever the witnesses saw or didn't see, one piece of evidence would seem pretty clear: As officers heard shots being fired near their border fortress, they rushed to assemble their companies—and took a count of their gathered troops. Everyone was there, and sergeants quickly "vouched for the enlisted men's presence during the shooting." On an army post where the government owned the ammunition, they also took a count of each soldier's issued rounds: none missing. Local civilians swore that soldiers had fired at them, but they couldn't identify any, while the soldiers had all been accounted for during the shooting and no rounds from the garrison had apparently been fired.

Investigators descended. From the army, Maj. Augustus Blocksom arrived to take sworn statements from every soldier in the implicated companies; from the Texas Rangers, Capt. Bill McDonald showed up to keep the peace, discovered it to be already pretty well kept, and assigned himself to a newly formed investigative committee of local citizens. Supporting the local inquiry, McDonald began making arrests and interrogating soldiers, the army remarkably allowing him to carry away a dozen privates and sergeants.

Meanwhile, Texas politicians successfully demanded that the black infantry companies be removed from the state—leading McDonald to accuse the army of interfering with his investigation by sneaking witnesses and suspects out of his jurisdiction. McDonald soon released his twelve prisoners, but not to their battalion. The army moved them under guard to Fort Sam Houston, military prisoners because they'd been arrested by a state official on the strength of personal hunches and no particular evidence.

The investigation turned into an inquisition, battering at men who wouldn't change their answer. Army investigators decided that they knew the soldiers had fired on the town, so they kept asking them the same question: Who fired? Finally, an outside force intervened, trying to force the answer. President Theodore Roosevelt sent written instructions to the War Department, directing it to give the men of B, C, and D Companies a clear choice between identifying the guilty parties and being purged from the army. They still wouldn't answer the question; the latest interrogator reported that his questions were consistently met by "a wooden, stolid look."

And so finally, after weeks of frustration, Roosevelt made good on his threat. On November 4, he signed an order dismissing 167 men from the army—dishonorably, and barred from reenlistment. No process preceded the order: no trial, no hearing, no chance to address a punishment that reflected no supporting evidence or testimony. A government that had labored to find some level of legal fairness for newly freed slaves was unable, forty years later, to manage any level of legal process at all for black soldiers. They could simply be punished, en masse, by the means of an arbitrary order. A new era in military justice had arrived.

7

"MANIACS OR WILD BEASTS"

Military Justice and American Expansion

DAVID FARIBAULT JR. WANTED MERCY. HE'D BEEN CONDEMNED TO death in 1863 by a military commission, convicted on murder charges for joining other Dakota Sioux warriors in a series of attacks on white settlers in Minnesota, and he hoped President Abraham Lincoln would spare him from hanging. But his bid for a pardon was based on a strange claim. As legal historian Carol Chomsky writes, Faribault spoke English, and knew that he was facing an army tribunal when he was brought before it. But he thought the commission was engaged in a fact-finding investigation, "and he did not know he was on trial for his life."

Implausible as it seems over the distance of a century and a half, Faribault wasn't alone in that misunderstanding. The same army commission sentenced hundreds of Dakota to death, in proceedings that often condemned dozens of men in a single day of perfunctory hearings—and most of them don't seem to have known that they were being tried as criminals. Thirty-eight actually went to the gallows together, executed as murderers when they thought they'd been fighting a war.

The verdicts handed down to Faribault and his fellow Dakota by the US Army were products of a nation that was trying to figure out what native lives meant to the rest of the country—where they fit, and how to understand their resistance to manifest destiny. Americans decided to make Indian war a crime, and to make Indian warriors into criminals. But that was only one of the many decisions they made, in a jumble of competing ideas that advertise their confusion. National expansion created questions that military courts tried to answer for many decades—not just across the continent but also with the eventual addition of territories around the world: Hawaii, Samoa, Guam, Cuba, the Philippines. Were native people conquered members of sovereign nations, simply incorporated into the nation that conquered them, or domestic enemies who had fought against what was effectively their own government? Could they live as separate people, or would they be forced to merge into the whole body of the nation?

For much of the nineteenth century, American military and political leaders could safely flounder between competing ideas. In practical terms, no one particularly knew what national policy toward native people was, though the certain idea of westward expansion clearly implied its basic form: They would be pushed west, somewhere, away from the advancing line of white settlement. Removal was both policy and evasion of the need to make policy, a way of not deciding. As the parallel channels of settlement and removal ran out of space and collided, though, it became harder to ignore the questions that manifest destiny posed. And so the question of the identity of conquered people— *who are they to us, and what are we to them?*—was decided, piece by haphazard piece, on battlefields and in treaty discussions. But it was also decided in military trials, sometimes on an extraordinarily dramatic scale. In that troubled forum, the answer kept changing.

AND SO DAVID FARIBAULT JR. stood before a military tribunal, tried for murder and sentenced to death, while no one bothered to tell him what the court was doing.

Faribault was a Dakota, and the Dakota people were part of the Sioux nation. The Dakota had once controlled much of the upper Midwest, before the westward expansion of the United States forced them to consolidate on "a narrow strip of land— about one hundred miles long and ten miles wide" in southwestern Minnesota.

But by 1862, as the Civil War occupied the full attention of the US government, the Dakota hadn't received treaty payments that had been promised in 1851. At the same time, more settlers pushed in on their remaining strip of land. The Dakota were a people who had lived by movement, traveling with the seasons and surviving off a massive, shifting base of food. Spring was for hunting parties, ranging far out onto the Great Plains; summer was for cultivating crops; autumn was for a great annual hunt in preparation for the hard winters of Minnesota.

Trapped in place, the Dakota lost the foundation of their system for survival. Government policy became a dependency trap, in this instance as in many others, forcing people with millennia of independence to rely on federal annuities to feed themselves. Officials used those payments to reshape Dakota culture, withholding payment as punishment or choosing to pay particular families and bands as a reward for settling down to farm on stable family plots—for, in effect, abandoning Dakota culture.

Resentment built, then burst. On August 17, seeing opportunity in the Civil War and the distraction of the US Army, a group of young Dakota men attacked white settlers in Acton, Minnesota. An act of overt violence by some Dakota threatened retaliation against the whole people, and the Dakota were forced to consider their response together. In councils of war, young men mostly argued for a war that would drive settlers away; older men mostly recognized the limited likelihood of success, and argued against fighting. Divided, with substantial dissent and trepidation, the Dakota chose war. The resulting wave of attacks targeted settlements that were often undefended. "Many of the settlers were unarmed and taken by surprise," Chomsky writes. "In most cases, the Dakota killed the men and took the women and children prisoners."

Internal disagreement ended the fighting, bringing on the predictable defeat. On September 23, Dakota opponents of the war took control of captured settlers held as prisoners, and sent word to Col. Henry Sibley—soon to be named a brigadier general, and the commander of the US Military District of Minnesota—that they were ready to surrender. On September 26, Sibley took 1,200 Dakota prisoner, and went on to capture another 800.

The scale of the violence had been serious enough to capture the government's full and infuriated attention. In just over a month of fighting, Chomsky concludes, the Dakota had killed a little over 100 soldiers and militiamen—and an estimated 358 settlers, many of whom had died with little opportunity to defend themselves.

As the army held its Dakota prisoners, senior officers traded letters—men within a formal institution, with rules, trying to define their circumstances. They defined them darkly. Sibley convened a five-member military commission to churn through the cases of hundreds of prisoners and "try summarily" those who had participated in "the present State of hostilities." The guilty, he informed Maj. Gen. John Pope, would be "promptly disposed of," whether or not he had the authority to dispose of them. He meant that he would dispose of them with a rope— mass executions, without delay.

Pope and Sibley weren't thinking about the rules that bound their actions. The major general wrote to his subordinate that Dakota outrages "call for punishment beyond human power to inflict." And the punishment he wished he could inflict went beyond the Dakota warriors who had killed settlers: "It is my purpose utterly to exterminate the Sioux if I have the power to do so. . . . They are to be treated as maniacs or wild beasts, and by no means as people with whom treaties or compromise can be made."

Dakota aggressors were to be wiped out—disposed of as animals. And they were to meet that fate in a military court, as if it mattered. Pope and Sibley managed their discussion in the language of legal systems and judicial procedure, talking about trials and executions. But they weren't actually talking about the law.

Sibley convened his military commission on September 28, and trials began that day. No investigation or preparation preceded them. "It appears that the Commission tried sixteen men on that first day," Chomsky writes. "Ten were convicted and sentenced to be hanged; six were acquitted and apparently released." Working closely in the records of the trials, Chomsky is forced to offer conclusions about what appears to have happened on that date because the rush job of the transcripts leaves behind a paper trail that requires educated guesses where errors and omissions cloud the surviving record. The army was in a hurry.

By October 7, the commission had condemned twenty Dakota men to death, and Sibley wrote to Pope that he planned to start hanging them soon—even if their trials weren't "exactly in form."

But it's not clear what the trials would have looked like if they were exactly in form, because the commission almost certainly wasn't doing anything it had legal authority to do; it wasn't *in form* from the moment it opened. Like Winfield Scott in Mexico, Sibley had decided to use a military tribunal to enforce prohibitions that didn't appear in military law. Proceeding on the view that the Dakota defendants weren't soldiers captured at war, the army was putting an armed band of civilians on trial on charges of murder, robbery, and rape. The institution had never done anything like that before with native people, and wouldn't again. "Many wars took place between Americans and members of the

Indian nations," Chomsky writes, "but in no others did the United States apply criminal sanctions to punish those defeated in war."

Proper or not, legal or not, the trials rushed on, "with as many as forty-two tried in a single day." Charges of murder were supported by specifications that rarely listed particular people alleged to have been killed by a particular defendant; the commission mostly established collective guilt through testimony about who had been present and not present in groups of attackers. Many witnesses were also implicated, and sought mercy for giving evidence against others. Their recollections were distinctly tainted with self-interest as they named names: condemn more fellow defendants, get more mercy. A mixed-ancestry Dakota named Thomas Robertson "testified in fifty-five of the trials." Deliberations resulting in death sentences lasted for minutes, for dozens of defendants being tried together. The military commission was sending captives to the gallows on a conveyor belt, in box lots.

Throughout the trials, no apparent legal standard was in operation; it's hardly appropriate to call them trials. In a later defense of the commission, Sibley remarkably insisted that "no doubt exists in my mind that at least seven-eighths of those sentenced to be hung have been guilty of the most flagrant outrages." Military officers considering life-and-death charges tried to get close enough, more or less.

"One of the mistakenly condemned, Chaska, had saved and protected a white woman from death or harm during her captivity," writes historian Michael Clodfelter. "She pleaded for his life, but several days after the mass hanging the woman found Chaska's name on the list of those executed, his name confused with that of Chaskadon, who had killed a pregnant woman and cut the fetus out of her womb."

In all, the commission tried "nearly four hundred Dakota men," and sentenced 303 of them to die. Lincoln commuted some of the death sentences, and postponed many more, properly uncertain about the fairness of their trials. Pressured by Minnesota officials, though, and warned that local mobs would inflict their own justice if the army flinched from the task, the president signed death warrants for 39 of the condemned men. Soon after, the army sent word that they weren't sure if one was actually guilty, and Lincoln suspended his execution.

On the morning of December 26, 1862, at Mankato, Minnesota, the remaining 38 were led as a group to a scaffold big enough to hold them all. As they fell through the trapdoor, a crowd of local witnesses sent up "a single prolonged cheer." The bodies were buried together in a common grave.

In the following years, the federal government went on examining the circumstances of men it had already tried and convicted. By March of 1866, President Andrew Johnson commuted all of the remaining death sentences, and ordered the release of every prisoner. Defeated, they were released to a new reservation in the Nebraska Territory.

In an initial rush to condemn, the US government had come up with an answer about native people who fought against white settlers and their army: They were ordinary criminals, beasts, and maniacs, subject to an invented military jurisdiction that wouldn't try them as enemy soldiers. Then the federal government backed away from that answer.

Ten years later, in California, it came up with a different one.

FIRST, THOUGH, the armed forces had another important decision to make about the place of native people before American military courts. Like the events of the Dakota War, the Sand Creek Massacre led the army to convene a military commission. But in this instance, there were no native aggressors to put on trial. Near the end of November 1864, a regiment of Colorado Territory volunteers had attacked a Cheyenne and Arapaho group camped peacefully and under a promise of army protection on the banks of a remote creek. With only the actions of soldiers and former soldiers to review, and native people as victims, the military commission convened to examine the massacre became fastidious about jurisdiction and legal authority—fading away with no result at all. This was the other way military justice could shape the American engagement with native people: by choosing to do nothing, creating space for soldiers to make their own answers without consequence.

The skirmishing in Colorado that led to the cavalry attack at Sand Creek had its origins in a gold rush, beginning in 1857 and taking off in 1858. It brought a flood of settlers into the territory, especially as men gave up on California's heavily mined gold country and looked for a new place to hunt wealth. A treaty signed in 1861 guaranteed the Cheyenne and Arapaho a reservation and federal annuity payments, but the native signatories didn't represent all of the native people. Others went on stealing cattle and attacking settlers, in the familiar exchange of low-intensity but persistent violence.

For white settlers in Colorado, the Civil War made the danger feel more acute. After 1861, most regular troops were called away from the territory to fighting farther east. And then came the Dakota War in 1862, an event watched closely from Colorado as newspapers filled with stories about the massacre of helpless Minnesota settlers. But the territory wasn't defenseless: It had its own volunteer regiments, which had fought well against Confederates in the Battle of Glorieta Pass, in March of 1862, permanently ending the Confederate hope of controlling the Southwest and its mineral resources. The same names show up at Glorieta Pass and Sand Creek, in heroism and in horror: Maj. John Chivington led cavalry in the battle, securing the victory with a shrewd attack on the Confederate supply train, and Lt. Silas Soule fought under his command. Both were promoted.

In June of 1864, hoping to establish some level of peace in a troubled territory, Gov. John Evans offered refuge to "the friendly Indians of the plains." Those waging war would be destroyed, the governor wrote, but he added that he didn't want to "injure those who remain friendly to the whites." So Evans directed native people who were not engaged in hostilities to report to army officials for resettlement under military supervision. "The object of this is to prevent friendly Indians from being killed by mistake; none but those who intend to be friendly with the whites must come to these places," he wrote.

The Cheyenne leader Black Kettle took the invitation, and led a group of Cheyenne and Arapaho to their designated settlement at Sand Creek—the place the army sent them, promising its protection. The native people at Sand Creek withdrew from the war that went on around them, comfortable in the knowledge that they had made peace with the settlers and their government.

But other native people remained at war, and refused to report to the governor's settlements. Throughout the summer, skirmishes continued, and settlers discussed rumors of massacres to come. On August 20, historian Duane Schultz writes, a messenger from the plains reached the governor's door in the middle of the night to deliver an emergency message: Soon, "every settlement between the Platte and Arkansas rivers would be attacked simultaneously by war parties." Small attacks two nights later were quickly defeated, but the atmosphere of understandable hysteria didn't cool. The white population of Colorado waited for a vicious Indian plot that would soon reveal itself, as it had in Minnesota.

In the face of the crisis, the territory's two volunteer regiments seemed inadequate to the task at hand, and were engaged in duties related to the Civil War. So the territory opened recruitment for the Third Colorado Volunteers, a cavalry regiment with a hundred-day commitment, and its ranks filled with men who hadn't responded to earlier calls for soldiers.

Discipline in the new regiment was nonexistent. "No one wanted to drill, guard duty was ignored, and none of the volunteers, apparently, obeyed any order unless the mood was on him and the tone of the command suitably civil," an observer wrote. It was an armed mob in uniform, tasked as a military organization. Col. George Shoup took command, but he did so under John Chivington's recent authority as a colonel and Colorado's overall military commander. When the regiment rode to war, Chivington would ride with it, effectively becoming its real commander in the field.

In the weeks leading up to the Sand Creek attack, Chivington made his command style abundantly clear. If all the "red rebels" could be killed, he wrote, "it will be a great savings to the government, for I am fully satisfied that to kill them is the only way to have peace and quiet." In August, Schultz writes, Colorado troops caught a band of twenty-two Confederate partisans who had been robbing trains and stagecoaches. Chivington put them on trial before a military commission, and informed his superior officer, Maj. Gen. Samuel Curtis, that he intended to execute the men at once. When Curtis wrote back that Chivington had no authority to order executions, the colonel agreed to turn over his captives to the custody of regular army troops at Fort Lyon, a hundred miles from his headquarters in Denver; on the way there, though, under the supervision of one of Chivington's captains, the manacled Confederate prisoners were all killed during a supposed escape attempt.

Visitors to the site of the supposed fight between the soldiers and their prisoners noted that every one of the twenty-two dead men had been shot through the forehead, and soldiers in Denver pointed out that no one taking the captives through a hundred miles of wilderness had bothered to draw provisions for them. But no formal investigation resulted, and Chivington appears to have taken a lesson from the experience about how much he could get away with in wartime.

In November, with the Third Colorado Volunteers about to dissolve at the end of their hundred-day enlistments, Chivington decided to act. He needed someone to attack, at the head of a regiment that had barely seen any action—the "Bloodless Third," as people had started to call it. On November 23, he took command of the 3rd and part of the 1st regiments, a force totaling 575 men. They rode toward Fort Lyon, out on the eastern plains, where Soule was stationed. Meeting with the commander of the fort, Maj. Scott Anthony, on November 28, Chivington said he was there to attack Indians; Anthony, who had recently met with the leaders of the native people camped with Black Kettle and assured them of his protection, offered Sand Creek as a site where he could be sure to find some. But he also gave Chivington a list of people at the Cheyenne camp, including Black Kettle himself, and three white traders who had gone to visit; they were to be spared, he said, with advance notice of the attack and a chance to escape.

With his target identified and his purpose settled, Chivington briefed his officers about his plans. For a while, many resisted. In an extraordinary series of discussions, several of the men tasked with leading troops into battle at Sand Creek argued with their commander, taking open positions against a decision they regarded with naked disgust. Quite a few of the officers under Chivington's command had participated in peace talks with Black Kettle and his warriors, meetings at which the army officers sent to join the discussion had been badly outnumbered—and had walked away without incident. The person pointed out to them as their enemy had met with them in peace, and assured their safety. "But there was more to their objections than a sense of gratitude," Schultz writes. "There was also a question of honor."

At the head of the officers trying to stop Chivington's attack, Capt. Silas Soule maneuvered not just within the colonel's command but also within the larger army. Meeting with the commander of Fort Lyon on the afternoon of Chivington's briefing, Soule reminded Anthony that the people at Sand Creek had been assured of the army's protection; Anthony replied with the promise that "the friendly chiefs . . . would be spared," and nothing more. Other men took Soule aside and warned him to stay away from Chivington, who had gotten word that the captain was trying to stop his planned attack. But he kept trying to impose sanity on the day. Soule carefully outlined his objections in writing, Schultz writes, "but the note was returned unopened." Several of his subordinates confronted him directly, in two different meetings; the colonel responded with threats and ranting, fists clenched. Chivington would not be stopped. The column marched.

On the morning of November 29, 1864, Black Kettle woke to the sound of worried voices, as the people camped around him shouted that soldiers were coming. He walked out of his lodge, saw the approaching columns of cavalry, and raised two flags: a white flag, and the flag of the United States. "The American flag had been given to him four years earlier by Commissioner of Indian Affairs A.B. Greenwood, who had instructed him to display it whenever he was approached by soldiers," Schultz writes. It would serve as a symbol of protection. He stood beneath it, telling people not to worry.

And then the soldiers opened fire.

Soldiers in the attacking force would later describe the chaos of their attack, a mob assault that poured down into the encampment with no particular order or plan. Firing wildly and running through the camp, soldiers accidentally shot other soldiers. Cramer, who had argued against the attack, led men into it, then lost control of them. He would later describe people "who started toward our lines with hands raised, as if begging for us to spare them." Unarmed, hands raised, they were killed in groups. Moments before sending his regiment into the camp, Chivington had shouted his final orders, which included the explicit directive to "take no prisoners." He was not just talking about the warriors among the Cheyenne and Arapaho on the banks of the creek below him. "I don't tell you to kill all ages and sex," men remembered him saying, "but look back on the plains of the Platte, where your mothers, fathers, brothers, and sisters have been slain, and their blood saturating the sand on the Platte." Which was true, but beside the point: Settlers had been killed, but not by the people who were about to be attacked.

Massacres are often strangely slow, and this one fits the pattern. The killing proceeded at a leisurely pace—first as some of the surprised men in camp put up a scattered fire and briefly held the soldiers back, and then as cavalrymen tracked down groups of people hiding in the brush and sand hills along the creek. Schultz has combed soldiers' testimony for the details of the killing as it was described by the men who did it. The wounded were shot and stabbed. Children wandering without their parents were finished off. A "little girl about six years old" approached a group of soldiers, waving a piece of white cloth; "she had not proceeded but a few steps when she was shot and killed."

"During the massacre," a soldier would testify, "I saw three squaws and five children, prisoners in charge of some soldiers; that, while they were being conducted along the road, they were approached by Lieutenant Harry Richmond, of the Third Colorado Cavalry; that Lieutenant Richmond thereupon immediately killed and scalped the three women and the five children while they were screaming for mercy; while the soldiers in whose charge the prisoners were shrank back, apparently aghast."

However much men were aghast, only one company held back entirely from the killing, as their commander ordered them not to fire or enter the encampment. Capt. Silas Soule would not be forgiven for his restraint.

With the encampment at Sand Creek wiped out, Chivington and his subordinates debated a continuing effort to track down and attack its survivors. But they had lost the element of surprise, and made their intentions clear. They would have to actually fight young warriors who knew they were coming. They decided to go home, triumphant after their assault on a peaceful camp.

It was a tactical joke and a strategic disaster. The attack on the peaceful camp at Sand Creek produced the very problem it was intended to solve, pushing the Cheyenne and Arapaho to unite with groups of Sioux warriors in Colorado for three years of devastating attacks against white settlers. Betrayed in peace, they abandoned peaceful relations altogether, bringing on a real and sustained war. It also divided the territory, the nation, and the army, leaving soldiers and politicians on both sides of the resulting debate over the regiment's actions.

Army officers were consistently among the men most disgusted by Chivington's attack—men of courage and honor who saw him for what he was. In congressional hearings and government correspondence, a parade of colonels and majors lined up to damn him as a coward who had attacked peaceful people. And the first of the official reports agreed, as the Joint Committee on the Conduct of the War assembled by Congress condemned the 3rd Colorado in a powerful statement. Chivington's attack, the committee concluded, "would have disgraced the veriest savage among those who were the victims of his cruelty"; knowing that the camp had been settled in peace, "he took advantage of their inapprehension and defenseless condition to gratify the worst passions that ever cursed the heart of man."

But the personal words never matched any institutional deeds. As the hundred-day men of the 3rd Colorado Volun-

teers went home at the end of their term of service, Chivington resigned his commission and became a civilian—and was
allowed to resign, freeing himself from military jurisdiction.
Soon after, on February 9, 1865, the army convened a military
tribunal in Denver to independently investigate a massacre that
Congress had already condemned. The panel of officers didn't
constitute a court-martial, or even a court of inquiry, since Chivington was no longer a soldier; instead, their whole purpose was
to produce a report, and to file it.

Still, the army's investigative hearing did something critically
important, staging a direct confrontation between two men who
were telling a radically different story. The proceedings of the
investigative commission that convened in Denver opened with
seven full days of testimony from Soule, Chivington's unyielding
nemesis, who sat calmly in front of his antagonist and looked
straight at him while he spoke. Then the captain went on attend-
ing the proceedings, carefully watching the testimony.

But then, halfway through the inquiry, Soule didn't appear in
court. After an uncomfortable silence, the president of the tribunal opened and closed the day's hearings in one short and awkwardly recorded statement, read into the record in "cold, clipped
tones":

"Captain Silas S. Soule, veteran battalion First Colorado
Cavalry, having—while in performance of his duty as provost
marshal—been assassinated in the streets of this city, the commission, in respect to the memory of the deceased, is adjourned
until 9 a.m. tomorrow morning, April 25, 1865."

The word was carefully chosen: "assassinated." The night
before, Soule had been walking in the city with his new wife
when he heard gunshots. He ran to investigate. But the shots had
been fired precisely in the hope that Soule would run toward
them; he rushed into the trap that had been laid for him by one

of Chivington's cavalrymen. Soule fired once, and struck Charles Squiers in the arm; Squiers, who had the advantage of surprise, shot Soule in the head.

A month later, the military commission ended its hearings and issued its report. It went into a file. "They issued no conclusions, no judgments of guilt or innocence," Schultz writes. Chivington went on his way, and lived long enough to visit the little unincorporated settlement that was founded in his name in 1887, ten miles from Sand Creek. He was an honored guest, and led a tour of the battlefield. Today you can find the decaying remains of Chivington a few miles from the Sand Creek National Historic Site, its few remaining buildings open to the elements.

The Sand Creek Massacre took one more life. In the summer after Soule's murder, Charles Squiers was caught in New Mexico. Lt. James Cannon went to bring him back to Denver for a court-martial. Back in town, Cannon was soon found dead in his hotel room, of no apparent cause. Squiers wandered out of army captivity and left the city on a horse that happened to be saddled and waiting near the jail. No one ever bothered to find him again.

IN 1873, SIX MODOC WARRIORS were put on trial before a military commission in Northern California. Unlike the Dakota, though, the Modoc were on trial as enemy soldiers; eleven years after the single instance in which a military commission tried native people for crimes, the nation experimented with a new answer to an old question. "It was to be the only time in this nation's history," writes historian Doug Foster, "that Native Americans were tried for war crimes."

Like the American conflict with the Dakota people, the Modoc War had deep roots.

In 1848, a carpenter found flakes of gold in a California river, and easterners poured into the state. The hunt for gold mostly happened to the south of the Klamath Basin, at least at first, and the Modoc Indians who called the basin their home weren't initially threatened by the wave of prospectors. But the gold rush drew more people than the gold country could support, and prospectors began to make a wider search. In 1851, near Yreka, California, they found what they were looking for, and the gold rush opened a second front.

Modoc warriors tried to drive out the new arrivals—opening a cycle of retaliation, atrocity for atrocity, that went on for more than a decade. In 1852, a Modoc attack on a settler wagon train killed sixty people, in response, a group of settlers from Yreka invited the Modoc to a peace conference later that same year—and ambushed them, killing forty-one. Two years later, their leader was appointed to be the regional Indian Affairs commissioner.

By 1864, worn down by a long cycle of conflict, the Modoc agreed to sign a treaty that committed them to giving up their ancestral lands and relocating to a reservation. But they were moved onto the Klamath Reservation—with the Klamath, who had signed a similar treaty. They had given up their land in exchange for a new home, but the new home wasn't theirs.

So they left. In short order, the young leader Kintpuash led a group of Modoc off the reservation and back to their old land. More hostilities followed between Modoc and white settlers; more negotiations ensued; Kintpuash agreed to return to the reservation. The Klamath went on mistreating them, and the federal government ignored the Modoc people's petitions for a separate reservation. At some point, the army gave Kintpuash an officer's uniform coat, and he took to wearing it, and so got the nickname from white settlers that he's mostly known by now: Captain Jack.

In 1870, disgusted yet again by conditions on the Klamath Reservation, Kintpuash led a band of Modoc back to Tule Lake.

The army returned in 1872 to take them back for still another return trip, supported by Oregon militia—and blundered into a battle as an argument at the opening of negotiations turned into shooting. Captain Jack's band of Modoc had a natural advantage in the resulting war: the lava beds of the Klamath Basin, rough terrain riddled with caves and rocky trenches. The Modoc retreated to an exceptional stronghold, a high point in the lava beds that gave them strong cover, good concealment, and clear fields of fire—and held out for months, turning back an attack on January 17, 1873, that left the army with thirty-five dead and the Modoc without a single injury. The Modoc War turned into a long stalemate, more than twenty years after the first violence between whites and the Modoc.

The federal government had been doing this performance for years, sending Modoc bands to the reservation and then going out and sending them back. It was a well-rehearsed duty. And so, to break the standoff, peace commissioners arrived and opened negotiations. But the talks broke down on the same subjects as always, in the same way as always: The government proposed that the Modoc move back to the Klamath Reservation, and Kintpuash and his band remained as enthused by that possibility as they had always been.

Finally, though—exhausted, and facing more of the endless same—a group of Modoc warriors proposed a horrible new plan, with the 1852 massacre in mind. Since peace talks could never lead to the outcome they wanted, they argued, the only alternative was to return to fighting. And the best way to resume hostilities was to kill the enemy leader—which could easily be accomplished by luring him in under a flag of truce, as the Yreka settlers had done to other Modoc, on the premise that they wanted to continue with the negotiations. Men in their twenties had never known life without the fading effort to hold off white settlers, and a sense of defeat hung over the proposal. "We just as well die in a few days from now, as to die a few weeks from now," the warrior Black Jim is supposed to have said. These weren't men who were offering a plan to defeat their enemy. Some accounts have Kintpuash saying it would be better to die by bullets than by starvation. Men at the end of defeat were suggesting a way to finally get to the denouement they had perceived to be inevitable for a long time.

On April 11, 1873, a team of government negotiators traveled to the negotiation site set up near the Modoc redoubt in the lava beds, led by Brig. Gen. Edward Canby. "All parties to the negotiations had already agreed that they would come to the meeting unarmed," Foster writes, but two of the peace commissioners, warned by their Modoc interpreter, may have had concealed pistols. It didn't help if they did. Two Modoc warriors hid behind nearby rocks with rifles. Like the other Modoc men gathered in the clearing, Captain Jack carried a hidden revolver, sitting for discussions but taking his feet again when the government negotiators rejected for the last time the list of places he said he would be willing to live.

"Well, he walked right up in front of General Canby," a witness would later testify, and drew his revolver from its hiding place under his shirt. "He pointed his revolver down at General Canby's face. His revolver hung fire, but he set the hammer again; that time it fired its shot and hit Canby under the eye." The other government negotiators ran for the soldiers waiting nearby, with the Modoc firing at their backs. Rev. Eleazer Thomas was shot and killed, his body stripped of its clothes. Alfred Meacham—shot five times and left for dead—survived after Toby Riddle, the commission's interpreter, shouted that more soldiers were coming, frightening off the men who were preparing to shoot him again.

Murdering a general, the Modoc brought a long stalemate crashing to a close. Canby was a well-regarded Civil War veteran, and newspapers screamed his betrayal and murder across the country. Canby and General of the Army William Tecumseh Sherman had been cadets together at West Point. Ordering reinforcements to join the assault on the Modoc, Sherman concluded his orders to Col. Alvan Gillem with the assurance—echoing John Pope's view of the Dakota—that "you will be fully justified in their utter extermination."

But their utter extermination didn't follow.

Gillem's eventual replacement, Jefferson C. Davis—the Civil War brigadier general, now a colonel in the far-smaller postwar army—took command, battered the Modoc into surrender, and prepared for summary executions. And then the War Department sent its orders: The leaders of the Modoc were to be charged with war crimes and put on trial.

It wasn't clear that the men to be tried as war criminals could really be called that. "A key issue was whether the conflict could rightfully be called a 'war' so that the Modoc defendants could be subject to military rather than civil law," Foster writes. "This was a troubling question, because only nations can engage in war."

Putting Captain Jack on trial for his life, the army was doing him a strange and ironic favor: It was treating him as the leader of a sovereign military, the soldier of a nation. The American war destroyed the Modoc as an independent people, and then their American war-crimes trial effectively declared them to be exactly that. An emerging Indian-rights movement, the heir to antebellum abolitionism, celebrated the War Department's decision. The trial would do for native people, declared the American Indian Aid Association, "what President Lincoln's emancipation proclamation did for the black men."

Precisely because it granted sovereign status to native people, the government's decision sailed into the wind of American public opinion. In an editorial, the *New York Tribune* pronounced the captured Modoc warriors to be "mere outlaws and marauders, no more entitled to belligerent rights than so many ruffians escaped from Sing Sing. There can be no war except between independent nations, or a government and its revolted subjects; to recognize the sovereign character of a band of two-score Digger Indians is preposterous."

The debate wasn't between policy and public opinion, though, since the government was equally divided. A series of official reports offered the view that the matter wasn't complicated; the Modoc were "in no sense citizens of the United States," and so could be treated as a foreign people engaged in a war against the country. Attorney General Charles Devens Jr. weighed in with a similar view. "Because Indian tribes had been recognized as 'independent communities' for treaty-making purposes and tribes frequently carried on 'organized and protracted wars,' he compared the Modoc to a foreign nation for purposes of waging war against the United States," Foster writes.

But soldiers on the ground with the Modoc couldn't begin to imagine the basis for treating Indians as sovereign people—a modern category, as they saw it, bizarrely applied to savages. Neither did it make sense to soldiers to bring them before a court-martial as soldiers. "These Modoc cannot understand what is meant by a court," Davis told a newspaper reporter. He had asked them; they didn't know. "They would regard a court trial, with its technicalities, its testimony, etc., as a kind of jugglery, and if convicted and sentenced to death, could not be made to understand that justice figured in the business at all."

The federal government was at war with its own premises, one set of officials shrugging at the process that another set of officials depicted as obvious.

As it was applied, though, the process was more theatre than trial, a pro forma bit of performance on the way to a hanging. In the days leading up to the event, more than 150 Modoc men, women, and children were held under guard at Fort Klamath, not far from the Klamath Reservation. But only six were taken before the military commission, identified as participants in, and advocates of, the killing of Canby and Thomas. The officer convening the commission had just said that the men appearing before it had no way of understanding what a trial was, but this view didn't lead to any suggestion that they should be represented by a lawyer. On the fourth and final day of the collective trial, a Yreka attorney appeared and asked to be allowed to represent the defendants, too late to matter.

Without a lawyer during testimony, the defendants were asked if they wanted to cross-examine prosecution witnesses; in response, Foster writes, "the six men sat in glum silence." Having said that the men on trial couldn't understand "what is meant by a court," no one from the institution putting them on trial bothered to explain any of it to them. The court proceeded as if its invitation to cross-examine witnesses had simply been understood and refused. None spoke English; invitations to perform legal procedure came through a Modoc interpreter, Frank Riddle, who couldn't read, write, or understand "military and legal jargon." The army was putting on a trial for the sake of putting on a trial, its defendants barely even engaged as spectators.

And then their guilt was judged by a five-member commission that included four veterans of the Modoc War, former subordinates of the general killed by the defendants. The uniform verdict and sentence weren't a surprise: six guilty verdicts, six death sentences. President Ulysses Grant commuted the sentences of the two youngest Modoc convicts to life imprisonment, a development the army kept from the men in question until the day they thought they would die.

Having staged a pro forma trial, the army prepared to make a spectacle of the execution. Three months after the trial, soldiers led the six condemned men to the gallows—the two commutations not revealed until the executioners were ready to begin—in front of an audience that included their own families and local children. "One school in Ashland, Oregon was given a weeklong holiday so the students could attend," Foster notes. But the spectators weren't just locals; the execution attracted a national audience, and people traveled from as far away as Cleveland and Pittsburgh to watch Captain Jack and his fellow Modoc die. It was, writes historian Boyd Cothran, "one of the most anticipated public executions of the 1870s," a thing to be consumed as performance.

And as product. Souvenir hunters began arriving before the spectators. Louis Heller, a photographer from Yreka, captured portraits of the condemned men, later printed and sold for "four dollars a dozen." An army officer "visited Captain Jack and procured a dozen autographs, which he later sold."

At 10:20 on the morning of October 3, 1873, Cothran writes, the trapdoor opened under the four men waiting on the gallows; "the wives and children of the condemned broke into anguished wails as a stifled cry of horror rose forth from many of the Indians in attendance." And then the bodies were cut down, and the captain in charge of the executions began to sell "lengths of the hangman's ropes and locks of the dead men's hair for five dollars a piece, the proceeds to be shared among the officer corps."

Conquered by force and reduced to spectacle, the Modoc passed through a display of law on the way to their fate—silent in a military courtroom, as if a war-crimes trial were under way.

In three Indian wars, military justice proposed three answers in response to violence. In one instance, army courts tried native people as common criminals, and killed some, and moved the rest to prisons and reservations. In another, army courts tried native people as enemy soldiers fighting for a sovereign nation, and killed some, and moved the rest to prisons and reservations. And in a third, soldiers just killed peaceful native people, declaring them by their action and the indifference of military justice to be outside the protection of the law. No single answer prevailed; no single policy cohered. But the effect in every case was the same, grinding down the independence and freedom of people who no longer had a place in the American order.

THE EVENTS CHANGED with each person who described them: The man was middle-aged, or old, or young and strong, and missing an eye, or not. He failed to help the soldier, or he actively tried to push the soldier under the water. He was sprinting to escape, or just standing there, or had taken a step. In any case, he was always unarmed, and the end was always the same: 1st Lt. Preston Brown drew his sidearm and shot the man in the back of the head.

In August of 1898, the month after the United States took Cuba from Spain, American troops defeated Spanish forces in Manila—and then stayed to occupy the Philippines. For three decades, the United States had been developing policy to build a bridge of colonial possessions across the Pacific Ocean to Asian markets, looking for coaling stations to service a navy that would protect the nation's global commerce. But President William McKinley insisted that the American occupation of the Philippines was a benevolent effort undertaken in the service of the Filipinos, "as our fellow-men for whom Christ also died." The recipients of McKinley's kindness didn't get the message: They fought for their independence.

So Americans ended their war with Spain and went to war with an independence movement. The primary American counterinsurgency effort in the Philippines lasted until 1902, though some of the islands weren't pacified until 1913.

Like Winfield Scott in Mexico, American commanders at war with Filipino insurrectionists used military commissions as a tool for producing order and submission. Legal scholar David Glazier has found evidence of 828 trials by military tribunal for serious offenses in four early years of the American occupation; most were for crimes against Filipino victims, many of them "Americanistas" attacked for supporting the US presence. Local tribunals called provost courts also heard cases involving minor offenses, and doled out modest punishments. The American military was performing the functions of government, policing crime and exerting sovereignty. Waging the symbolic effort now known as lawfare, the tribunals conducting trials for Filipinos gestured carefully at the kinds of procedural fairness they weren't legally obligated to deliver. Commanders disapproved sentences won through hearsay evidence and self-incrimination, working at a politically astute performance that showed the American determination to provide "exemplary due process." Military commissions worked to send a message: American governance was reasonable and measured.

But the performance of order and structure wasn't a reflection of the whole effort. For Americans fighting in the Philippine War, counterinsurgency was as clear an undertaking as it tends to be. Insurgents hit and run, vanishing back into the rest of the population. Or violence just arose from what could seem like the population as a whole: In Balangiga, a seaside town on the island of Samar, a company of the 9th Infantry was having breakfast on the morning of September 28, 1901, when they were attacked without warning by hundreds of local men. The 74 soldiers stationed in the town took nearly total casualties; 54 died, and only 2 walked away unwounded.

Like soldiers in the Indian wars back home, troops fighting Filipinos tried to force clarity onto the landscape, relocating and concentrating the population of hostile areas into camps with clear boundaries. For soldiers, the result was supposed to be a simplification of an endless muddle: People inside the camps were pacified, people outside the camps were insurgents. For Filipinos, displacement came with hunger, insecurity, and the destruction of the homes they were forced to leave. Seeking further clarity, soldiers turned to torture, subjecting captured enemies to the "water cure" to make them talk. Information was the thing they most lacked; Lt. Col. Arthur Wagner described the army as a "blind giant."

In December of 1900, the blind giant was hungry. A few days before Christmas, six men from a company of the 2nd Infantry went foraging outside their camp, hoping to catch chickens for their holiday dinner, and came under fire. Stationed nearby, Brown responded to the call to arms, and led twenty-five men to the river where the shots had been fired. The soldiers from the foraging party pointed Brown to the origin of the gunfire on the opposite bank of the river, and he waded in with his men. They reached an island and stopped, then waded back into the main channel of the river to reach the opposite bank. But the water got too deep for wading, and soldiers were carried away by the river.

Meredith Mason Brown, a historian and retired lawyer—and the great nephew of Lt. Preston Brown—has researched the incident in the army's records, and describes it in detail in a 2006 article. The lieutenant swam for the opposite bank, he writes, and other men swam up behind him, but Cpl. Charles Weidner "was swept downstream and drowned." Brown would later report that he had come under fire as he reached the other side of the river, and killed nineteen insurgents with his men before forcing the rest to retreat.

As the firing died down, though, a private dragged a Filipino to the lieutenant. The man, "wearing only a breechcloth," was unarmed and alone; the private told Brown he had seen the man sitting on the riverbank as Weidner drowned, and saw that he could have saved him if he had bothered to try. Brown questioned the man for a few moments, in Spanish and Tagalog phrases, without any signs that the other man understood anything he was asking. Everything that followed would be contested, but within a few moments, Brown had killed him—firing at an unarmed man who had his back turned. Back in his camp, Brown wrote an after-action report for Capt. Francis Fremont, carefully describing everything but the killing of the Filipino prisoner. But later testimony would reveal that the lieutenant did tell his company commander about that killing—and Fremont had agreed that it wasn't the kind of detail that should go into a written report.

An unnamed, unarmed man, killed casually and dumped where he fell, his death mentioned to a superior but not officially reported. Literary scholar Louise Barnett approaches Preston Brown's court-martial as literature, probing at the things people said and didn't say. Brown reported that he and his men had killed nineteen insurgents, Barnett notes, but he couldn't explain that number at his trial. "I did not see nineteen men, myself; but I questioned and asked several men, and took the average as nineteen, as near as I could figure it." He produced a number by storytelling, not by counting bodies.

Another lieutenant had also joined Brown, leading a group of men from a different company. Lt. Paul McCook had gone with Brown as they pursued the men fleeing from the gunfight at the riverbank, chasing them to a nearby village—and helping to burn it to the ground. When his report mentioned the destruction of the village of Pamplona, though, Fremont returned it to him and said to take out the part where they set fire to a whole community. "No doubt the burning of towns suspected of being hostile was part of the conditions of making war in the Philippines," Barnett concludes, "understood by all but equally understood to be best confined to oral communication."

The men of the 2nd Infantry were engaged in careful performance, rewriting in real time to shape a story about what they were doing in their war. In his later court-martial, Barnett notes, Brown described the death of the man on the riverbank without including the action of killing: "I pulled my revolver, the double action, the man fell, and was shot through the head." It was, Barnett writes, as if Brown had been "merely an onlooker rather than the principal actor in the scene."

But McCook rewrote the battle again, appearing more than two months later with a new report and a large set of signed affidavits from men in both his company and Brown's company. He turned it all over to the regional inspector general, alleging the murder of a noncombatant. It was a personal project; he had been working for some time against his fellow officer, making the rounds and convincing other men to join his cause. The background behind McCook's choice threatens to overwhelm the main action: The army's investigative report describes him as "peculiar and eccentric to the point of being unreliable," and also describes Brown as "no diplomat" in talking to other men who angered him. At the resulting court-martial, Brown notes, McCook testified that he had nothing against the other lieutenant, "except the uniform discourtesy with which he has usually treated me." It's at least possible that one army officer accused another army officer of murder in the pursuit of a personal vendetta, not as an expression of concern for the life of a man killed for sitting next to a river.

The personal feeling behind the charges traveled downward. At trial, men from McCook's company told a story about an old man who had tried to help the drowning soldier—before being gunned down by a lieutenant who had motioned that he was free to go. But men from Brown's company told an entirely different story about a young man, healthy enough to fight as an insurgent, who had tried to push the drowning soldier down into the water, or had done nothing to help him. Then he ran for the bushes, trying to escape, and their lieutenant fired at a fleeing prisoner.

The court seems to have believed a little of each story: Hearing charges of murder, "with malice aforethought," it returned a guilty verdict on a single count of manslaughter. But that conviction would be enough to destroy Brown's career and cause him considerable hardship, as the court sentenced him to a dishonorable discharge and five years imprisonment at hard labor.

Brown would never serve any of that time, and he wouldn't have to face dismissal. The great-grandson of a senator, the grandson of a judge and a congressman, the nephew of a senator and governor, and the son of a Union Army colonel who had been "a leading lawyer in Lexington and Louisville," the lieutenant was politically positioned to protect himself from the burdens of military justice. He had been tried in the Philippines, by men who had fought under the same conditions he faced in combat; his fate would be decided by politicians who were friends and the old political allies of his family.

Shortly after Brown's conviction, Secretary of War Elihu Root got a polite letter from William Howard Taft, the American commissioner of the Philippines, who hoped he could be indulged in putting in a good word "on behalf of a son of an old and cherished friend." Taft's letter joined similarly supportive others from Supreme Court justices and friends from both houses of Congress. Justice Henry Brown "noted that Preston Brown's father had been a classmate of his at Yale." On January 27, 1902, President Theodore Roosevelt reduced Brown's sentence; for killing an unarmed man, the lieutenant was moved down thirty spaces on the promotion list for first lieutenants, and fined half his pay for nine months. He retired as a major general.

As the War Department and the president considered Preston Brown's fate, the war in the Philippines was growing rapidly uglier. After the Balangiga Massacre, the American counterinsurgency effort took on a harder edge; torture and reprisal killings became more routine. In the fall of 1901, Marine Corps major

Littleton Waller was sent to Samar with his battalion to help the army bring the island under control. At the end of December, Brig. Gen. Jacob Smith sent him on a march across the island to find a route for a telegraph cable that could connect military camps separated by dense jungle. When Waller's men staggered out of that jungle three weeks later, ten had been left behind to die. Again, different men told different stories. The Filipino porters carrying gear for the marines had either mutinied and withheld food from sick and weakened men, or had helped to get those men to safety under brutally difficult circumstances. Waller decided to solve the puzzle with strength and decisiveness: He had the porters shot, eleven men killed without trial.

Court-martialed for murder, Waller was acquitted. Along the way, though, the major rebutted prosecution testimony from Smith by revealing the orders his temporary commander had given him when he arrived on the island, in words that echo John Chivington's orders to the 3rd Colorado: "I want no prisoners. I wish you to kill and burn, the more you kill and burn the better it will please me." Pushed for clarification, Waller said, Smith had set a limit, telling the major to kill every Filipino from the age of "ten years and older."

Samar, Smith had said, was to be turned into a "howling wilderness."

Tried by his own court-martial, Smith was sentenced to be "admonished." Root and Roosevelt, under political pressure as word spread at home about brutal counterinsurgency tactics in the Philippines, insisted that the sentence was inadequate. They went as far as they could go against the outcome of a military trial, politically rejecting a sentence they could only legally reduce: They told the brigadier general that they expected him to retire.

Having given orders for mass murder, Jacob Smith got about the same punishment as John Chivington, but with an added feature: He was sent home on a pension.

PART THREE

POWER AND PLURALISM

*World War I
to 9/11*

The twentieth century was the era of the institution, centered on the long materialization of the bureaucratic spirit and the creation of vast systems of control. Historians of the century have described the social vision of "high modernism," a rage for systematized order that could be devastating to ordinary people. In America's twentieth-century armed forces, though, the debate over the rational production of modern order also produced successful arguments for a more balanced justice. Modernization wasn't an inevitable process in which the individual was always ground down by the metastasization of institutional force. For one thing, people attempting to modernize and rationalize military law had to figure out what it meant to do that. They had to make an explicit argument, in public, and debate their premises. The result was a system of justice that became less arbitrary, more clear in its operation, and more restrained in its application of power.

But the road to that new balance and restraint passed through a wilderness of great pain and violence. Over the course of thirty-five years in the middle of the century, American military justice produced giant show trials, a mass execution carried out in secret, towering acts of racial injustice, routine cruelty, and a set of procedural rules that finally made courts-martial so much more fair for defendants that the scope of the change can hardly be exaggerated. During those three and a half decades, military law and courts changed far more significantly than they had in the previous 140 years. In effect, World War II closed the eighteenth cen-

tury in the system of American military justice. When we look closely at the things real people actually did to other real people, the evidence points us in many directions at once, creating a story defined by paradox and complexity.

The high modern project was contested from below as it was debated within itself. The objects of bureaucratic order remained all of the things that state planners didn't want them to be; the pluralism of the human world declined its orders to neaten up into straight lines. High modernity fragmented internally, but it shattered against the demands of an insistent humanity. "All areas of military life—training, leadership, combat, discipline, race relations—became battlegrounds where citizen-soldiers and army officials vied for the upper hand," writes historian Jennifer Keene in a history of World War I. Those officials would be quite surprised to find themselves vying for the upper hand; they had assumed that they just had it, because they were the officials. Total war and vast institutional mass bore downward on human lives; human lives shoved upward, fighting for human dignity and the joyful mess of its own hierarchy-destroying spontaneous order.

8

"WE RETURN FIGHTING"

Black Soldiers in the Jim Crow Era

ON THE LAST NIGHT OF NOVEMBER IN 1917, TRUCKS DELIVERED
lumber to a clearing at Camp Travis, a new US Army post near
San Antonio. Army engineers went to work by the light of two
bonfires, moving quickly to build a new structure that would
be gone just a few hours later. Shortly before dawn, the trucks
returned, and thirteen shackled men were led to the newly built
gallows. One whispered, "Good-bye, boys" to his guards as they
positioned him over a trapdoor. None of the others spoke, or
spoke loud enough to be heard. A minute before sunrise, the
traps were sprung, and all thirteen men "plunged nine feet to
instant death." Then the engineers broke down the gallows, as
the rest of Camp Travis woke to begin the day.

Through much of the twentieth century, and particularly
between the start of the First World War and the desegregation
of the armed forces in 1948, the American military descended
into constant racial conflict—and American military justice
descended into racial farce. Mass mobilization and the rapid
growth of military organizations put millions of Americans in
uniform, a process that brought the urgent controversies of the
larger society pouring through the gates of army camps and
navy bases. The combination of wartime service and social

oppression galled black troops, men who offered their lives to a country that denied their full citizenship. They fought racial injustice in the army, and then left to join and often lead the burgeoning civil-rights movement at home. But many black men, and smaller numbers of black women, were punished for their resistance in the ranks.

Jim Crow went to war, black soldiers and sailors fought back—and courts-martial worked to contain their resistance, producing still more anger and conflict over increasingly naked forms of injustice. Just as the Civil War brought African Americans into the military in large numbers, bringing black men into the rhetorical mainstream of an ideal that had always taken military duty to be a foundation of manhood, African American involvement in the wars of the twentieth century took a wrecking ball to the foundation of white supremacist authority. In ways we haven't fully examined, war made freedom.

The First World War started that destruction, and did so in shockingly painful ways. The summer and fall of 1919 are remembered as America's "Red Summer," a period soaked in blood by a wave of race riots as soldiers returned from war. Black soldiers went home with the powerful political sense that they had fought for democracy, and earned the right to equality; as W.E.B. Du Bois famously wrote in the pages of *The Crisis*:

> *We return from fighting.*
> *We return fighting.*

But the assertion of rights and status by black veterans produced a calamitous backlash across the country, in a concentrated period of white supremacist violence aimed at protecting the racial status quo. Still, the moment can't be isolated. The Red Summer came from somewhere, and it echoed; a focus on the summer of 1919 erases years of critical context. White mobs burned the black-majority city of East St. Louis in 1917, and the African American district in Tulsa in 1921. In 1923, the black community of Rosewood, Florida, was entirely destroyed: buildings burned to ashes, many residents shot and buried, survivors permanently driven away.

Alongside the crisis in American society, a racial crisis grew in the nation's military. Like the infantrymen stationed near Brownsville in 1906 (who were discussed in Chapter Six), troops serving in African American regiments during World War I found that the army was more concerned with white anger than justice for black soldiers. In Houston in 1917, an exchange of rage and violence was turned into an unambiguous crime—entirely an attack by black men on white men. And the outcome was not only unjust in a larger sense but also almost certainly illegal under the Articles of War.

In 1917, the 24th Infantry had been a busy regiment in a small army, one of the regiments made up of black privates and sergeants but led by white officers. It spent much of the first half of the decade in the Philippines, and had served on the Mexican border. But when the United States entered World War I in April of 1917, the War Department initially decided to send only white soldiers to fight in Europe—a policy that would soon change under pressure, but that still decided the question of where the 24th was to go. The regiment was divided, its battalions sent to different posts for stateside guard duty at camps being prepared to train white soldiers for war. Third Battalion drew the new Camp Logan, a mile from what was then Houston city limits, and reached the camp in Texas at the end of July.

Like the 25th Infantry in Brownsville eleven years earlier, they weren't welcomed. The 18th Amendment was being debated in Congress, as prohibitionist sentiment swept the country. Even though the city already had an African American population of 30,000—rigidly segregated in neighborhoods with their own bars—Houston "dries" grabbed the arrival of black soldiers to advance the cause, printing newspaper advertisements to ask white citizens if they wanted the new arrivals wandering drunk through their city. From the moment of their arrival, white citizens saw black soldiers as social disorder embodied.

Feeding that impression, some of the men of 3rd Battalion, 24th Infantry, or the 3/24, rejected the rules and symbols of Houston's firmly established segregation, defiantly challenging the color line. On streetcars, passenger seating was marked with a divider to separate sections for white and black riders; on the evening of the regiment's arrival, soldiers began to tear down the partitions. Infantrymen serving in wartime, they expected better. The next night, historian Robert Haynes has written, dozens of black soldiers crowded onto a streetcar, completely ignoring their inability to fit the whole group behind the Jim Crow divider. Thrown off, they piled onto another streetcar—and announced that "they would just like to see the first son of a bitch that tried to put them off."

Mutual hostility metastasized. Soldiers assigned to guard duty were required to identify the civilian construction workers building the camp before letting them through the gates, a form of authority that gave black men control over the movement of white men. "Workmen coming to and from the camp demonstrated their resentment by making snide comments as they passed," Haynes writes, "or by blatantly addressing the guards as 'niggers'." Soldiers responding to the provocation with "the slightest sign of discourtesy" were punished; the abusive civilian workers were unrestrained by any threat of consequences.

Pushing back against the threat of official discipline, the men of the battalion became increasingly intolerant of disrespect. The paymaster of the Houston Lighting and Power Company would later tell investigators that a black guard had responded to him sharply after he had spoken to him in his usual way: "Look here. I want you to understand that we ain't no niggers. I am no nigger." Other white visitors to the camp would later describe the guards with a battery of loaded words: "impertinent," "impudent," "insubordinate." Meanwhile, in town, black soldiers were harassed by white city police. There was nowhere to go to escape degradation and harassment.

Terrible decisions compounded the rising tension, though some had their origins in authentic progress. In May of 1917, responding to protest from black leaders and civil-rights organizations, the War Department opened its new Colored Officer Training Camp at Fort Des Moines, Iowa. But that positive development was matched by a devastating loss for an infantry battalion: The 3/24 lost its sergeant major, several first sergeants, and several of its other sergeants to officer training. An infantry battalion lost its foundation: no sergeants, no order. Officers picked replacements, but the most experienced NCOs were gone for good, replaced haphazardly with less experienced soldiers. Meanwhile, while the leaders responsible for keeping daily order in the battalion were shipped away to another state, the battalion commander addressed the concerns of city officials about armed black troops on their streets by agreeing to disarm his military police. Now the battalion had inexperienced sergeants, ineffective MPs, and more than 600 increasingly bitter soldiers.

Confrontations piled up. On August 14, a white construction worker loudly discussed the racially distinct cures for a "nigger snakebite"; a guard from the 3/24 raised his weapon, warning the workman to watch how he spoke. On August 18, black and white civilian workers brawled over their place in a payroll line; a white worker stabbed a black camp employee to death while black soldiers assigned to the area as guards looked on in disgust. On August 20, a white contractor backed his car into a black civilian taking a nap under a tree; Pvt. Pat McWhorter leveled his rifle at the driver and called him "a vile name." The private was court-martialed and sentenced to three months at hard labor.

Throughout those confrontations, and others like them, the enlisted soldiers of the battalion reached a devastating consensus: They agreed that their officers were weak and useless leaders who weren't protecting them against a growing attack on their dignity as men. The battalion commander, Lt. Col. William Newman, got a new nickname: "Sissy Bill." The vacuum of leadership grew more dire, as a battalion without an established corps of NCOs also lost the sense that its officers were fit to lead.

Finally, black empowerment and the arrogant posture of white supremacy slammed together in a decisive way—beginning with an event that had nothing at all to do with the army or its soldiers. On August 23, two white Houston police officers came across an illegal craps game in a black neighborhood, and chased the teenagers who ran from them. One officer fired a shot, though he said later that he had fired into the ground. The same officer, Lee Sparks, burst into the home of a black woman, Sara Travers, and began tearing through it in search of his fleeing suspects. "Did you see a nigger jumping over that yard?" he asked her. Travers complained about Sparks being in her house without permission, and from here the surviving accounts split. Sparks, ranting about "God damn nigger bitches," responded that "we don't allow niggers to talk back to us"—but then Travers says the officer "hauled off and slapped me," an allegation the policeman denied. In any case, the officer and his partner agreed that Travers needed to go to jail for talking back to them, and they hauled her—from her living room, barely dressed—into the street.

Resistance to oppression and misconduct can be planned by established groups, but it can also arise as the spontaneous manifestation of local order or a shared grievance. That's what happened to Lee Sparks and his partner: Sara Travers had neighbors, and they began to assemble. Among the crowd was a soldier from the 3/24, Pvt. Alonzo Williams, free from duty on a pass from his company. Williams, "visibly annoyed" by the way the two white police officers were treating a black woman, walked up to them and tried to intervene. Sparks wasn't in the mood for a discussion; he drew his revolver and beat Williams with it, hitting him in the head "about four or five times." Then the officers arrested Williams too, and packed him off to jail with the woman he'd been trying to protect.

Black soldiers and white policemen were consistent in their responses to each other. Later that afternoon, another soldier stopped Cpl. Charles Baltimore, "a senior member of the provost guard," on the street, and told him about the beating and arrest of a fellow soldier. The officers pointed out to him, Baltimore approached them and demanded an explanation, a noncommissioned officer asserting his status in a confrontation with local authority. Just as he'd done with Williams, Sparks drew his revolver and struck the unarmed corporal in the head—then fired three shots as Baltimore ran away, the second time the officer had fired his gun that day. He missed; Baltimore was soon tracked down and taken away to jail.

The exchange between Sparks and Baltimore was one of those historical moments when people were using different scripts, operating on assumptions so fundamentally different that they could only have created more anger and conflict. Charles Baltimore was a uniformed soldier, a noncommissioned officer with his rank on display, and a member of the provost guard, empowered with multiple forms of authority. He asked a question he had the power to ask, military police inquiring about the arrest of a soldier. Sparks bristled at the idea that a black soldier could hold any status that would give him a right to demand an explanation for something. "I don't report to no niggers," he responded, shortly before he drew his weapon. His authority was in his badge

and skin, as a city police officer and as a white man in a confrontation with a black man. A black noncommissioned officer had
no claims to status that Sparks was prepared to recognize.

Baltimore arrived at the city jail covered in bruises and lacer-
ations; Sparks reported that the soldier had accidentally run into
a wall. In a telling deviation, the other policeman backed every
part of Sparks's story but the claim that Baltimore "had used pro-
fanity." One officer was trying to tell a particular story about the
soldier who confronted him, making him insolent and uncon-
trolled, but his partner couldn't bring himself to go that far.

A series of disasters coalesced. While Baltimore and Williams
sat in jail, other soldiers ran back to camp with the story of an
incident they had just witnessed. But they hadn't seen the ending,
and they guessed wrong at what had happened. A white Houston
police officer had fired shots at a black corporal, they said, and
probably killed him. As the story circulated, two city police detec-
tives showed up at the camp to investigate an unrelated theft, and
soldiers saw them arrive. Men guessed at the meaning of their
appearance, adding details to an invented story: *The police killed
one of ours, and now they're gathering on our camp to do something more
to us.*

The story picked up so much momentum that it could survive a development that should have served as a brake. A captain
had gone into the city to meet with police, and he came back
around five thirty in the evening in the company of a soldier
from the battalion: Cpl. Charles Baltimore, back from the dead.
Maj. Kneeland Snow summoned the first sergeants from their
companies, and displayed the corporal like a piece of evidence.
"Here is Baltimore. You can see he is not shot," he told them.

They had disproved the stories racing through their camp,
so the battalion's officers believed the problem was solved. Snow
released Baltimore and the first sergeants, confident that he
had quieted the battalion. But he hadn't. Baltimore, who had

been beaten and nearly shot, wasn't soothed by the fact that the police who tried to kill him had missed. He went back to his company in an entirely understandable state of rage. Haynes notes another remarkable failure of communication, as a police commander had promised the captain that they would punish Officer Sparks—and even consider criminal charges—for his obvious and dangerous misconduct. But the captain neglected to mention it to Baltimore, or to any other enlisted soldier in the battalion.

Weak leadership, unjustified brutality, horrible communication: Violence was growing from a long chain of avoidable causes. Still armed only with the information that police had beaten a respected NCO and tried to kill him, the soldiers went on gathering in angry clusters, trying to decide what to do. Vida Henry, the acting first sergeant of Company I, approached the battalion commander with a warning that his soldiers were spinning out of control. Again, in a battalion that had lost many of its leaders, the commander was new to the job; Lt. Col. Newman had left for a new assignment, and Snow was in his second day at the head of the battalion.

And then it came. Around eight o'clock in the evening the major went to investigate Henry's warning, a late moment in a long day of conflict. Snow found men inside a supply tent—taking rifle ammunition. The implications were immediately clear. "He instantly ordered the first sergeants to search the men's tents for loose ammunition," an order that he might have been expected to issue under the circumstances. But again, the order mattered less than its interpretation. After weeks of unrelenting abuse, and knowing that city police had just tried to kill a fellow soldier, the men of the 3/24 suddenly found their leadership trying to disarm them—*for what purpose?* With that, a private from Company I ran through the camp, shouting the alarm: They're coming. A white mob was about to attack. It wasn't, but men from every company exploded out of control, storming their supply tents and grabbing ammunition to defend themselves against an assault they had invented in the absence of leadership and clear information.

No one is sure how many men left the camp, but Haynes estimates the size of the group at 75 to 100. Threatened with attack, infantrymen went on the offensive, charging into Houston and bringing the fight to the men who had become their enemy. They meant to find particular targets, since the men who made it back to camp were able to describe the particular policemen who had arrested Williams and fired at Baltimore; the soldiers were hunting Houston police officers, not just storming the city. The police responded in kind, as officers came under sudden fire and urgently called for help.

In short order, the army and the police department were engaged in a running gun battle on the city streets, and men began to die. One of the first was Officer Rufus Daniels—the partner of Officer Lee Sparks, and one of the men the 3/24 was looking for. For reasons no one will ever know, Vida Henry—the first sergeant who had warned Major Snow about the building anger in his company—became one of the leaders of the men who ran into the city. But Henry tried to lead other men further than they would go; he began to lose support as he tried to get men to follow him in an assault on a police station. Soldiers began to hesitate, then to withdraw. The column fighting its way through Houston petered out, and the gunfight stopped by stages.

As the wave broke, Henry watched it ebb. It was over. He "shook hands, one by one, with his fellow soldiers" as they broke away and returned to camp. He was saying goodbye. Children found his body in the Fourth Ward the next day, a rifle at his side and the back of his head blown away—an apparent suicide. An explosively initiated insurrection had faltered into its conclusion. Violence had begun in anger; peace returned in sorrow and worry. Men who had found the limit of their willingness to tolerate abuse had gone on to find the limit of their willingness to kill other men in the streets of an American city.

But first they had fought. In the end, Haynes concludes, "the men of the Third Battalion had to decide whether to accept the oppressive conditions of Houston or to fight back. A sizeable number chose the latter course."

Abused and attacked, and left without support from the institution at the center of their lives, they'd had to look to themselves for an answer. They made their choice, in stages, on bad information and understandable principle. Charles Baltimore was alive, and no mob was coming for them, but their decision to resort to violence followed a long chain of thoughtlessness and cruelty.

The resistance of black soldiers to racial injustice had always forced military institutions and individual officers to reveal themselves. The need for order could stand alongside the recognition of a deeper justice; during the Civil War, Sgt. William Walker's regimental leadership had simultaneously pursued capital charges against him for mutiny and petitioned national leaders to address his grievance. It was possible for a commander to forcefully oppose mutiny and allow himself to understand what real kinds of injustice had caused it. In Houston, though, wartime politics and prevailing racial sentiment coalesced to destroy any possibility of understanding. The army needed the camp, and Houston's white political leaders wanted the attack on its police punished by the harshest possible means. Addressing a political crisis, Maj. Gen. John Ruckman convened a series of mass courts-martial that—like the military commissions that tried Dakota warriors—tried soldiers in large groups on capital charges.

The first trial opened on November 1, 1917, to hear charges against sixty-three soldiers: a sergeant, four corporals, "two cooks,

one bugler, and fifty-five privates." They sat on an elevated platform, in rows, spectators and spectacle at the same time. All faced
the same four charges, accused of disobeying orders to remain
in camp, mutiny, conspiracy to commit murder, and assault. The
trial centered on a set of handwritten checklists, hurriedly com-
piled by officers at Camp Logan as men fought the police in the
streets of Houston. Men on the checklists were taken to have
been inside the camp during the fighting; men not on the lists
were taken to have been in the city, firing at the police.

The defense of all sixty-three men was in the hands of Maj.
Harry Grier, a career infantry officer—with no legal training or
experience—who had been appointed to the task by the army's
Southern Department. He was given two weeks to prepare the
defense. But Grier approached his duty with unmistakable seriousness, against a haphazard prosecution that assumed guilt
more than it offered proof. Merely by bothering to try, he won a
few points in favor of the men on trial.

Under cross-examination, officers testifying for the prosecution had to agree that their lists of men found inside the camp
may have been incomplete. Tents and latrines went unsearched,
and parts of the camp outside the battalion's assigned area mostly
went unchecked; officers made up their own procedures as they
went along, and were "vague about the time the checks were conducted and about the number of men missing at the time." Men
were on trial for their lives, and the witnesses were taking rough
guesses about the lists they scribbled in a panic.

Then, for a week and a half, forty-four Houston residents
testified about the gun battle as eyewitnesses—though "none of
them could identify a single soldier." One, a black man named
Courtney Clark, testified that he had helped to arrest a private
named Terry Smith; asked to identify him in court, he "pointed
to Private Douglas Bolden." Then came members of the Illinois

National Guard, men assigned to the camp for training who had been sent to help make arrests as rioters returned to camp. They were equally unsuccessful in identifying particular defendants in court.

Finally, the army's prosecutors called seven men from the 3/24 itself, witnesses who had either not left the camp with the rioters or been offered lighter punishments in exchange for helpful testimony about the attack they had joined. On the witness stand, Pvt. Lloyd Shorter lost his memory of the events he was describing—but then the judge advocate read him a list of names, and he placed nearly two dozen in the midst of the riot. Pvt. Cleda Love had been in the battalion for less than three months, but remembered the names of most of the men who went into town with him; offering his testimony, he "rattled off a total of forty-one," including men known to have been in camp the whole time.

Against the shambles of the prosecution's case, only sixteen of the defendants testified on their own behalf. Pvt. William Hough said he had spent the evening hiding behind a tree on Camp Logan. Others said their names weren't on the lists of men found present in camp because they spent the evening under a cot or behind an icebox.

But the particulars of the testimony didn't matter much in an event that was mostly a show trial. A total of 194 witnesses testified, producing nothing much. Prosecution witnesses mostly couldn't identify any defendants as participants in the fighting; defense witnesses mostly offered uncorroborated alibis that the court could easily ignore if it wished to do so. None of that mattered. The prosecution's case didn't rest on individual proof about personal acts. In his closing statement to the court, Maj. Dudley Sutphin argued for the collective guilt of the defendants: "Where a number of persons conspire together to do an unlawful act, and death happens in the prosecution of that common design, all and each one of the conspirators is guilty of murder," he argued. It was the winning argument.

The court didn't proceed with care. Having adjourned late on Tuesday afternoon, and returned to court on Thursday morning with a complete set of verdicts, it spent only Wednesday considering the testimony of 194 witnesses on a set of charges against sixty-three defendants. Fifty-four were found guilty of every charge. A lucky five were found not guilty. The remaining four were found guilty on a single charge of disobeying orders by leaving camp.

A final decision made the court's disregard for the men on trial remarkably clear: On November 29, the verdicts and sentences were delivered in a closed session, outside the presence of the defendants. Thirteen men were sentenced to death, but weren't there to find out about it. Neither was the news delivered to them outside the courtroom. The defendants had written a statement to the court, stating a shared preference: If they were sentenced to death, they asked to be shot by firing squads as soldiers, not hanged. The court turned aside the request, and sentenced the condemned men to die on the gallows. Forty-one of the others were sentenced to life imprisonment at hard labor. A single court-martial had disposed of dozens of lives with a single day of deliberation.

Warehoused, knowing their trial was over but not knowing the outcome, the men sentenced in the first court-martial found out on the evening of December 9 which of them had been sentenced to death. But they still hadn't learned how they would die. The next day, their guards transferred the thirteen condemned men to new barracks. The legal path to their execution was supposed to travel through a long and slow process, as their verdicts and sentences went up the chain of command for careful review—but that's not what happened. Ruckman had decided to move quickly.

On the night of December 10, as the condemned men slept, army engineers built a scaffold by the light of several bonfires. Finishing the structure, they prepared thirteen nooses over two large trapdoors, each big enough for a group of men. The site of the execution had been chosen with great care, a hidden site for secret killing; the men were to die on the remote banks of a creek outside San Antonio, far from any possible outside witnesses and surrounded by heavy brush. On the morning of December 11, they were awakened before dawn, ordered into uniform, and loaded onto trucks. Their arrival at the execution site gave them their first indication of how they would die: They saw nooses by the light of bonfires, and understood they had been denied their request for firing squads.

On the gallows, the men spoke quietly to the ministers who had been chosen to comfort them as they awaited death. Two were army chaplains, and white; without black chaplains to attend the mass execution of black soldiers, the army had also invited a civilian to attend, a black minister who joined the white officers on the platform. As the nooses were adjusted, the condemned men sang together quietly. A ring of white infantrymen surrounded the gallows, ordered into place to prevent the escape of men manacled at the hands and feet. The men of C Company, 19th Infantry, had guarded their fellow soldiers for months, and the other infantrymen on the gallows called out to them, quietly saying goodbye—reflecting the strange respect that had grown between men who were about to be killed and the men who were responsible for making sure of it.

Then the commander of the execution detail gave the signal, and all thirteen men dropped through the trapdoors. Their necks snapped at the end of the long fall. Their bodies were quickly moved into the graves prepared nearby—the transfer delayed only by a struggle with some of the knots around their necks, jammed tight from the jolt. The burial sites were marked by numbers. As the burial detail worked, the engineers tore down the gallows and disposed of the lumber. The army was hiding the signs of its already hidden execution.

"An hour after dawn," Haynes writes, the only remaining evidence of the execution was "thirteen anonymous markers protruding from freshly dug earth." Later that day, Maj. Gen. John Ruckman publicly announced the executions—for the first time, waiting until the men were dead to disclose his intention to carry out the sentences.

Two more mass trials followed, with more convictions and more death sentences. Of the 118 soldiers who faced charges, Haynes writes, "only seven were acquitted." Twenty-nine men were sentenced to death; fifty-three to life in prison.

But the verdicts weren't the end. For a decade, African American civil-rights organizations successfully lobbied successive presidents—Wilson, Harding, and Coolidge—for clemency, in a series of partial victories that accumulated slowly. Six more soldiers were executed, and many remained in prison well into the 1920s, but some were spared from death sentences imposed by military courts, and others were released from long prison terms. By the end of the 1920s, "only a handful" were still in prison; the last was paroled on April 5, 1938, as life sentences broke against the reality of organized, systematic, sustained black activism.

The effects on American political culture were profound. The fate of the men from the 3/24 was an early and important test for organizations like the NAACP, which had only been founded in 1909. Throughout the early 1920s, African American activists rallied to a cause that had originated in military courts; the Houston rioters became the subject of a national NAACP petition drive in 1921, a massive effort that produced 50,000 signatures. On September 28, Haynes writes, "a delegation of thirty prominent black Americans met with President Harding." By 1924, the

NAACP leaders meeting with President Calvin Coolidge were able to hand him a petition signed by 124,000 people.

The power of black activism grew behind the engagement of civil-rights groups with the failures of military justice. Decades before the lunch counter sit-ins and Freedom Rides that are widely seen as the heart of the civil rights movement, African American groups demanding equal justice for black soldiers led national civil-rights campaigns and expected to be received at the White House.

THE SECOND WORLD WAR brought far more Americans into uniform, and far more African Americans among them. Military justice was no more fair to black soldiers in World War II than it had been in World War I, but race didn't just determine the outcomes of courts-martial; it was an important weight on the scale, but not the only one.

One of the most famous conflicts over racial inequality that led to a court-martial began late on the night of July 6, 1944, when an army lieutenant got on a bus at a post in Texas that was then called Camp Hood. In his civilian life, the athlete and UCLA alumnus Jackie Robinson would integrate major league baseball; as a soldier, though, Lt. Jack Robinson wasn't yet a Brooklyn Dodger or a national symbol of racial equality. Drafted in March of 1942, Robinson had applied for Officer Candidate School, with four years of college (that stopped short of a degree) and strong performance in basic training on his side. But his application was summarily rejected, and he was soon "assigned to help take care of horses in the stables" at Fort Riley, Kansas. As his biographer Arnold Rampersad has written, Robinson's experience reflected the racial views of military policymakers. "Leadership is not imbedded in the negro race yet," argued Secretary of War Henry Stimson, "and to try to make commissioned officers to lead men into battle—colored men—is only to work a disaster on both." But a happy accident brought Robinson to Fort Riley alongside the boxer Joe Louis, "then at the peak of his national fame." Louis put his renown to use with a call to the office of the secretary of war, and Robinson found himself accepted to a newly integrated OCS class.

Having become an officer against considerable odds, Robinson struggled to make that status meaningful. He held a commission in an army that remained mostly segregated; the athlete who would play for the Dodgers was turned away from the all-white army baseball team at Fort Riley. To the army, he wasn't an officer—he was a black officer. That distinction was written on every moment of his experience: At the moment he got on the bus, Robinson was on his way back to his quarters from the colored officers' club. But he also knew that a recent army order had officially desegregated army transportation, and he was ready to insist on the point.

Robinson's choice of a seat carried an extra bit of danger: The white bus driver thought he'd taken a seat next to a white woman. He hadn't. Virginia Jones was the light-skinned wife of another black army lieutenant, and Robinson knew her. But the driver, Milton Renegar, demanded that Robinson move away from the white woman and go to the back of the bus. Not debating the details, the lieutenant flatly refused. "The Army recently issued orders that there is to be no more racial segregation on any Army post," he said. "This is an Army bus operating on an Army post." At the bus station soon after, another white passenger joined the argument. Elizabeth Poitevint, a civilian army employee, "let Robinson know that she herself intended to press charges against him." The bus dispatcher called for the military police. Robinson heard the dispatcher's question to the driver: "Is this the nigger that's been causing you trouble?"

The growing bluntness of the racial hostility made Robinson increasingly direct about his refusal to tolerate it. Two MPs drove the lieutenant to their headquarters—not yet officially under arrest—so he could be questioned. But as they arrived, a third military policeman walked up to the car to greet them. Pvt. Ben W. Mucklerath asked the other MPs if they had the "nigger lieutenant" with them. Seething, Robinson told the private he would "break him in two" if he used the word again.

Inside the building, a series of conversations were similarly hostile. As Robinson was questioned by the assistant provost marshal, Capt. Gerald Bear, a white civilian stenographer interrupted to bark questions at the lieutenant: "Don't you know you have no right sitting up there in the white part of the bus?" Bear invited Mucklerath to sit down as he made a statement for the record, then insisted that Robinson stand. His social status was being made perfectly clear for him: A black officer was inferior to a white private, inferior to white officers, and inferior to white civilians. He had no rank or standing the others would respect.

Robinson understood the meaning of the performance. Bear, he said later, "did not seem to recognize me as an officer at all. But I did consider myself an officer and felt I should be addressed as one." The subtext was fundamental, penetrating to a basic fact of identity. Robinson had fought to become an officer; having achieved that status, he had to fight to actually occupy it. He had to become the rank he wore, and to hold it against a determined effort to take it away. If the other men in the room with him didn't have to address him as an officer, then he effectively wasn't one. They were trying to take what he had worked to earn. Robinson responded angrily, and his anger became a crime. He was, Bear would later testify, "disrespectful and impertinent," and lacking the comportment of an officer in the presence of enlisted soldiers—at least one of whom had just called him a nigger in his presence. The confrontation reached its climax, as Bear told

Robinson he was to return to his quarters and consider himself under arrest.

Jim Crow wasn't a monolith; a series of quiet struggles began over the charges the lieutenant would face. Robinson was being treated for an old athletic injury, so he was temporarily quartered at a hospital off-post. When he returned there under guard, word of the conflict had gotten there ahead of him, and "a white doctor who knew Jack warned him that a report had come in about a drunken black lieutenant trying to start a riot." The doctor took a blood sample, securing helpful evidence that Robinson hadn't been drinking. Then, when the provost marshal sent his complaint to Robinson's battalion commander, Lt. Col. Paul Bates "refused to endorse the charges," blocking a court-martial. Before the end of the month, though, Robinson had been transferred to a different battalion, and his new commander agreed to the charges that Bates had brushed aside.

Everyone involved understood that the coming court-martial was a political event. Robinson wrote to the NAACP, asking for help that didn't come. A letter from the organization, dated the day after the court-martial, declined the lieutenant's request for help in finding a civilian lawyer. Meanwhile, as Robinson's biographer Rampersad has written, army records describe a phone call between two colonels at higher echelons discussing a case that was obviously "full of dynamite." The army as a whole was watching, knowing that the outcome of Robinson's court-martial wouldn't be just a local matter.

When it came, Robinson's trial was carefully circumscribed, a wide-ranging list of five charges whittled to just two. Neither of the surviving counts related to the events on the bus, moving that confrontation out of the court's deliberations. As the late historian Jules Tygiel noted, the paring back of the charges had an ironic effect: A reduction of Robinson's legal jeopardy "also made his defense more difficult." The court-martial would hear about the lieutenant's angry demeanor toward a group of MPs and the assistant provost marshal, but they wouldn't be asked to consider the proximate cause of his anger. The trial would begin with a story about an angry lieutenant at the military police head-quarters, being hostile to authority for reasons that were moved outside the legal matter at hand. "Robinson was no longer on trial for refusing to move to the back of a bus, which was within his rights, or for responding to the racial slurs of a civilian," Tygiel wrote, "but for acting with 'disrespect' toward Captain Bear and disobeying a lawful command given by that officer."

The reshaping of the charges allowed the prosecution of the case to elide testimony that would have explained Robinson's behavior—such as the charge that the lieutenant had disre-spected another officer, Capt. Peelor Wigginton, who had ini-tially questioned him. The specific act of disrespect alleged in the count was that Robinson had said this: "Captain, any Private, you, or any General calls me a nigger and I'll break him in two." Testimony on that statement would have opened an inquiry into the reason Robinson would tell an officer he wasn't willing to be called a nigger; the charge evaporated. Another abandoned charge accused Robinson of cursing Renegar and Poitevint, sup-posedly telling the latter that "you better quit fuckin' with me, or words to that effect." Again, the charge opened the door to a series of uncomfortable questions about why Robinson would be telling another passenger on a bus to stop fucking with him. The lieutenant was angry for a good reason, but the reason could be left unspoken.

It didn't work. At Robinson's trial on August 2, the court-martial heard testimony from Mucklerath, who under cross-examination "denied that he had called Robinson a nigger." Then another MP, Cpl. George Elwood, testified that Mucklerath had done just that. The court-martial was figuring out the context for the defendant's anger. At the same time, the two surviving charges were collapsing into a muddle. Bear testified that Robinson had disobeyed his direct orders, but gave confused and contradictory answers about what those orders were supposed to have been. Similar contradictions crept into his testimony about the lieutenant's demeanor, and a member of the court voiced his doubts about one of the supposed signs that Robinson had been insolent: "I do not see the manner in which he leaned on the gate had anything to do with you." Robinson's trial told half a story, and told it badly. He was acquitted of both charges.

In a contest over status, a series of soldiers had revealed themselves. A military policeman got caught lying; a captain, supposedly in charge of an interrogation in his own office, had been rude, flustered, and unprofessional. And a lieutenant, treated poorly by a series of other men, demanded to be treated like an officer. He earned the status he claimed.

Robinson was not the only black soldier who would fight to preserve a hard-earned status.

One important thing had changed in the army: By 1943, women enlisted in substantial numbers, joining the new Women's Army Corps. The American military had already struggled to decide how women would be treated in the ranks. During World War I, the navy had allowed women to enlist, serving in support roles to free men for combat jobs. Then, in the summer of 1918, Yeoman First Class Barbara Foss decided she didn't want to be a military stenographer after all, and she went home. No one knew what to do. A story in the Chicago Tribune explained that Foss was "technically" a deserter who should "technically" be arrested, but naval officials had no desire to throw women in the brig. They quietly discharged her, in one of the first instances of the American military's effort to figure out the place women should occupy in the ranks.

No such problems interfered with the willingness of military authorities to court-martial black women. In early 1945, sixty

WACs assigned to an army hospital at Fort Devens, Massachu-setts, as trained medical technicians were ordered to perform the duties of unskilled orderlies: scrubbing floors, washing windows, serving food to white WACs in the same hospital. The hospital commander, Col. Walter Crandall, talked openly in the halls of the facility about his unwillingness to use "nigger Wacs" or allow black women to work directly with white patients. A delegation of African American servicewomen met with the commander—who insulted them and dismissed their protest. "In response to his remarks," writes historian Leisa Meyer, "most of the sixty black Wacs stationed at the hospital walked out of the meeting, and the next morning they all refused to report to work."

Threats broke most of the resistance, as both the colonel and Maj. Gen. Sherman Miles ordered the strikers back to work. Six refused. Then Miles sent a white WAC lieutenant to warn them that wartime mutiny could be punished by death. Two returned to their duties; threatened with execution, four stayed. Like Sgt. William Walker eight decades before them, who had refused to fight for unequal pay even as his regimental commander warned him he was committing an act of mutiny, Pvt. Alice Young, Pvt. Anna Morrison, Pvt. Johnnie Murphy, and Pvt. Mary Green were willing to insist on equality at any cost.

They should have found support outside the military. As the Fort Devens WACs were charged with disobedience, African American civil-rights organizations were three years into a pub-lic "Double V" campaign that called for two victories: one victory against fascism overseas, and one victory against segregation and white supremacy at home. And that activism had already achieved substantial wartime gains, as the labor organizer A. Philip Ran-dolph's threat of a massive march on Washington led President Franklin Roosevelt to issue Executive Order 8802 in June 1941, prohibiting racial discrimination in defense industries.

The problem, though, was the premise of the Double V campaign. The message African American organizers wanted to send was that black service members were actively fighting for both of its intended victories, waging simultaneous war on fascism and racism. Refusing to perform duties assigned by their commander during wartime, the Fort Devens WACs threatened that narrative. Civil-rights groups crab-walked away from four black women who faced severe punishment for their decision to resist racial inequality. Fort Devens sat thirty-five miles from Boston, the nearest city with an NAACP chapter. The chapter president, Julian Steele, issued a public statement pronouncing the WACs "misguided" and deploring their refusal to work. As the four women awaited trial, black newspapers across the country "expressed sympathy for the situation which had prompted the strike, while not supporting the strike itself." They were mostly alone, trapped on the outside of an emerging movement that would go on debating what causes to adopt and how to speak about them. They would face a court-martial without support.

But then the court-martial itself was the very thing that made civil-rights activists realize they could no longer keep their distance. Tried together at Fort Devens, all four WACs were charged with refusing to obey orders. The court—which included two black officers—turned aside the defense argument that they had been improperly assigned to menial labor on account of racial discrimination. The sentence was the same for all four: a year in prison at hard labor, with a dishonorable discharge. Murphy was dragged from the courtroom by military police, sobbing. Civil-rights leaders had been expecting convictions and some form of punishment, but—not quite thirty years after the navy had decided it couldn't possibly imprison a woman for wartime desertion—a harsh sentence involving prison terms and hard labor came as a shock.

A carefully maintained posture of distant disapproval vanished in an instant. The army suddenly faced a nationwide storm of protest from the NAACP, the ACLU, and Mary McLeod Bethune's National Council of Negro Women. Most powerfully, they turned the tables: If Young, Morrison, Murphy, and Green had disobeyed orders, so had Colonel Crandall, who had violated army regulations with punitive and discriminatory work assignments. Petitions demanding Crandall's prosecution poured into the War Department. "We have made personal contacts with Mrs. Roosevelt," Bethune wrote shrewdly. The pleas of the petitioners, Meyer writes, "were joined by letters from hundreds of individuals, white and black, who felt the women's sentences were wholly unjust." Some made a disturbing point about the sentence, asking military officials to consider the effect it would have on morale— and so obedience and commitment to duty—among a million black men in uniform.

An array of activists and organizations hit the army in many places at once, from many directions and with a whole battery of claims and threats that spoke directly to the fears that plague a bureaucracy. The campaign that suddenly sprang to life was tough, shrewd, and too diffuse to easily counter. It was the kind of activism that foretold the civil rights movement of the 1950s and 1960s. In fact, though, it *was* that movement, and it was well under way in 1945.

Two weeks after the four WACs were convicted and sentenced to prison, a brief story in the *New York Times* opened with the actions of an officer who had just recently sent a lieutenant to threaten the Fort Devens WACs with mutiny charges and death: "Four Negro members of the Women's Army Corps were restored to duty today after Maj. Gen. Sherman Miles, commanding officer of the First Service Command, voided court martial proceedings against them." It worked.

Civil-rights organizations were building a mass movement, and learning the politics and tactics of that movement along the way. They stood aside, and Young, Morrison, Murphy, and Green were convicted; then they organized a rapid, coordinated, and furious response, and the army backed down in a matter of days. "In addition," Meyer writes, the army issued orders "to stop assigning African-American Wacs at Lovell Hospital to menial duties, and clearly delineated the types of jobs enlisted women were not required to perform, including scrubbing floors." But Colonel Crandall wasn't there to enforce those orders.

He'd been offered a chance to immediately retire.

THE INJUSTICE of World War II military courts had a long echo.

In a familiar cycle, manpower demands gradually ground down the boundaries of segregation in the wartime navy. After April 1942, black sailors began to break out of the role of messmen. Navy leaders "reluctantly agreed to accept blacks for general service, but within a completely segregated system of training and assignments." Then that limit was abandoned, late in the war, as the navy "announced that it was abolishing segregated training camps and assignments." Along the way, the service commissioned its first black officers in 1944, the "Golden Thirteen" who broke a barrier in the navy that had long since been breached in the army.

But if progress was the trend, segregated service in non-combat roles was the most common station for most black sailors during the war. The experience of several hundred of those men led to the largest mass trial in navy history, as fifty sailors were tried for mutiny in a single courtroom.

Port Chicago sits thirty miles from San Francisco, along an industrialized strip of the Suisun Bay. During World War II, the navy used the busy port to feed the war in the Pacific, cramming bombs and other war materiel into an endless stream of Liberty and Victory ships. Black navy crews loaded explosives under the supervision of white officers, endlessly pressured to hurry; accounts from men who worked on the docks describe a series of reckless practices, as officers bet one another to see who could load a ship faster, or encouraged their crews to race. The same officers assured sailors on the loading teams that their work was safe. Bombs and artillery shells went into ships' holds without detonators, and an explosion was supposed to be unlikely.

On July 17, 1944, that promise turned out to be wrong. The Victory ship *Quinault Victory* and the Liberty ship *E.A. Bryan* were being loaded on opposite sides of the same pier, each with several thousand tons of ammunition and explosives, in a day-and-night effort. At 10:18 that night, men from daytime crews asleep in barracks more than a mile away were thrown from their bunks by a massive explosion that collapsed buildings and sprayed glass through the air. Decades later, historian Robert Allen interviewed survivors of the explosion—who had been sure, at first, that Japanese bombers had somehow reached the mainland. As they realized what had really happened, men raced for the docks to help the survivors.

But there were no survivors there to help, and no docks at which to help them: The explosion had evaporated everything along the waterfront, including the ships. "The *E.A. Bryan* was literally blown to bits," Allen writes. "Very little of its wreckage was ever found that could be identified." At the railhead that served the docks, train engines and boxcars "disintegrated into hot fragments flying through the air." The 1,200-foot wooden pier where loading crews worked "simply disappeared." The nearby civilian town of Port Chicago was damaged as if by bombing. Walls buckled, windows imploded, and streets and buildings were hit by "falling debris from the ships, including undetonated bombs and jagged chucks of smoldering metal." People in town who had turned to look toward the flash from the docks were blinded as the blast threw glass into their eyes.

The death toll comes mostly from the comparison of personnel lists to living bodies, since most of the dead vanished with the pier and the ship that had been the source of the explosion: 320 dead, mostly at the docks, and 390 wounded, mostly at barracks and other buildings farther from the blast. Black men were the entire enlisted force that made up the loading crews, so they represented the majority of the casualties: 202 of the dead, 233 of the injured.

A court opened in the ruins. Even as hospitals treated the wounded and the Red Cross rushed in lumber to help rebuild the ruined town, the navy convened a court of inquiry to discover the cause of the explosion. It opened on the morning of July 21, and took testimony for a month. The inquiry quickly discovered that officers had discussed safety problems on the loading pier for months before the explosion, and a Coast Guard loading detail assigned to supervise the work had withdrawn, unwilling to be responsible for the working conditions they had witnessed. Officers were implicated, and the navy itself; the testimony pointed to serious failures of leadership.

But that's not where the court wished to look. With that testimony in hand, the judge advocate assigned to the inquiry offered the court his extraordinary conclusion, which it mostly accepted: "The consensus of opinion of the witnesses—and practically admitted by the interested parties—is that the colored enlisted personnel are neither temperamentally or intellectually capable of handling high explosives."

Though the court of inquiry reached no firm conclusion about the source of an explosion that had killed all of its close witnesses and vaporized most of the immediate physical evidence, one possible cause went entirely missing from their list of possible causes. They didn't mention the routine and officer-sponsored races to load ships, despite having heard testimony that they were a regular event on the docks. The intellect and temperament of black sailors had become a significant part of an official explanation that carefully ignored much of the available evidence.

Soon after, the surviving members of Port Chicago's navy loading crews were transferred to barracks down the bay in Vallejo, near the Mare Island Ammunition Depot. Waiting to find out what the navy had in mind for them, the men began to discuss their future—and they decided that they were done with the work of loading explosives onto ships. They prepared a petition, and destroyed it, trying to find a way to present their grievance without signaling a conspiracy to engage in disobedience. Many requested combat duty, preferring to take their chances at war.

And then, on August 9, they were issued work gloves, and marched toward the docks until they all stopped together, simultaneously, at a critical juncture in the road that led to the docks.

Unsure how to proceed, navy officers ordered 258 mutineers confined to a floating barge, locked into tight quarters for three days. While they waited for the navy to decide what to do with them, the men talked—in conversations that would be reported, soon after, by informants. Men who spoke up became ringleaders, organizing the wartime mutiny.

Soon enough, and inevitably enough, the men were given "The Talk"—the same one that William Walker had received during the Civil War, and the same one the Fort Devens WACs would get the following year. On August 11, armed guards led the men from the barge to a baseball field, where Rear Adm. Carleton Wright harangued them over the familiar themes. "I want to remind you men," he told them, "that mutinous conduct in time of war carries the death sentence, and the hazards of facing a firing squad are far greater than the hazards of handling ammunition."

Then Wright left the field, and officers ordered the men to fall into one group or another: Willing to obey all orders and load explosives, or not willing to obey and to load explosives. It

was time to make a final choice, under the fresh threat of execution. "It was an incredibly difficult moment," Allen writes. "Several men wept openly as they chose one side or the other. Two
brothers separated and took opposite positions. Many men vacil-
lated, going first to one group, then to the other." Finally, from a
group of 258 men, 44 stood in the group that was still not willing
to load explosives again. Another 6 were soon added to the group
from work crews that hadn't been present on the barge or the
baseball field, and the navy had its 50 mutineers.

Wright ordered two sets of courts-martial. Men who at first
refused to work but later returned to the docks were given summary courts-martial on a single charge of refusing to obey an
order. A total of 208, from the men on the barge and other crews,
were sentenced to bad-conduct discharges and the forfeiture of
three months' pay.

The other fifty faced a general court-martial, and the possibility of death sentences. As in the Houston riot and the Dakota War
trials, the army produced its justice in box lots: The mutineers
were tried together, fifty men in one courtroom. And again, as in
the aftermath of the Houston riot, much of the thirty-two days of
testimony described events in the aggregate, as witnesses struggled to identify any particular acts by any particular sailors. Lt.
Ernest Delucchi heard a voice say, on the baseball field, that "the
motherfuckers won't do anything to us; they are scared of us;
they won't even send us to sea." A defense objection that this testimony was "hearsay from unidentified speakers" was overruled.
Unattributed, the statement had been effectively attributed to
the whole group.

But evidence was almost beside the point. The court deliberated for a little less than an hour and a half—including a lunch
break—before finding all fifty men guilty, and sentencing them
all to fifteen years in prison. Aggregated evidence established
guilt in the aggregate, which led to an aggregated application

of common justice. Applying a more focused personal evaluation after the trial, Wright reduced the sentences for forty of the men, lowering prison terms to as little as eight years. They were shipped together to the Terminal Island Disciplinary Barracks, in San Pedro, and began to serve their time together.

As in the case of the Fort Devens WACs, the harshness of the sentences led to protest from the NAACP—led by civil-rights lawyer Thurgood Marshall, who had attended some of the court-martial. Marshall won an audience with the navy's Office of the Judge Advocate General, and presented an argument that the case had been won with hearsay testimony and weak evidence; the JAG office suggested to Wright that he reconvene the court to reconsider its verdicts without the questionable witness statements. The court met for a single day, and then announced its decision: The verdicts and sentences stood.

But the end of the war changed the environment in which the NAACP's argument was received, and continued activism did its work. By January 1946, like the Houston rioters sentenced to life and released under later political pressure, forty-seven of the Port Chicago mutiny defendants had been freed from prison. And there was one more act of mercy to come, very modest and very late. On December 24, 1999, President Bill Clinton signed a pardon for Freddie Meeks, one of the two surviving defendants (and the only one to apply for a pardon). Fifty-five years after the event, a single Port Chicago defendant found some form of belated justice.

Nine years later, another president engaged in a similarly belated act of justice.

In August of 1944, a fight between Italian prisoners of war and African American soldiers at Fort Lawton, Washington, had left several seriously injured. The next morning, the body of an Italian prisoner named Guglielmo Olivotto was found hanging from a noose on the post. Forty-three black soldiers were tried for rioting, and three for murder, in a court-martial that saw the prosecution refuse to turn over all of its evidence to the defense. Twenty-eight of the men were convicted on rioting charges, and two were found guilty of manslaughter, despite the inability of most witnesses to identify any of the defendants.

Decades later, the journalists Jack and Leslie Hamann revisited the trial in a years-long investigation, writing a book that cast serious doubt on the convictions. Pressured by members of Congress, the army revisited the court-martial—and overturned every conviction. One of the convicted soldiers, Samuel Snow, got a check from the army in 2007, back pay for the time he had spent in a military prison: $725. Finally, though, President George W. Bush signed a bill into law in 2008 that awarded interest payments to former prisoners convicted after the Fort Lawson riot, and the army awarded honorable discharges and written apologies to the two remaining survivors. At a ceremony in Seattle, Snow was finally given his honorable discharge, at the age of eighty-three. He clutched it to his chest—and died a few hours later.

Resistance to injustice wore down the military's version of separate but equal. William Walker destroyed inequality in the American armed forces; so did Charles Baltimore, and so did Alice Young, and so did Jack Robinson. They destroyed military segregation, together, in the aggregate, over time and by pieces. American society followed, and civil-rights organizations outside the armed forces joined the fight. But the military was first.

The particularly galling racial injustice that followed the gun battle between black infantrymen and white police officers in Houston would also have one other surprising effect: It would make the application of the law a bit less arbitrary for every American who served in the army.

9

"AN EMERGENCY CONDITION"

World War I and the First Debate over Reform

IN THE TWENTIETH CENTURY, TWO WORLD WARS BROKE THE American system of military justice, or appeared to have broken it. Millions of men and tens of thousands of women twice left the armed forces with personal memories of military discipline. Many had experienced courts-martial—as defendants, witnesses, court members, or friends of others who had been put on trial— and the experience was often a bad one. As historian William Generous Jr. writes, the results of wartime military trials were "frequently a shame and a sham." Sentences were grossly inconsistent, particularly across the ranks. "Soldiers' letters to the *Stars and Stripes* in Europe complained voluminously that enlisted men were court-martialed for offenses which officers committed with impunity or a reprimand," a news story noted in 1946. Commanders influenced verdicts, or just steered them like a bus on a schedule. Hurried and pressured, courts guessed at defendants' rights and procedural rules as they went along. As always, no court of appeal offered military personnel a chance to legally challenge an unfair trial.

The scale of twentieth-century war forced a debate. In a few months during 1916, the Battle of the Somme left more than a million men dead or wounded. Americans watching Europe descend into a grotesque paroxysm of mass destruction had to face the possibility that they would be dragged into a conflict that required massive armed forces of ordinary citizens. Robert Penn Warren was right: The Civil War had been a warning. In the age of industry, war would consume populations with startling efficiency. The world would need bigger armies, and a growing number of citizens would be subject to the full scope of their authority.

During the Civil War, Jennifer Keene writes, the Union Army "ultimately only drafted 8 percent of its wartime force," turning to conscription only as the all-volunteer model failed to produce the required numbers. The Americans who served in World War I, on the other hand, "served in the country's first national mass army, of which 72 percent was conscripted." The timing isn't an accident: 1916 was the first year in the century in which Congress significantly revised the Articles of War. A country watching the growth of modern war began to think carefully about its implications for their countrymen who might come to fight it.

The first substantial changes Americans made to their military code in the twentieth century reflect the extraordinary degree to which the earlier laws of the armed forces had been an arbitrary instrument of power; the revised requirements of 1916 are most notable for the fact that they hadn't already been required. "For the first time," writes historian John Lindley, "the code specifically granted the accused the right to be represented by either military or civilian counsel of his own selection." Another article now specifically forbade "compulsory self-incrimination," as if forced confessions had been acceptable for a century and a half.

Still another change precluded witness testimony from members of a court; no longer would it be possible for a person voting on the guilt of a defendant to also be permitted to take the witness stand and offer evidence for his own consideration. And commanders convening a court-martial would finally be explicitly required to tell the defendant what the charges would be before a trial began, rather than being permitted to announce what the charges were after several days of testimony. A soldier defending himself before a court-martial would always know what he was defending himself against.

Congress had given soldiers some extraordinarily basic legal protections—for the first time in American history—a decade and a half into the twentieth century. But these early changes went only so far: Congress debated, and rejected, the creation of a court of military appeals. And it's unclear how deeply the revisions penetrated into the actual functioning of courts-martial. A soldier on trial for serious offenses often didn't seem to know that he had "the right to be represented by either military or civilian counsel of his own selection." Rights on paper weren't consistently rights in practice.

The practical reform of military justice could also serve institutional needs, protecting the armed forces from their own laws. In the months after the United States declared war on Germany in 1917, Acting Judge Advocate General Samuel Ansell noticed a spike in serious offenses in the army. As the nation prepared to join the war in Europe, violations of the Articles of War that resulted in dishonorable discharges "were averaging more than 100 per week." The court-martial had become an escape hatch for men who didn't want to serve in combat. A series of memoranda from Ansell and Secretary of War Newton Baker warned commanders not to reward military offenders by sending them home or to prison, a safer destination than the battlefield. Less punishment was more punitive: Shirkers were forced onto the battlefield because their chain of command had been warned to overlook their calculated transgressions against military law.

Ansell's position as the acting head of the army's legal branch led to one of the most important events in twentieth-century military law, the Ansell-Crowder dispute. During the First World

War, the army had two men who thought they had the same job and the same authority. The judge advocate general of the army, Maj. Gen. Enoch Crowder, was ordered to oversee the wartime draft, a set of duties that left Ansell—a brigadier general—to run his office. As the acting judge advocate general, Ansell regarded himself as the army's top legal officer. But Crowder was only on a temporary reassignment, and hadn't surrendered his title and permanent office; he was still the army's judge advocate general, even as he wasn't in place to do the routine work of that office. A perfect bureaucratic fog settled over the army: Setting out to reform military justice, the person running the JAG office found himself in a long dispute with the person who was in charge of the JAG office.

The Ansell-Crowder dispute was a battle of templates and a struggle for institutional power. As a lawyer, supported by a staff of young lawyers who had joined the wartime army from careers as prominent civilian practitioners and law-school professors, Ansell set out to modernize and rationalize a capricious system—by taking it out of the hands of line commanders and bringing it under his control. Imagine how that proposal would read to a career infantry officer: An office full of lawyers told an organization full of warriors that they wanted to remove authority from the backward and unjust people who had always run it, and instead move it under the authority of people who were capable of balanced action and rational thought. Lawyers said that a thing would work better if it were run by lawyers; they told military commanders that the thing would become more wise and fair if it weren't run by military commanders.

And so a new attempt to reform courts-martial became a struggle over the location of power in the military. In a series of briefs circulated through the top levels of the army and the War Department in 1917 and 1918, Ansell argued that his department should have the direct authority to review court-martial proceedings for legal errors. Finding those errors, JAG lawyers would have the power to overturn unfair verdicts and sentences; their authority would no longer be advisory, and the final decision would no longer belong solely to commanders. The Office of the Judge Advocate General would become a kind of review board, the ultimate judicial destination for military defendants.

If legislation was needed to give him that power, Ansell wrote, "I hope its exercise will not be subjected to General Staff supervision. Such supervision, it seems to me, would necessarily destroy the judicial character of the power." Lawyers, he hoped, would wrestle an area of direct authority over the discipline of soldiers from the officers who ran the rest of the army. Lindley drolly calls Ansell's argument for separate power "a potential irritant" to other power centers in the institution. It was certainly that. The officer acting as the army's top legal official asserted explicitly that courts-martial "are not based upon, but indeed are independent of, command power as such"; though military courts were military, they were "courts all the same." He could not have wandered farther outside the long-established institutional lines.

The institution guarded those lines fiercely and instantly. Replying to the army's top legal officer as the army's *actual* top legal officer, Ansell's primary antagonist made the traditional view of courts-martial explicit. "War is an emergency condition requiring a far more arbitrary control than peace," Crowder wrote. "The fittest field of application for our penal code is the camp. Court-martial procedure if it attains its primary end, discipline, must be simple, informal and prompt." Courts-martial were precisely not "courts just the same," judicial creatures like civilian courts in which the rights of defendants were fundamental; rather, they were an instrument of command authority, designed to stomp out disobedience and slack discipline. Lawyers weren't supposed to run them.

Crowder had more rank, more authority, and more political allies. For the time being, he won. Or at least he mostly won, because a shocking event intervened in the middle of the argument. In Texas, black soldiers from the Third Battalion, 24th Infantry had been tried for their role in the Houston riot, and sentenced to death. Then the War Department and the uniformed leadership of the army had received shocking news from the commander of their Southern District: Thirteen men had already been hanged, without the formality of an approval from anyone outside that military district. A local commander was executing American soldiers in lots without having mentioned the death sentences to the army or its civilian chain of command. Baker issued a general order requiring commanders to submit court-martial proceedings that resulted in death sentences to the judge advocate general. They would at least be checked for serious errors before the sentences could be carried out, though the JAG office wouldn't have the authority to unilaterally overturn verdicts and sentences. The order, Lindley writes, "established some level of appellate review in courts-martial," a change for all soldiers that resulted from the capricious punishment of African American soldiers alone.

AT WAR IN EUROPE, officers of the American Expeditionary Forces (AEF) brought surprisingly few serious charges against their subordinates. More than 2 million Americans served overseas during World War I; only 6,873 were tried by general courts martial. Few were sentenced to death, and fewer still were actually executed: Between 1917 and 1919, the AEF carried out a total of 11 death sentences—fewer than the number executed on a single morning in Texas. But these numbers were the product of personal choice and command decisions much more than they reflected the formal operation of a legal system, and they reflected the institutional defeat of a leader who wanted to create an easier path to the firing squad.

In the first days of January 1918, a US Army court-martial convened behind the trenches in France to conduct the trials of two privates who had refused an order to participate in training. Both soldiers would later say that they had disobeyed their orders because they were physically incapable of obeying—they had been exhausted and almost too cold to move. That same fatigue was written all over their perfunctory trials. Everyone was tired; everyone just wanted to get it over with. A second lieutenant briefly left his infantry platoon to serve as defense counsel, and a hastily chosen handful of officers shambled into place as a court. Shrugging at the charges, the lieutenant suggested to the accused that they just plead guilty and hope for the best. Without a hint of objection or explanation, they did exactly that. And then, after the briefest of deliberations, the court sentenced them both to death.

The soldiers who became symbols of the debate over the forms and boundaries of military justice were ordinary men of very little status. Their personalities were not examined; their names had limited meaning to the men of higher status who would debate their fate.

It started with simple exhaustion. On the evening of December 29, 1917, two privates in the 1st Infantry Division were brought before a general court-martial in France, one after the other, to be tried for sleeping at their posts. Both Pvt. Jeff Cook and Pvt. Forest Sebastian had been assigned to forward positions as sentinels, and both were found asleep—standing up, arms thrown over the forward walls of the trenches—by corporals. Both had gone almost entirely without meaningful rest through the week leading to their shifts on guard duty. In brief trials on a single evening, both were tried and sentenced to die in front of a firing squad.

A few nights later, another general court-martial in the same division tried two more privates, Olon Ledoyen and Stanley Fishback, over their refusal to drill. Together, the two separate trials took less than two hours; a court haphazardly made up of four inexperienced lieutenants and a single colonel barely deliberated over the sentence. And they hadn't needed to deliberate over the verdict. "The second lieutenant who acted as defense counsel allowed both privates to plead guilty to a capital charge and asked only one question in cross-examination of the prosecution's witnesses," Lindley writes. "He had nothing in defense or extenuation to offer." Two more men were condemned to face the firing squad by an indifferent and hurried process.

At first glance, these four trials suggest the level of justice available from a drumhead court-martial in an army exhausted by its conditions on the battlefield. But two of the men sentenced to death had done their own part to exhaust the army that sentenced them to death. For Ledoyen, the court-martial and guilty verdict in January of 1918 were his fifth; for Fishback, they were his fourth. The court that tried to send them to the firing squad reviewed those prior convictions as they deliberated. Both men had made themselves easy to kill; they had offered their own argument that they were beyond the possibility of redemption through mercy.

And then the four death sentences became political symbols.

First, though, all four cases raced through a series of reviews without meeting an obstacle, being approved by the division judge advocate and the division commander before passing through the hands of the AEF commander, Gen. John Pershing, who had no legal authority to review them. The court-martial files from all four cases arrived at army headquarters in Washington, DC, with a note from Pershing all but demanding that the sentences be approved by the president. And he was in a hurry: "I recommend that the sentences in these cases be confirmed and that I be advised by cable of such action." Pershing wanted to get a sharp message to his army about the discipline he expected from its soldiers, and quickly.

At army headquarters, the four cases kept racing toward confirmation. Crowder, as the judge advocate general, pronounced all four to be legally solid: "The court was lawfully constituted," he wrote in each case. "The proceedings were regular. The record discloses no errors." Crowder sent the cases to the army's chief of staff, their next stop on the way through the chain of command to the president, with a covering memo that offered no recommendation about the sentences. But he warned about the institutional politics of the whole affair. "Undoubtedly Gen. Pershing will think, if we extend clemency, that we have not sustained him in a matter in which he has made a very explicit recommendation," he wrote. The lives of four soldiers were on the scale against a general's sense of his political support on the battlefield.

Suddenly, though, two very distinct memoranda appear in the printed records of World War I army justice published by the Senate Committee on Military Affairs after the war. On April 10, 1918, Lt. Col. Alfred Clark, an officer assigned to the Office of the Judge Advocate, took up an extra review of the four death penalty cases sent from France. "All of these cases were tried with an expedition which does not give, on the face of the records, any appearance of deliberation," he wrote. "Counsel for the accused made no statement or argument" in two of the cases, and barely any argument in the other two.

Then Clark went through the brief testimony, noting obvious vagueness in critical answers from witnesses. Finally, he turned to other cases tried by the same court, with similar testimony on similar charges and under similar circumstances. With all that overlap of fact and substance, he wrote, verdicts and sentences landed all over the map: some acquittals, some light sentences, and some death sentences—for the same thing, and in one pair of mismatched cases with nearly identical testimony from the very same witnesses. In cases that had traveled all along the chain of command, earning easy approval, something had gone badly wrong. And no one had apparently bothered to notice.

Five days later, Ansell weighed in with his own memorandum. It wasn't an ordinary piece of institutional writing, and it didn't follow an ordinary review. Addressed to Crowder, Ansell's memo opened with a paragraph explaining its own existence. "After reading these records I said to you the other day that were I the confirming authority, I would not confirm these sentences, and that for the same reason I could not, were I you, recommend confirmation," Ansell wrote. "At your request I shall now state very briefly my reasons as I then stated them to you orally."

An argument had broken out inside the Office of the Judge Advocate General, split between two different conceptions of duty and authority. It was the same argument Crowder and Ansell had been having about process—and that they would go on having—but with four human beings attached to it. An abstract debate over systems and procedures had been turned real. Ansell turned to the "human facts" of the cases, coupling lawyerly argument to a demand for the consideration due to fellow soldiers. "Disapproval need not be based on strict legalism," wrote the army's number-two lawyer to the army's top lawyer. In the age of rising institutional power, in a mass army built through conscription, officials at the top of a bureaucracy were arguing for human specificity—for the salvation of particular, individual lives.

But Ansell was still arguing like a lawyer. Ledoyen, on the advice of the second lieutenant defending his case, had pleaded guilty to a charge of refusing to drill. Then he told the court, in a casual and unsworn statement that wasn't treated as testimony, that he hadn't been *refusing* to drill—but rather had been trying to explain that he was physically unable to drill, after being wet and cold under horrible conditions for a long time. "This statement was plainly inconsistent with his plea of guilty," Ansell wrote, but the court didn't pursue further evidence of the claim. In the cases of Sebastian and Cook, he added, testimony showed that both men had gone days without a chance to sleep. "These are matters of extenuation, the truth of which the court made no effort to prove or disprove." Rushed, shoddy, inattentive, a pair of courts-martial voted to take the lives of their fellow soldiers without noticing the evidence put in front of them. "These cases were not well tried," Ansell wrote.

A powerful sense of responsibility pervades Ansell's memo to Crowder, with not a little self-righteousness; at one point, he writes that a new concern is "finding lodgment in my conscience," and must be expressed. "Were I charged with the defense of such a boy on trial for his life, I would not, while charged with that duty, permit him to make a plea that means the forfeit of his life," Ansell wrote, the government should always have to prove serious charges, and not just have a legal victory handed over without effort. "Court, judge advocate, and counsel should all endeavor to see that there is a full trial as well as a fair trial, and that no matter of defense, including extenuation, be omitted."

Though Ansell mostly lost his wartime dispute with Crowder over systemic court-martial reform, he won the argument about these four men. The very next day, Crowder—who had already argued in writing that the sentences should be approved—began to circulate new arguments against carrying out the executions. "I regret exceedingly that in each case the accused was allowed to make a plea of guilty," he wrote in a long memorandum to the army chief of staff. Ansell had argued with force and conviction, but Crowder had shown the strength of character to discover he had been wrong about a consequential matter of his professional responsibility.

But the lawyers didn't own the whole argument. They could

only offer advice, and weren't alone in being able to offer it. On April 17, immediately responding to Ansell's memorandum and Crowder's change of heart, Chief of Staff Peyton March argued forcefully for the appropriateness of the sentences. March was a highly regarded artillery officer of long service, a worldly man with deep experience as a soldier. As chief of staff, he would modernize the army in lasting ways. His argument for the execution of the four men condemned by hasty courts-martial at the front was a traditionalist's brief for stern military justice, but it didn't come from a merely reflexive traditionalism.

March knew the battlefield, knew the institution, and knew the context of the surrounding events; he minutely picked apart the comparisons to other cases advanced by the JAG lawyers, showing the differences between men condemned to die for sleeping at forward observation posts on the battlefield and men condemned to lighter punishment for sleeping on guard duty in the rear. None of that information had been provided to him— he pieced together a full picture of the cases from the names of the reviewing authorities, knowing which generals were responsible for which duties and areas. It was a brilliant performance of practical knowledge. Then he went on to the particular circumstances of the four cases at hand.

"Before daylight on the morning of November 3, 1917, the first attack by the Germans upon the American lines took place," March wrote. "A salient near Artois, which was occupied by Company F, of the Sixteenth Infantry, was raided by the Germans, who killed 3 of our men, wounded 11, and captured and carried off 11 more. The very next night, that is, the night of November 3–4, 1917, Pvt. Sebastian was found sleeping on his post, and on the night of the 5th Pvt. Cook was found sleeping on his post. This condition of affairs presented an absolute menace, not only to that portion of the line held by the American troops but to the French troops in the adjacent sectors." A combat veteran of two wars—three, if we count his service as a battlefield observer in the Japanese Army during the Russo-Japanese War—March saw the events under discussion with a clarity and a tactical specificity that was missing from the debate between lawyers.

"The safety not only of the sentinel's company but of the entire command is absolutely dependent on the vigilant performance of his duties as a sentinel," March argued. Mercy for failed sentries was cruelty to the men who had relied on their protection.

The same death sentences simultaneously became the subject of a discourse that pushed aside any level of specificity at all. While Ansell, Crowder, and March argued over the four courts-martial, the cases had become public sensations, covered loudly and often in the newspapers. Letters poured into the War Department; civic groups circulated petitions, fighting to save the lives of American soldiers. Many of the letters, Baker explained to Wilson, were from "mothers of soldiers," horrified by the thought that their own sons might stand before a firing squad for a moment of exhausted weakness. Baker had become secretary of war with no military experience; he was a lawyer and old college friend of Woodrow Wilson, and had served as the mayor of Cleveland until 1915. He could not possibly have seen the four cases in front of him more differently than Peyton March had seen them.

"Many of the letters are from serious and thoughtful men," Baker went on, "who argue that these cases do not involve disloyalty or conscious wrongdoing, and that whatever may have been the necessities of military discipline at other times and in other armies, the progress of a humane and intelligent civilization among us has advanced us beyond the helpful exercise of so stern a discipline in our Army in the present war."

At the highest levels of the American military, harsh justice on the battlefield was either seen as a necessary condition to maintain discipline under conditions of great danger—or as a rejection of progress and civilization itself.

Baker did notice one remarkable thing that no one else had thought to mention: Fishback and Ledoyen, who had refused an order to drill, "were members of a company commanded by Capt. D. A. Henckes." The secretary of war had misspelled the name, but he was right about the circumstances: Two privates sentenced to death for disobeying orders at the front had served under the command of the German American army captain David Henkes, who would be sent home from Europe and sentenced to twenty-five years in a military prison for his persistent refusal to fight against Germans. "I cannot force myself to the conviction that I am capable of making war on my kindred upon their soil in a manner that would become my duty and station," Henkes had written to Baker a year earlier, while he was still stationed in Texas, asking to be released from duty. The army had refused his resignation, and sent him to the battlefields of France as a company commander.

"I confess I do not see how any soldiers in his company could have been expected to learn the proper attitude toward the military service from such a commander," Baker concluded.

Perhaps predictably, Wilson sided with his old friend from Johns Hopkins. He granted Cook and Sebastian "full and unconditional" pardons, and commuted the sentences of Fishback and Ledoyen to three years in prison. But the debate over their fate leaves us with a rich record of competing values in the evaluation of military justice, and of the ways that people arrive at those competing values. Newton Baker and Peyton March lived very different lives, and so saw entirely different things in the same set of courts-martial.

For military traditionalists, harshness was mercy: "I recommend the execution of the sentences in all these cases," Pershing wrote, "in the belief that it is a military necessity and that it will diminish the number of like cases that may arise in the future." Exemplary justice prevented future failures of discipline, which prevented future acts of punishment. Kill a bad soldier, save many others from being punished. There were no mere sadists, no naked martinets in the discussion at the highest levels of government; every one of the competing arguments over the lives of four soldiers had some quality of mercy to it, even as men argued for death.

Wilson pardoned Forest Sebastian and Jeff Cook on May 4, 1918; returning each man to his company, he wrote, would give him "the restored opportunity of his forfeited life as a challenge to devoted service for the future." Cook was soon sent home, twice wounded seriously in combat. Sebastian died fighting on July 2, not quite two months after the president spared him from the firing squad. Baker sent Wilson a note bearing the good news. "It will interest you to know that upon restoration to duty both made good soldiers," he wrote.

The president was pleased. "It is very delightful to know that they redeemed themselves so thoroly," Wilson wrote back, "and it was very thoughtful of you to give me the pleasure of learning about it."

An argument about individual lives had proved a structural point: Men forgiven for serious offenses on the battlefield could go on to reestablish a disciplined service. The powerful men arguing for legal formalism and the institutional expression of a civilized mercy were only so invested in the actual lives of the men who had become their symbols.

IN THE FACE of a debate over legal formalization, social judgments still mattered. Even in the comparatively egalitarian US Army, class and status influenced discipline in significant ways. For American officers fighting in the First World War, military justice was often an avoidable embarrassment. While 1,105 AEF officers were tried by general courts-martial—the only tribunal that could try an officer—a hard-to-determine but probably sizable number were removed from the army by the quieter intervention of efficiency boards that had the authority to evaluate officer performance.

Failed privates went to trial; failed officers were often given a gentle hint about their failure through poor performance evaluations that encouraged them to resign their commissions. "The postwar testimony on the efficiency boards in the AEF indicates that even when there were triable offenses, well within court-martial jurisdiction or purview, as a matter of policy most commanders used the efficiency boards, which were clearly designed to deal with sins of omission rather than commission, with inefficiency rather than criminal conduct, to get rid of offenders," Lindley writes. The perception that officers and enlisted men faced different forms of justice was mostly correct.

Still, American enlisted soldiers faced far less severe discipline than privates serving in European armies—to Pershing's lasting disappointment. The AEF commander tried to convince the War Department to give him the authority to approve executions himself, in the field, sparing the need for presidential review. The British and French, he argued, had discipline in the field down to a crisp and brutal science, executing several men for desertion every week. "Beyond doubt punishment for desertion or misconduct must be almost summary if it is to have a deterrent effect," the general wrote in response to Baker's general order requiring the legal review of death sentences before they could be carried out. Pershing never got the power he sought; American soldiers were subject to a system of justice that was far more harsh and arbitrary than civilian justice at home, but far less harsh and arbitrary than military justice in other armies.

But Americans weren't interested in that comparison. When the war ended in November of 1918, criticism of wartime military justice burst open. Ansell appeared before what was then

the Senate Military Affairs Committee in February 1919 to offer
testimony that was widely reported. He didn't hold back. "The
whole system is wrong," he said, describing the very system he
had just been responsible for managing. "For the sake of our men
and their families we must put an end to this cruel system, and
we must do it at once." Ansell's comments met a warm reception in Congress; the chairman of the committee that heard his
testimony had recently spoken from the Senate floor to say that
Americans "have no military law or system of administering justice which is worthy of the name of law or justice. We have simply
a method of giving effect to the more or less arbitrary discretion
of the commanding officer."

As they had in the four death penalty cases, newspapers
picked up the emerging controversy and amplified it—and sim-
plified it, shaving off the complexities of thoughtful positions.
The long debate between Ansell and Crowder, Lindley writes,
"was no longer an argument and discussion confined to a limited number of officers in the War Department." The structure
and process of military justice had gone fully public. The army's
top two lawyers essentially repeated their wartime debate all over
again in a postwar setting, but for a much larger audience. And
the defenders of the status quo didn't just leave the debate in
printed form to the newspapers. At Baker's urging, Crowder had
a subordinate write a long defense of the existing court-martial
system; then the army printed 70,000 copies, under Crowder's
name, and mailed them to the members of state bar associations
all over the country.

The end of the war also implied the arrival of the usual
moment of musical chairs. A peacetime army would be a much
smaller army, with far fewer officers. "Between the Armistice and
June 30, 1919, over 2.7 million officers and men received their
discharge papers and returned to civilian life," Lindley writes.
Officers who stayed on reverted to their peacetime ranks, in an

army that needed far fewer senior officers; Ansell, a brigadier general during the war, was returned to the rank of lieutenant colonel. His supporters assumed the reduction in rank had been a sneaky form of punishment.

Needing to be reappointed to a second term as judge advocate general, Crowder began maneuvering to secure his office against his leading rival, sending out inquiries to find Ansell a job at a law firm—a thing that Ansell had never asked him to do, and that he didn't know his antagonist was doing. Crowder tried a similar tactic for at least one of Ansell's supporters in the office, asking around the army to see if anyone needed a colonel. By polite and indirect means—or by passive-aggressive means—he was cleaning out his old office as he settled back into it.

While Crowder maneuvered against Ansell, Ansell did some maneuvering of his own. In the spring of 1919, two military-justice reform bills—one introduced in the House, one introduced in the Senate—embodied Ansell's list of suggestions, offered directly to members of Congress "without War Department approval." Restrained by a military hierarchy in which his status was declining, he just decided not to bother with it. As always, the question of military appeals was front and center. So was a proposal to assign a legal officer to courts-martial who would control trials like a judge. Another Ansell proposal, a requirement that enlisted men be tried by courts that included enlisted members, Crowder viewed—in the immediate wake of the Russian revolution—as "bolshevism."

Against Ansell's departure from military propriety and his chain of command, the War Department did some maneuvering of its own. A board made up of two major generals and a lieutenant colonel—called the Kernan Board after its president, Maj. Gen. Francis Kernan—reviewed the state of military justice and pronounced it to be just fine. Ansell's proposals, the board warned, would take "the power to discipline our armies" out of the hands of the men who commanded them. With congressional hearings planned to hash out the differences between the Crowder and Ansell camps, the lower-ranking and more radical officer freed himself from institutional restraint so he could fight freely for his cause. Ansell resigned his commission on July 21, 1919, leaving the military in the service of military reform.

At last, the denouement came: The Senate voted on the bill that embodied Ansell's proposals. But the vote, when it came, was a vote on an amended bill; the single amendment was the complete removal of Ansell's proposals, and their entire replacement with a set of reforms proposed by Crowder. The House followed suit, and the revised Articles of War were signed into law in June 4, 1920. The reformers had been outmaneuvered.

"Crowder's handiwork lasted for nearly thirty years before giving way to the Uniform Code of Military Justice," Lindley concludes.

The changes in the Articles of War that Crowder had submitted to Congress as an alternative to Ansell's proposals were relatively modest, but nevertheless important in a few ways. The revised articles forbade a convening authority to send back an acquittal or a light sentence and demand that the court revise their decision; a general could no longer just tell a court that he wanted a do-over with a conviction or a harsher sentence. Other changes required pretrial review of charges by the local judge advocate, and "stipulated that a thorough and impartial preliminary investigation precede all trials."

The military also moved in the direction of a figure who would be like a judge: A trained "law member" would offer rulings on legal questions during courts-martial. But his rulings would be mostly advisory, and could be overturned by the officers who made up the court. Moving in the direction of having judges, the army also moved in the direction of having a court of appeals. A formal board of review created in the JAG Office would "review all sentences of death, dismissal, or dishonorable discharge for the legality of the proceedings," with the authority to recommend to the judge advocate general that the results of a court-martial should be vacated. Baker's wartime general order had been validated as law, and formalized in an official board.

But Crowder meant to block serious reform, and he did. The underlying substance of the 1920 revisions to the Articles of War is that they adopted limited adjustments to defuse a fierce and public criticism that threatened more serious changes. The judge advocate general and his allies largely preserved the existing system of military justice by appearing to modify it. The new articles masked a traditionalist position behind the language of reform, offering change to prevent change. That victory would last all the way through the next world war.

THE COURT-MARTIAL remained useful as a political weapon. Between the wars, one of the most famous military trials in American history addressed questions about the right of American armed forces personnel to publicly criticize the institutions they serve. On September 3, 1925, the US Navy airship *Shenandoah* was ripped apart in a storm over Ohio and fell 6,000 feet to the ground, killing fourteen members of its crew. The navy had also recently lost a trio of seaplanes during an attempt to fly from Los Angeles to Hawaii.

In San Antonio, Col. Billy Mitchell watched these military disasters as the celebrated commander of American World War I air combat forces and the most persistent advocate of air power in the armed forces. Mitchell's career was already in decline, as he embarrassed and frustrated more powerful officers with his unyielding insistence that aircraft would become central to the task of making war; in 1921, he had led a series of tests that showed warships could be destroyed by aerial bombing.

But his successes were taken by other military leaders as failures. In a moment when the US Navy had become a global power, it wasn't helpful to argue that the battleship had been rendered obsolete by a new threat. Mitchell was also known for radical claims, like the one about American military facilities at Pearl Harbor being vulnerable to attack from the air. In the 1920s, everyone knew what nonsense that was. And so Colonel Mitchell lost the rank he had earned in wartime. Then he was sent in exile from Washington, DC, where he had been deputy commander of what was then the Army Air Service, to Texas, where he became air commander to an army corps.

Watching a series of air crashes that were likely to be taken as proof of the limits of air power, Mitchell was unable to stay silent. He called a press conference, and handed out a mimeographed statement: "These incidents are the direct result of the incompetency, criminal negligence and almost treasonable administration of the national defense by the Navy and War Departments."

The 96th Article of War was a catchall, tacked on at the back to allow the army to try soldiers who did something improper or disturbing that wasn't otherwise defined by any particular provision. It prohibited "all disorders and neglects to the prejudice of good order and military discipline," as well as "all conduct of a nature to bring discredit upon the military service." As journalist Joseph DiMona noted, Mitchell described Article 96 with derision; under its terms, he said, "an officer could be tried for tickling a horse." He had done quite a bit more, and he was quickly brought to trial by the army leadership he had denounced as almost treasonous.

The army tried Mitchell in a converted warehouse near the Capitol, bringing him back from Texas to face the institutions he'd attacked. Both sides put on a show. Mitchell, defended by Rep. Frank Reid of Illinois, tried to defend himself by proving he had only been speaking the patriotic truth to a nation that needed to hear it. A parade of defense witnesses testified about the military potential of air power. Will Rogers appeared at the defense table, making a show of patting Mitchell on the back.

On the other side, the judge advocate prosecuting the case closed with an interminable gust of oratory that compared Mitchell to Aaron Burr—"except for a decided difference in poise and mental powers in Burr's favor." The colonel, he warned, was "of the all-too-familiar charlatan and demagogue type," a "loose-talking imaginative megalomaniac." The court, composed entirely of general officers—including Maj. Gen. Douglas MacArthur, a friend of Mitchell's—found Mitchell guilty, and sentenced him to a five-year suspension in rank, duty, and pay. It was the end of Mitchell's career; disgusted, he resigned.

The military had successfully defended its honor against the kind of wild-eyed megalomaniac who would go around saying that Pearl Harbor could be attacked from the air.

10

"WE'VE GOT TO LIVE WITH THIS THE REST OF OUR LIVES"

The Deadly Justice of World War II

WE'RE STILL MOSTLY IN THE DARK ABOUT MILITARY JUSTICE during World War II. Close to 2 million court-martial records remain almost entirely unexamined, leaving us a daunting task that will require many hands and a long effort. But a few broad outlines are coming into focus. In the most serious instances, we've been in the dark about World War II military justice because the federal government has worked to keep us there, condemning soldiers to an obscurity they were reasonably believed to have earned. At the Oise-Aisne American Cemetery in France, the US government's American Battle Monuments Commission runs four burial plots that are open to the public: plots A through D. They hold the honored remains of Americans killed fighting during World War I. But Plot E is from a later war, the closed "fifth field" in a four-section military cemetery. It's locked away behind walls and hedges, where the graves of ninety-six men are marked only by numbers. Deprived of names in death, the soldiers buried in Plot E are the men who shamed their army, the rapists and murderers—and one deserter—whose graves are meant to be hidden.

And then Col. French MacLean found them. He wasn't the first, but he was certainly the most thorough. As an infantry officer nearing retirement and teaching at the National War College after the 9/11 attacks, MacLean sat down to do historical research in army legal records. That's when a friendly clerk asked him an extraordinary question: "Would you like to see the death book?"

The death book: a "green, oversized ledger book, with handwritten entries concerning capital crimes cases involving Army personnel in World War II." He began to go through the entries and the court-martial files, thinking about ways to study the cases in more detail, but found himself overwhelmed by the dimensions of the task. He put them aside and finished his military career.

In 2008, though, now retired, MacLean went back to the cases "in earnest," as a problem to be solved. He had names and court-martial records, but he discovered he had "a paucity of data about the background of the executed soldiers." So he turned to the military personnel records that the government maintains at a facility in St. Louis.

Or, rather, he tried to. Military personnel records are "non-archival," treated as personal files with privacy protections until sixty-two years have passed since a service member's separation from the armed forces. But even when those dates passed for the men in the death book, the records weren't made public. Army personnel officials in St. Louis marked them as "vault files," locked away from ordinary research access. Finally, though, in 2011, the records were moved to a National Archives facility, and the archivists opened the files the personnel clerks had held back. As MacLean pulled the files, he discovered why he'd had so much trouble getting his hands on them. Each had the same thing written across the cover:

Reasons for retention in classified file are
<u>EXECUTION</u>

And so, in an effort that took a decade to really begin, it was a retired army officer who waited out the bureaucracy to put together our first clear look at the ninety-six men the army executed at war in Europe and later moved to a hidden plot at Oise-Aisne. In 2011, it became possible to fully study the most serious matters of military justice in the early 1940s.

The path to Plot E is still a mystery; many more men could have ended up there but didn't. As MacLean writes, "between December 1941 and April 1946, the Army charged 2,799 American soldiers with rape and/or murder," both punishable by death. Many charges were dropped in the chaos of war, and some trials resulted in acquittal, but 1,136 were found guilty of those capital charges. Most were sentenced to prison, while "226 initially received the death penalty, but had this sentence commuted." The soldiers actually executed for rape and murder were exceptions in an army that mostly didn't punish rape and murder with death. What was different for these men? Eighty of the ninety-six graves hold the remains of black soldiers, and that number has been suggested as an answer. "That means that 83 percent of the men executed in Europe, North Africa and the Mediterranean Theaters of Operation were African-Americans, in an Army that was only 8.5 percent black," literature professor Alice Kaplan has written.

There's no question that racism shaped American military justice during World War II. But MacLean's work in the archives shows with appalling clarity that the executions of the men buried at Plot E mostly weren't unjust, even if others got away with similar crimes because of their race, rank, or location. The crimes of the men buried in hidden graves at Oise-Aisne make up a parade of mostly unambiguous depravity, though the resulting trials were sometimes uncomfortably casual for the capital charges they examined. Pvt. James Kendrick was a white soldier hanged in Algeria; he raped and sodomized a nine-year-old girl, suffocating her as her nose and mouth were driven into the ground by his weight. Her body was found five days later, her face eaten entirely away by maggots, after her sobbing mother passed a picture around an army camp and officers sent out search parties.

The crime wasn't a whodunit. Witnesses had spotted Kendrick driving an army truck with the girl and her brother riding as passengers. The brother told investigators that the soldier had sent him away to get him some wine, but was gone when he came back with it. Caught, Kendrick first said the girl had accidentally fallen out of the truck as he was driving it, and was crushed by a wheel. Asked about rape, he responded, "I won't say I did it, but I won't say I didn't do it; because I was too drunk to remember." Then he changed his story, and the new account had the nine-year-old dying of a sudden seizure during consensual sex.

Kendrick was caught at the end of May, 1943, tried quickly in June, and hanged on July 17, a white soldier rushed to the gallows by an appropriately horrified army. His death wasn't a tragedy or an injustice.

Similarly, Pvt. William Harrison Jr., "a white soldier from Ohio," raped and murdered a seven-year-old girl in Ireland on September 25, 1944. "He admitted to being with the girl and desiring sexual contact, but claimed he passed out," sociologists J. Robert Lilly and J. Michael Thomson have written. "He did, however, tell CID officers where to find his boxer shorts at the crime scene." He was hanged on April 7, 1945.

The same month Kendrick was hanged in Algeria, four African American privates in a quartermaster battalion "took turns raping a Sicilian woman in front of her husband and infant child." Again, the crime wasn't difficult to solve: Both the woman and her husband separately picked the same four men out of a lineup of a dozen soldiers. All four admitted it, but blamed the others for the idea. They were hanged the next month.

The list goes on like this, bad men doing horrible things to innocent people and getting caught in generally quick and clear ways. Pvt. Louis Till was hanged by the army on July 2, 1945, along with Pvt. Fred McMurray. Together on the Italian coast, they had robbed a sailor, raped two pregnant women—causing one to miscarry—and murdered a third woman in another house after she tried to close her door to them.

By itself, the presence of Louis Till among the dead men in Plot E is particularly suggestive of a story about racial violence; his son, Emmett, would infamously be murdered ten years later in Mississippi at the age of fourteen after making a show of flirting with a white woman on a dare. Alice Kaplan has argued for Louis Till's death as an artifact of the Jim Crow military. "An Army where black soldiers were classified by race, badly trained, poorly led and treated as less than human encouraged violence among those soldiers," she wrote. "We recently remembered the 50th anniversary of Emmett Till's murder and unjust trial. We also need to remember Louis Till's trial, not because he was innocent, but because we as a nation were guilty."

The example doesn't serve the principle: However guilty we were in the general matter of racial injustice, America "as a nation" wasn't guilty of anything in the case of Louis Till. He was a rapist and a murderer, and met the same fate as white soldiers like James Kendrick and William Harrison Jr. In this case, at least, a black soldier was executed because of what he did, not because of who he was.

Still, some of the ninety-six men buried in the hidden plot at Oise-Aisne were executed following questionable courts-martial, and some of those procedurally defective trials were probably marred by racial prejudice. But the army was at least gesturing at fairness in some of those cases. Pvt. Walter Baldwin, for example, was a black soldier executed by the army; his case suggests several larger conclusions about military justice during World War II.

A postwar criminology study tried to reach an educated guess about the number of people in the wartime armed forces who would have been likely to engage in crime if they had spent the same years as civilians; though it can only be a guess, the likely reality is that the military's criminals are the people who would have been criminals anyway. The nation needed a big army, and quickly. Draft boards culled as well as they could, and one draft-eligible man in eight was released from service "for reasons other than physical." As author William Bradford Huie wrote, "their number was 1,532,500—the temperamentally unstable, the maladjusted, the sexually perverted, and the overly nervous." But induction standards didn't automatically bar people with criminal records from enlisting or being drafted. "Moreover," Generous writes, probably describing every army in history, "the military population was heavily skewed towards males between the ages of seventeen and forty, the largest crime-producing segment of the society at large." The army had a population of criminals because society had a population of criminals, and armed forces recruited soldiers from the heart of that population—with an urgent need to fill up the ranks, and increasingly little time as the war went on to screen for personal character.

In Baldwin's case, a single arrest as a civilian preceded a disastrous series of encounters with military justice. Like Olon Ledoyen and Stanley Fishback in the First World War, a soldier executed by the army gradually reached the gallows by way of *many* courts-martial. He had been inducted in March of 1941, and was executed in a cold morning rain on January 17, 1945. In the short period between those two dates, MacLean concludes, Baldwin was court-martialed "at least" six times. In 1942, the army sent him for a psychiatric evaluation; the resulting report pronounced him to be "a constitutional psychopath with emotional instability and inadequate personality." He was promptly shipped out to France.

William Harrison's personal history had been about the same: five courts-martial before the one that condemned him to death, and a nearly identical diagnosis of a "constitutional psychopathic state, with inadequate personality." The injustice done to these soldiers is in the historical record, but it's not most prominently located in the courts-martial that condemned them to death. They didn't belong in a wartime army.

In August of 1944, Baldwin went AWOL, and not for the first time. Five days after he walked away from his company, he walked into a barnyard and fought with the husband and wife he found there, the French citizens Adolpha and Louise Drouin. He shot both; Adolpha died. Soon after, he "walked in to an American unit bivouacked nearby and admitted that he had just shot a Frenchman."

Under the uncomplicated circumstances of his crime and confession, Baldwin was likely to have come through a court-martial with an easy conviction and a severe sentence. Still, the court-martial convened to try him was composed with some effort to be fair; two of its ten members, 1st Lts. Charles and Benjamin Smith, were African American officers. In a curious reversal, though, the two black officers appointed to sit on the court-martial of a black soldier were challenged and removed from the court by Baldwin himself, at the request of the officers appointed to serve in his defense. The reason given makes little sense from the available records and across the intervening decades: Baldwin's defense team asked that the two black lieutenants be removed from the court "due to the unusual diction of the accused." As the defense motion cryptically explained, "this man has a very unusual diction for a colored person." They didn't elaborate.

Baldwin was convicted on every charge he faced, and sentenced to be hanged. Reviewing his trial, the staff judge advocate for the region where the court-martial took place complained about the poor quality of the proceedings. Lt. Col. Dean Ryman had been "reading records of courts-martial and Boards of Officers with considerable frequency for over a quarter of a century," he wrote, but couldn't remember another court "which shows such a lack of comprehension by all concerned of what the tribunal had to do, or how to go about doing it."

Understandably, Ryman was particularly baffled by the decision to challenge the two black officers who had been added to Baldwin's trial by the explicit order of the general officer who convened the court. For all that, though, he was sure "the correct result has been obtained." Baldwin was executed a few weeks later, his court-martial a strange but not unheard-of shambles. He had received a more serious trial than Ledoyen and Fishback, white soldiers in a previous war whose defense counsel had told them to just plead guilty to capital charges.

ALONE AMONG THE MEN buried in Plot E, Pvt. Eddie Slovik wasn't a rapist or a murderer. He was just a deserter—and, famously, the only deserter executed by the American military during the twentieth century. It was a sign of the army's desperation that he was even there: A petty criminal with a prison record and a distinctly anxious temperament, Slovik had been classified as 4-F, unsuitable for military service, before manpower shortages late in the war forced draft boards to scrape the bottom of the barrel. Shipped into France and the battered 28th Division as a replacement in August of 1944, Slovik fled before even reaching his company. He attached himself to a passing Canadian unit, hanging out for six weeks as a cook and a forager. Eventually, he and another man who had deserted with him returned to their own company. The other man joined the fighting, and wasn't court-martialed; redemption could be earned instantly by picking up a weapon and doing the job.

But Slovik wouldn't earn that redemption. He began thinking about leaving again from the moment he returned to the American lines. Openly and directly, he asked officers if he would be considered a deserter if he walked away from his company. Then he did it, in just as open and direct a way: Slovik approached an officer he thought was an MP and asked to surrender to him as a deserter. That lieutenant sent for someone from Slovik's own 109th Infantry, and 1st Lt. Wayne Hurd arrived. It was October 11, 1944, at Rocherath, Belgium, near the German border.

The US Army had tens of thousands of deserters during World War II, and it executed precisely one. The Articles of War allowed a general court-martial to impose the death sentence for desertion, and forty-nine deserters were sentenced to death during the course of the war—out of 2,864 who were convicted. But the army declined to apply that sentence to every other one of the men convicted of Slovik's offense. Accounts of the execution all take a stab at an explanation, but they miss the background in the events leading up to Slovik's death.

Slovik handed Hurd a handwritten note, a plain confession: "I, Pvt. Eddie D. Slovik #36896415 confess to the Desertion of the United States Army." The note went on to describe Slovik's single experience under enemy artillery fire, shortly after arriving in Europe, when he was "so scared nerves and trembling." He narrated the rest of his experience through the moment that he asked his commander if he would be considered a deserter for leaving his company, and concluded with a signed promise to do it again: "He said their was nothing he could do for me so I ran away again AND I'LL RUN AWAY AGAIN IF I HAVE TO GO OUT THEIR." Hurd delivered Slovik and his note to the private's battalion commander, Lt. Col. Ross Henbest.

The moment that followed is extraordinarily telling, a human instance in a century of mechanized mass killing. It was just this, a single gesture: Henbest tried to give back the note to the man who had written it. Holding signed evidence of a capital offense, a written confession of wartime desertion by a private who was known as a coward and a prior deserter, a battalion commander in the US Army responded by trying to spare the other man any punishment at all. Henbest told Slovik to tear up his confession and go back to his company. The whole thing would just be forgotten. A field-grade officer in combat tried to protect a private from his own bad judgment, in a situation that required absolutely no patience or restraint at all from a military commander.

Henbest wasn't a bleeding heart, and he wasn't trying to nurture Slovik. He wanted him to do the same job, with the same danger, as the men who were at war alongside him. The exchange between this particular battalion commander and this particular deserter gives us a flash of insight into the culture of an army that had tens of thousands of deserters from combat, but only put a few thousand of them on trial: Commanders just wanted men to get back to work, in a climate of shared obligation. Men enduring hardship and danger expected other men to just do the same.

Selfishness galled. A soldier who ran from combat left another man to stand in his place—and possibly to die in his place. Henbest was a high school history teacher; when the war started, he had been on the faculty at the Gulf Coast Military Academy in Mississippi, where upper and lower divisions taught students in kindergarten through twelfth grade. He left to lead a battalion in war, watching young men die in combat after a career teaching young men. Two months later, outside the Belgian town of Bastogne, Henbest would be badly injured; under fire, he ordered his subordinates to give him a rifle and leave him behind. He was the kind of man who wouldn't burden others, at whatever cost, and he was suddenly faced with a man who wanted to run from combat without ever having fired a shot. And so he took Slovik's note, read it, and tried to hand it back. He didn't want to punish him; he wanted Slovik to go stand with other soldiers and fight.

Slovik refused to take the note, and so refused to take the offer of mercy. Moving ahead with a process they had tried to avoid, Henbest and Hurd both signed the back, giving witness to the statement, and Henbest asked Slovik to write an additional statement on the back of the note acknowledging that he understood the legal jeopardy it created for him. Then he tried to give the note back yet again, and Slovik still refused to take it.

The story of military justice is the story of a system, a set of rules and procedures managed by institutions. But it's also, and more powerfully, the story of millions of moments of personal choice, decisions between people who are cold and tired and far from home. A soldier—a brave man, relentlessly committed to his duty and responsible for hundreds of lives in a horrible war and a ravaged division—tried to protect another soldier, a man whose personal history couldn't reasonably be expected to summon the protective instinct. Henbest tried to give Slovik a chance at redemption. The judge advocate of the 28th Division, Lt. Col. Henry Summer, later made Slovik the same offer: Tear up the note and go back to your company, and then we'll forget the whole thing.

Slovik refused again, surely aware that no deserters had been executed, looking for a path to a military prison far from the battlefield. Years later, Huie interviewed a soldier who had guarded men in the custody of the 28th Division as they waited for trial. Sgt. Edward Needles remembered Slovik watching as other deserters came back from their courts-martial, "happy as hell," gleefully announcing that they'd been sentenced to long prison terms that would probably be reduced in peacetime. "He and the kids around figured he might be stuck in jail for two or three years after the war was over," Needles said. In the meantime, prison wasn't a battlefield; they were safe. Slovik insisted on a court-martial as he watched the deserters around him successfully avoid the danger of war. Officers offering him a way to escape a court-martial thought they were offering mercy; Slovik thought they were offering him a way to escape safety and go back to war. Their offer of clemency required his courage, and he didn't have any to give.

The army killed Eddie Slovik, but first it tried not to punish him at all. He insisted.

In the previous war, reformers like Secretary of War Newton Baker had argued with military traditionalists over the fate of men sentenced to death by drumhead courts-martial. Gen. Peyton March, the army chief of staff, had argued for severity as a harder kind of mercy: The exemplary execution of four men who committed serious military offenses would prevent the frequent recurrence of those offenses. Order would prevail in the army, and fewer men would do things that led to courts-martial. Over time, harder punishment would mean less punishment. The reformers won; the executions stopped. In World War II, American soldiers in Europe joked about desertion, and at least 40,000 walked away from their fellow soldiers on the battlefield. In a sense, Newton Baker killed Eddie Slovik; the argument that armies had outgrown severe punishment led to a circumstance in which men leading soldiers at war needed to impose severe punishment to remind men of the possibility. To understand Slovik's choices is to understand a background in which his army had made the punishment of his crime into a joke.

With a signed confession admitting repeated acts of desertion, and a written promise of his intention to desert again, a trial was pro forma. The court-martial that convicted Slovik couldn't have found their way to another verdict.

But then came the sentencing. As serious as the decision was, the members of the court-martial knew the same thing that

Slovik had known as he refused to take back his written confession. After the war, Williams told an interviewer that none of the officers voting to sentence the private to death believed that he would actually be executed. Struck with the seriousness of merely saying that another soldier should die, though, they took a cigarette break to think again about consequences they didn't even think they were really imposing.

Henbest and Summer weren't anomalies: The officers of Slovik's army weren't enthused about imposing the death penalty on him, and didn't reach their decision casually. Lt. Col. Guy Williams, the president of the court, "insisted on three ballots" when it was time to decide on a sentence. "The first was unanimous for death," French MacLean writes. "He then suggested that the panel take a cigarette break. The panel returned and took a second vote. Again, it was unanimous for death. Finally, Williams told the group, 'Well, gentlemen, this is serious. We've got to live with this the rest of our lives. Let's take a third ballot.' Again, the panel voted and again the vote was unanimous."

This is not what we regard as the course of the twentieth century, an era of increasingly callous state violence on a rapidly growing scale. Courts-martial in World War I had pronounced the death penalty on privates in the time it would take to eat lunch; not quite three decades later, a whole series of army officers hesitated to punish a private who couldn't have been more obviously hostile to his most basic duty. A giant government institution, notoriously bureaucratic and petty, was becoming more and more hesitant about taking the lives of its lowest-ranking members.

Slovik's death before a military firing squad was probably secured by a civilian agency. As his chain of command considered whether to grant clemency or carry out the sentence, the FBI sent Slovik's civilian criminal records to army officials in Europe. They hadn't known, and would have gone on not knowing without the outside intervention. Before he became a soldier, and before he became a military convict, Slovik had been a persistent petty criminal at home in civilian life. A thief several times over, he had spent several years of his short life in prison.

To an organization that regarded punishment as exemplary and found itself in the midst of a desertion crisis, Slovik's past made him an easier man to kill: a criminal, a coward, a man of no account, and a soldier who had turned aside the army's several attempts to give him mercy. In a letter to Gen. Dwight Eisenhower that misspelled the general's name, Slovik acknowledged that he had been offered redemption and refused it. "Then I wrote my confession," he explained. "I was then told that if I would go back to the line they would distroy my confession, however if I refused to go back on the line they would half to hold it against me which they did." Eisenhower approved his execution.

Slovik seems to have understood why he had been chosen as the deserter who would serve as an example. On the morning of January 31, 1945, a military police sergeant supervised the soldiers tying Slovik's hands behind his back before leading him to the courtyard where he would be shot. Sgt. Frank McKendrick whispered to Slovik to "take it easy," trying to calm him in the moments leading to his death. MacLean records the condemned man's response: "Don't worry about me; I'm okay. They're not shooting me for deserting the United States Army—thousands of guys have done that. They're shooting me for the bread I stole when I was twelve years old."

He was at least partially correct. But Eddie Slovik never looked outside himself; obsessed with his own fear and his own self-preservation, he never noticed the discussion other men were trying to have with him. They were trying to tell him that he was a part of something, connected to the lives of other men and obligated to fight for them at least as much as he looked after his own safety. Ross Henbest had something in his own character that allowed him to see the importance of other lives, even as he thought his own was ending; wounded in combat, he told other men to leave him behind and worry about themselves. Whatever it was in Henbest that gave him the strength to make that choice, Slovik didn't have it. Huie, in a surprisingly sympathetic account, called Slovik "a little man who would never know serenity," hobbled by personal weakness.

At war, watching men die, the officers responsible for Slovik's death had no patience for that little man's selfish weakness. In his message about the private's execution, the commander of his regiment would explain that he had been shot "for deserting his unit and his fellow man." Guy Williams, talking to Huie after the war, didn't regret that Slovik was shot, even as he expressed surprise that the sentence was carried out. The court-martial had reached the right sentence. "I didn't think I had a right to let him get away with it," he said.

And he probably didn't.

THE COURTS-MARTIAL of men like Louis Till and Eddie Slovik seem to tell a story of a harsh justice that mostly rolled downhill, inflicted by men of high rank on men on low status: privates, at the bottom levels of a mass army, chewed up and spit out by a giant institution. But the political vindictiveness and procedural unfairness of World War II courts-martial is illustrated well by the trial of a defendant whose rank and status were worlds apart from those examples. The strange and cruel trial of Capt. Charles McVay, the commander of the heavy cruiser *Indianapolis* when it was torpedoed and sunk by a Japanese submarine on July 30, 1945, would remain a topic of political debate for many decades after the event.

The fate of the *Indianapolis* is grimly famous. Struck by two Japanese torpedoes, the ship sank in a few minutes. Survivors would guess that about 300 men from a crew of 1,196 went down with the ship; the rest mostly ended up in the water without lifeboats, because they didn't have time to launch them. A series of oversights meant that no one reported the failure of the ship to arrive at its destination in the Philippines, so the men stayed in the water for five days while no one went searching for them. While they floated in their life jackets, the crewmen from the sunken ship were attacked by sharks, relentlessly, in wave after wave of powerful strikes that pulled screaming men under the water in a wet blossom of blood. On the fourth day, at long last and wholly by accident, a navy pilot flying an antisubmarine patrol noticed an oil slick in the water below him. He flew lower to investigate, saw men in the water, and sounded the alarm about the sinking of the *Indianapolis* for the first time.

The rescue that followed is a story of courage several times over. First, a seaplane pilot sent to drop rafts and rescue equipment saw men being attacked by sharks and disregarded a standing order not to land in the water; Lt. Wilbur Gwinn and his crew pulled fifty-six men out of the ocean, bobbing defenseless on the surface and unable to fly while overloaded with survivors. A few hours later, the first rescue ship arrived: the *Cecil Doyle*, a destroyer. "Disregarding the safety of his own vessel," reads one account, "the *Doyle*'s captain pointed his largest searchlight into the night sky to serve as a beacon for other rescue vessels." In a place where an American ship had recently been sunk by Japanese torpedoes, American sailors revealed their position at sea— while stationary in the water. This is the navy at its best, a picture of men risking their lives in service to one another. Together, the rescuers saved 317 men; somewhere around 600 had died while they were helpless in the water.

The events that followed still don't make much sense. During World War II, several hundred US Navy vessels were sunk by enemy action. It's an ordinary consequence of war: navies fight at sea, and ships are sunk. But McVay was tried by a court-martial, a decision that makes him the only US Navy commander ever put on trial for losing his ship to an enemy attack. The irony of the *Indianapolis* is that Americans were able to consider the full horror of its sinking, and demand accountability for the seriousness of the loss, because the war was over when the news first broke. The *New York Times* editorial calling the sinking of the ship "one of the darkest pages of our naval history" ran directly below the editorial on the postwar closure of the federal government's Office of Censorship. It was suddenly not possible to limit discussion of the event.

The many histories of the *Indianapolis* all note that the uniformed leadership of the navy, along with the civilian leaders of the Navy Department, gave an unexplained series of contradictory recommendations about the possibility of a court-martial for McVay. They were under pressure, and making decisions with one eye to the newspapers; in a memorandum to Secretary of the Navy James Forrestal, Judge Advocate General Oswald Colclough justified the charges against the captain "from the fact that this case is of vital interest not only to the families of those who lost their lives but also to the public at large." The navy was having a court-martial for the newspapers.

In May of 1999, trying to restore McVay's reputation long after the captain's death, the US senator Bob Smith decried the unseemly rush to judgment that followed the sinking of the *Indianapolis*. The loss of the ship and the delayed rescue of its crew was an embarrassment to the navy, and at least partially the result of several bad decisions that weren't McKay's to make. Four days before the *Indianapolis* left Guam, another navy ship had been sunk by a Japanese submarine along the route McVay would be taking; navy officials on Guam knew about the sinking of the *Underhill*, but didn't tell him about it.

Officers on Guam even knew the particular submarine—the

I-58—that was waiting in the path of the *Indianapolis,* since the ULTRA code-breaking system had allowed the navy to decipher the Japanese navy's encoded radio traffic. Again, no one told McVay. Since his ship wasn't equipped to detect the presence of submarines, the captain asked in Guam to be escorted to Leyte by a destroyer. His request was denied—by an officer who knew about the submarine revealed by the ULTRA intercepts. Then, in another intercepted and decoded message, naval intelligence heard the *I-58* reporting it had sunk a ship. The message wasn't passed on to potential rescuers. Imputing criminal negligence to McVay's failure to keep a Japanese submarine from sinking his ship, the navy was assigning full blame to one officer for a series of choices that passed through many hands.

The navy's desire to avoid a thorough discussion of such a serious loss—and the horror of 600 men being killed by sharks and ghastly thirst while no one looked for them—is suggested by the timing of the public announcement that the ship had been sunk. The *Indianapolis* was torpedoed on July 30; the navy learned no later than August 2 that the ship had been sunk. And yet the navy first acknowledged the loss on August 15—after the atomic bomb attacks of August 6 and 9, and on the day Emperor Hirohito announced that Japan would surrender. The news of the loss was released into the noise of bigger news, unsuccessfully brought before a public awash in information.

While those final events brought the war toward its close, the survivors of the *Indianapolis* were separated by different rescue vessels that went to different places. The whole group of surviving crew members wasn't available to discuss the events surrounding the loss of the ship. But the navy quickly went ahead with a court of inquiry on Guam, where McVay had been taken, and the inquiry recommended a court-martial on the limited information it had. McVay's supposed failure was that he had disregarded orders to zigzag his ship in good visibility and at his discretion, and had stopped zigzagging shortly before the torpedoes struck—a point that would become critical in his court-martial. The Pacific Fleet commander, Adm. Chester Nimitz, didn't agree that the loss of the ship warranted a court-martial, and sent navy headquarters a recommendation that McVay just be given a letter of reprimand. For reasons they didn't explain, though, Secretary of the Navy James Forrestal and Chief of Naval Operations Ernest King demanded that McVay be brought to trial. The court-martial was to convene on December 3, 1945, at the Washington Navy Yard.

The orders didn't specify one thing, however: They didn't say what charges McVay was supposed to be facing. He had committed a crime of some kind, and would be tried for it, with the actual crime to be determined at some future point. Four days before McVay's court-martial opened, the navy finally provided him with the charges he would face: "failing to issue timely orders to abandon ship," on a ship that had been ripped in half by torpedoes and sunk without power in a few minutes, and "hazarding his vessel by failing to zigzag during good visibility." The officer appointed to defend him, Capt. John Cady, had four days to prepare.

The trial that followed was both an unambiguous travesty and a strange piece of theatre. Capt. Oliver Naquin, the officer on Guam who had denied McVay's request for a destroyer escort, had known about both the sinking of the *Underhill* and the ULTRA intercept that showed the *I-58* in the path of the *Indianapolis*. In his testimony, he didn't mention any of that; in his judgment, he told the court, the risk of a submarine attack on the Indianapolis had been "very slight," justifying the ship's unescorted transit. It was a bizarre claim to make after the ship had been sunk by a submarine, and in support of a charge that McVay had failed to protect his ship against the threat of a submarine attack.

More strangely, a highly regarded navy submarine commander, Cmdr. Glynn Donaho, was called to establish that McVay was negligent in failing to zigzag. Asked if it would have been more difficult for him to hit a zigzagging ship with a torpedo, though, Donaho said no: "Not as long as I could see the target." Again, his answer was somehow taken to support the charge.

But finally, in one of the really bizarre choices in American military history, the navy put its star witness on the stand: Capt. Mochitura Hashimoto, the commander of the *I-58*—the man who had given the order to fire the torpedoes that sunk the *Indianapolis*. The US Navy's case against an American naval officer depended on the testimony of a recent enemy, whose personal actions had killed hundreds of American sailors. Hashimoto described for the court the way he had sunk the ship—in testimony meant to establish a crime by the man commanding the ship he had sunk. It was like charging George Patton for the loss of some tanks, and summoning Erwin Rommel as a prosecution witness.

McVay was partially acquitted, partially convicted, and entirely destroyed. Found not guilty of failing to give timely orders to evacuate the ship, he was found guilty on the charge that he had hazarded the *Indianapolis* by failing to zigzag. It was his fault the ship sank. His sentence, a long reduction of place on the promotion list, ended his career. He retired—then promptly returned to active duty the next year when Forrestal, who had insisted on McVay's court-martial, commuted his sentence. McVay retired in 1949 as a rear admiral, shamed and cast out and called back.

But the shame lasted. In November of 1968, at home with his wife, McVay shot himself in the head. A desk drawer in his office was filled with letters from the families of men killed on the *Indianapolis*.

In McVay's absence, the survivors tried to clear their former captain's name. In 1996, responding to demands for his posthumous exoneration, the navy's judge advocate general announced that the verdict would stand. "The conclusion reached is that Captain McVay's court-martial was legally sound; no injustice has been done, and remedial action is not warranted." Four years later, a joint congressional resolution declared that "Captain McVay's military record should now reflect that he is exonerated for the loss of the U.S.S. *Indianapolis* and so many of her crew." President Bill Clinton signed it on October 30, 2000. But the navy has never taken any further action. The conviction stands; in the records of navy courts-martial, Charles McVay caused the *Indianapolis* to be sunk.

HERBERT HAUPT was the twentieth century's Lambdin Milligan, the American who planned to attack America. In military terms, the effort undertaken by Haupt and his fellow plotters was close to meaningless, and began to fail as soon as it began. But their legal legacy is still with us, shaping the debate over the way military justice deals with captured enemies who aren't uniformed soldiers.

The path eight saboteurs took to a military commission and the Supreme Court began on a beach. Chief Radioman Harry McDonald was supposed to be tracking German submarines for the Coast Guard. When his moment came, it wasn't a difficult one: On the night of June 12, 1942, a German submarine got stuck on the sandbar just off the coast of Amagansett as it dropped a team of saboteurs on the coast. As journalist Michael Dobbs has written, "McDonald no longer needed his sophisticated tracking equipment to find a submarine in the middle of the ocean: he could both hear and smell the roar of U-202's diesel engine." The German navy was parked next to the beach.

Not far away that night, Coast Guard seaman John Cullen was assigned as a lone "sand pounder," walking an unarmed foot patrol up and down Amagansett Beach to look for signs of an enemy naval presence or violations of coastal blackout requirements. Shortly past midnight, he saw a group of men climbing out of the waves, dragging duffel bags; one was wearing a fedora. He asked who they were, and one of the men broke away from the others to answer his questions. They were fishermen from East Hampton, he said, and they'd accidentally run aground. Cullen spent a few moments trying to convince the stranger to walk with him to the nearby Coast Guard station, but the man resisted. Finally, as Cullen took him by the arm and told him "you have to come," the other man made himself absolutely clear: "Look, I wouldn't want to kill you." The stranger stuffed some cash into his hand and told him to forget he'd seen anything. Alone and unarmed, Cullen ran for help. Amazingly, they didn't try to stop him.

McDonald and Cullen had spotted the first signs of Operation Pastorius, a German plan to land eight saboteurs in the United States, equipped with explosives and a list of important economic targets. The saboteurs were all German-born, but all had also lived in the United States, and spoke English well; one, Haupt, had become a US citizen. They were expected to pass as Americans while striking from within, sustaining a campaign of psychological terror and material harm.

The men arrived by submarine in two teams, one on Long Island and one in Florida, and the first team reached New York City while the Coast Guard was digging their buried explosives out of the sand. But two decided not to go through with the plan, and George Dasch—the man who had tried to bribe Cullen on the beach—traveled to FBI headquarters to reveal the operation. He initially had some trouble getting the FBI to hear him out; his first move was to call the FBI switchboard and ask to speak to J. Edgar Hoover.

Soon enough, though, the FBI had enough information to arrest the remaining saboteurs. All eight were in federal custody by June 27, ending a campaign of military sabotage before it actually resulted in any military sabotage. The men were held and interrogated by the FBI; the matter was, initially, a civilian effort during wartime, a criminal investigation against enemies who hadn't been caught in military uniforms and weren't regarded as prisoners of war.

President Franklin Roosevelt changed the government's course with a pair of proclamations on the topic of enemy saboteurs, both issued on July 2. The first declared that all "subjects, citizens or residents of any nation at war with the United States," who enter the United States "to commit sabotage, espionage, hostile or warlike acts, or violations of the laws of war, shall be subject to the law of war and to the jurisdiction of military tribunals." Though the saboteurs had been caught by a civilian law-enforcement agency while they lived as apparent civilians, they wouldn't be tried by civilian courts. In his second proclamation, Roosevelt appointed a panel of seven army generals to try the eight erstwhile attackers, and assigned Attorney General Francis Biddle and Judge Advocate General of the Army Myron Cramer to prosecute them.

Moving the trial out of open civilian courts and into a closed military tribunal accomplished two things for Roosevelt and the government. The first had to do with the sense among officials that the law wouldn't do the necessary job. Judge Advocate General of the Army Myron Cramer warned the administration that federal law and the rules of evidence in federal court "would make it difficult to obtain a conviction for sabotage." After all, no sabotage had taken place. The most likely outcome of a civilian trial would be conspiracy convictions and short prison terms.

At least as important, though, was the value of secrecy in protecting a story the government was getting away with telling. German submarines had driven up very nearly to the beach, dropped off trained attackers equipped with explosives, and slipped away back to sea—despite the fact that one spent some time trapped on a sandbar, engines roaring as it worked its way free. Neither had been sunk; neither had been fired upon. In an open trial, writes historian Jonathan Lurie, "it would become clear to all just how easy it had been for two German submarines to land German nationals on the East Coast in 1942, totally undetected." Then the attackers had left the beaches, reached major cities, found apartments, and settled in comfortably. The FBI only began to investigate after one of the men insistently worked to turn himself in and identify his fellow saboteurs; undetected, the conspiracy walked itself into an FBI office and sat down. The government hadn't protected the coastline, or the country, very much at all.

The story in the press, though, was a story about extraordinary heroism and brilliant investigation. "Lone Coast Guardsman Put FBI on Trail of Saboteurs," the *New York Times* reported, and "FBI men under J. Edgar Hoover took up the chase from there." They didn't, and a trial in federal court would show that they didn't. So there would be no trial in federal court.

The alternative trial by military tribunal began almost immediately, conducted in secret inside the headquarters of the Department of Justice, and was essentially pro forma: The explosives had been recovered, and the men had been identified by one of their own team leaders. There wasn't much to prove.

But then the legacy of the Civil War got in the way. Roosevelt had appointed a team of army lawyers to defend the saboteurs before the military tribunal. Among them was Col. Kenneth Royall, a Harvard Law School graduate who was also a combat-wounded veteran of World War I. Royall looked to precedent, and saw the bright lights of *Ex Parte Milligan*, the 1866 case that established the constitutional limits on the use of military commissions when civil courts were open and functioning. In 1942, civilian courts were open throughout the United States; there was a place to bring the captured men to trial, with the protections of due process and the ordinary functioning of law. The Supreme Court had spoken, nearly eighty years earlier: Military commissions were not supposed to operate under those conditions. The government had to take its eight prisoners down to the federal courthouse and file charges with the Article III courts.

But Royall had orders from the president of the United States. The civilian courts were closed to the saboteurs, and they were to be tried by the military, period. So he invited Roosevelt to change his order. In a letter sent to the White House by messenger, Royall and another army lawyer told the president directly and personally, "There is a serious legal doubt as to the constitutionality and validity of the Order." A court should hear the matter, they argued, but the president's order forbade them to bring the case to the courthouse. And so, they concluded, "We respectfully suggest that you issue to us or to someone else appropriate authority to that end." Summoned to the White House the next day, the two lawyers sat "for what seemed like an eternity" without meeting Roosevelt, until a secretary emerged with the final word: "The President does not wish to discuss the matter with you." In the absence of a directive from above, the president had suggested, Royall "should act in accordance with his own judgment."

Royall gave Roosevelt one more chance to stop him, sending the president a letter warning him that he had decided to go forward with a legal challenge. "I will so proceed unless specifically ordered otherwise," he wrote. He got no response.

Before he brought his argument to court, though, Royall asked one more time for permission to make it. Standing before the military commission in the makeshift courtroom where it was conducting its trial, the colonel announced that he had "prepared papers for an application for a writ of habeas corpus, the purpose of which is to test the constitutionality and validity of the

President's Order." The other army officers appointed as defense lawyers took to their feet to distance themselves from Royall's statement, declaring themselves unable to oppose an order from their commander in chief. Undeterred, Royall explained that he would stand alone in the matter. "I am not asking anybody to take any part of my responsibility," he said. "I will do that and suffer the consequences."

After an adjournment for deliberation, the members of the tribunal returned with a statement: The commission, they announced, "does not care to pass on that question." Royall was on his own. He filed a motion for a writ of habeas corpus, and a district-court judge in Washington, DC, denied the petition. The military trial went on.

Royall was in a race, worried that his clients would be convicted and executed before he could even finish making his argument about jurisdiction. He wanted to bring the case before the Supreme Court, trying to stop a military proceeding that was drawing to a close. But it was summer: the court wasn't in session. He would have to convince the justices to convene. The colonel started in the obvious place, knocking on Associate Justice Hugo Black's front door. As lawyer Pierce O'Donnell has written, Black "was widely regarded as one of the Supreme Court's staunchest champions of the Bill of Rights," and was likely to see the constitutional issues clearly.

"The president had unilaterally decreed that the federal courts were off-limits to this class of enemy saboteurs," O'Donnell writes. "Even in time of war, this was an audacious power grab that shifted the balance of power from Congress to the president."

But Royall never even began to make his argument. A few steps inside Black's home, he announced the reason for his visit—and the justice threw him out. "I don't want to have anything to do with that case," Black announced, opening the front door he had just closed "in a clear demand that the unwelcome visitor leave at once." Royall left.

His next step would require a visit to the countryside. On July 23, a military plane made an extraordinary flight from DC to Philadelphia, where FBI agents were waiting to drive Royall, Biddle, Cramer, and another defense lawyer to the farm outside the city owned by Associate Justice Owen Roberts. Another visitor was already there, waiting for them to arrive: Hugo Black, who had come at Roberts's request. The Supreme Court justice served cheese and crackers to his guests, with glasses of milk from his own cows. Biddle thought they were arguing about nothing, debating a matter of undisputed wartime power. "The position of the Attorney General," an early law review article reported, "was that the President could lawfully have ordered the prisoners shot as soon as they were arrested, that trial before the Military Commission was given as an act of grace and not of necessity, and that as belligerents the prisoners had no right of access to any court." But Royall and Biddle went for a walk around the farm while Black and Roberts debated the request and phoned their colleagues, and the private discussion brought them to a conclusion: The Supreme Court would convene to hear arguments.

The court moved with remarkable speed while the military tribunal paused for its decision. Briefs were filed on July 29, and the court immediately heard oral argument the same day and the next. Royall appeared in the Supreme Court with Col. Cassius Dowell, one of the army lawyers who had declared to the military commission his unwillingness to challenge a presidential order. "In conscience," O'Donnell writes, "he could not abandon Royall as their against-all-odds struggle approached its climax." He was a lawyer; he would serve his clients.

Personally arguing the government's case, the attorney general continued to insist that there was no role for the courts in a matter that strictly involved military conflict. "The United States and the German Reich are now at war," Biddle began; the East Coast, he argued, "is a theater of operations." War is the business of the president and his military subordinates, not subject to the authority of judges.

Royall argued *Milligan*: The military was holding trials on American soil while the civilian courts were open.

The court issued a succinct order on the very next day. The charges brought against the defendants, the order concluded, "allege an offense or offenses which the President is authorized to order tried before a military commission." The military trial was lawful, and could proceed. It promptly did, and condemned all eight captured saboteurs to death.

On August 8, almost immediately following the conviction, six were executed by electric chair at the District of Columbia Jail. Roosevelt commuted two death sentences. Dasch, who had revealed the operation to the FBI, would serve thirty years in prison, and Ernest Burger, who had also assisted in the investigation, would serve a life term in prison. Both were released from prison in 1948 and sent home to Germany.

Three months later, the unanimous Supreme Court released a full opinion in *Ex Parte Quirin*. We're still arguing over what it means. *Milligan* didn't matter, the court decided, even for the US citizen Herman Haupt. Lambdin Milligan had been a citizen of long standing, resident in the United States; the saboteurs were subjects of a foreign state at war with the United States and entered the country to attack it.

More simply, though, the Supreme Court had allowed enemy agents into the courthouse. While Roosevelt had the authority to order the trial of the saboteurs by military commission, the majority opinion concluded, "neither the Proclamation nor the fact that they are enemy aliens forecloses consideration by the courts of petitioners' contentions that the Constitution and laws of the United States constitutionally enacted forbid their trial by military commission." Adversaries held by the military could ask the courts to consider their cases; even if the courts answered that their trial by the military was permissible, they at least had the right to ask the court to consider the question.

The *Quirin* decision has usually been considered a capitulation to executive power, allowing the president's military commission to get back to its job—and allowing the government to promptly execute its prisoners without fear of further legal intervention. The Supreme Court, O'Donnell argues, "failed most miserably in preserving the delicate balance between security and liberty. . . . More than anything else, allowing the prisoners to be executed without a fully reasoned opinion was a gross dereliction of duty later acknowledged by several justices."

But another view, forcefully expressed, is that *Ex Parte Quirin* set aside a long understanding of the nature of war, allowing the nation's enemies to challenge national authority in time of war. The courts had rejected the attorney general's argument for summary executive action. Enemies could sue.

"*Quirin's* holding on court access for undisputed enemy fighters was contrary to practice and precedent, is not supported by substantial reasons, and interferes with a detailed framework of international law and diplomacy that has long governed detention and treatment of captured enemy combatants," legal scholar Andrew Kent argues.

In just a few years, the *Quirin* ruling produced effects that would have looked indescribably strange to the earlier Americans who had run military commissions in Mexico, Minnesota, California, and the Philippines. It was in that latter place that Gen. Tomoyuki Yamashita was on trial on war-crimes charges before an American military commission in 1946—when he petitioned the federal courts for a petition of habeas corpus. Yamashita had argued that he wasn't personally responsible for massacres committed by soldiers serving under his command, since he hadn't affirmatively ordered them to commit those acts.

The Supreme Court's decision in *In re Yamashita* established the "Yamashita Standard," holding a military commander responsible for the actions of his subordinates whether or not they were following his orders. He was executed. But the more remarkable fact was simply that a Japanese general had appealed to the US Supreme Court, and had found the court willing to consider his case. The Modoc leader Captain Jack could not have imagined that possibility.

More than seventy years after the court's decision, the argument over the effects of *Quirin* is far from being closed.

WHILE AMERICANS DECIDED how to bring their enemies to justice, they were also asking sharp questions about the way their own military personnel had been treated during the war. Even before World War II ended, the army and navy began to examine the effectiveness and fairness of wartime military justice. A profusion of institutional committees reviewed the records of courts-martial and found their proceedings to be a recurring disaster; in 1946, a postwar army panel declared that court-martial sentences had been "fantastically" excessive. A War Department clemency board, with the recently retired Supreme Court justice Owen Roberts serving as chairman, reviewed tens of thousands of courts-martial, "remitting or reducing" 85 percent of the convictions and sentences it evaluated. A similar navy study reviewed 2,115 wartime trials, and found that "almost half" involved "flagrant miscarriages of justice."

As William Generous has noted, the committees that examined wartime military justice were made up of a diverse set of panelists—men from different backgrounds and professions: judges, law professors, prominent lawyers in private practice, and a mix of senior and junior officers drawn from the armed forces. And there was, between them, a "general agreement among the majority." In World War I, the contest between lawyers and warriors had produced sharp divisions in the evaluation of courts-martial and their work. In the next war, those divisions became far less pronounced. People from a range of backgrounds, approaching the topic from different starting points, reached something far closer to consensus:

American military justice was broken.

II

"You Cannot Maintain Discipline by Administering Justice"

The Cold War and the UCMJ

THE SPRING AND SUMMER OF 1952 WERE A CONFUSING TIME FOR the men who found themselves hanging out with Capt. Fred Chewning, a Signal Corps officer stationed in Georgia. Soldiers and their civilian friends kept suddenly and inexplicably finding themselves engaged in forbidden sexual acts with the captain. They weren't sure why, though Paul Kessler thought it was maybe the beer. "Sometimes when I am under the influence of alcohol, I am homosexual myself and I followed him and committed an act of sodomy," he explained. Sober, though, he realized that he hadn't meant it; like Cpl. Donald Charnetzky, who had also accidentally engaged in sexual acts with his company commander, Kessler reported Chewning's crime to the army. The captain was sentenced to three years in prison at hard labor, an outcome that survived command approval and appellate review.

By the end of World War II, the armed forces had long since developed a vague social tradition of looking away from many kinds of sexual offenses. As James Valle wrote about the court-martial of Marine Corps Pvt. George Crutch for an attempted act of shipboard sodomy in 1805, or the trial of a navy lieu-

295

tenant with a taste for young boys, courts-martial had no appe-
tite for detailed testimony about illicit sex. They often rushed
through trials, cut short the testimony, and got right to the not-
guilty verdict—which would be followed soon after by the quiet
departure of the acquitted defendant.

The soldierly distaste for allegations of illicit sex could even
lead to charges against people who made commanders consider
an uncomfortable allegation. In 1879, in a notorious incest trial,
Brig. Gen. Edward Ord had convened a court-martial to try Capt.
Edward Geddes on false-accusation charges. From a small post
in West Texas, and with support from other witnesses, the captain had reported that he saw 1st Lt. Louis Orleman having sex
with his own daughter, Lillie, as she begged him to stop. Geddes was convicted, though President Rutherford Hayes threw out
the verdict; Orleman wasn't charged. To their commander and
the court-martial, the captain had committed the more serious
offense, making his fellow officers consider events they didn't
want to notice.

In the military as in the larger society, violations of discretion
became simply *false*, facts notwithstanding, as a way of shunting
aside an ugly story. "The easiest attitude for a public that never
spoke about such things was to assume that an accusation of
incest could not be true," literary scholar Louise Barnett writes in
her study of the trial. "Even if it were, bringing it to light was the
greater scandal, a corruption of public discourse." For a century
and a half, military commanders and the courts they convened
didn't want to hear about this stuff.

And then, suddenly, they did. The Cold War had sex on its
mind, in a long panic that tied communist ideology to homosexual desire—seeing intertwined threats in behavior regarded
as political perversion and sexual perversion. Courts-martial
aggressively policed the sexual acts and sexual preferences of
armed-forces personnel, in a long campaign meant to shape a

culture for its dangerous political and military struggle with a terrifying enemy. The legal historian Elizabeth Lutes Hillman appropriately titled her book on Cold War courts-martial with a double meaning in mind: *Defending America*. The military was defending the country, and the military justice system was defending its values. Courts-martial joined the culture war.

In that choice, the military was just doing what the rest of the federal government was doing at the same time. In 1953, President Dwight Eisenhower issued Executive Order 10450, requiring federal agencies to investigate civilian employees who might present a security risk. On the one hand, the order required the investigation of federal officials who might have "a sympathetic association with a saboteur, spy, traitor, seditionist, anarchist, or revolutionist, or with an espionage or other secret agent or representative of a foreign nation." But the order also required that agencies be on the lookout for "criminal, infamous, dishonest, immoral, or notoriously disgraceful conduct, habitual use of intoxicants to excess, drug addiction, sexual perversion."

As historian David Johnson has written, these weren't really separate Cold War categories; *seditionists* and *sexual perverts* were widely thought to be the same people, or at least good friends. Johnson describes a "lavender scare" that intertwined with the red scare of the 1950s, leading to a purge of gays and lesbians from the federal government. A rising wave of repression produced an emerging gay rights movement, embodied in organizations like the Mattachine Society—and, finally, in the Stonewall Riots of 1969.

In this moment as in others, the American military was America. The Cold War armed forces were guided by the same ideas about security and subversion that prevailed in the larger culture. Historian Kellie Buford has described the growing obsession of courts-martial in the second half of the twentieth century with "adultery and bigamy, same-sex sodomy and 'unnatural' sexual relations, servicemen's consummation of marriages to non-American women in host countries without command approval, pornographic consumption, prostitution and pandering, indecent exposure, and window peeping," all rapidly growing categories of military crime.

Sex was more than just sex. For people living through the dark hours of an emerging arms race, a series of scandals about internal subversion and Soviet espionage, and the potential threat of nuclear annihilation, actions perceived as sexual perversion weren't merely frightening because of their sexual menace. An understandable panic for order turned domestic disorder into a problem of national security; politically, and therefore culturally, it wasn't a time for recklessness.

But while a whole variety of illicit sexual acts produced a military backlash, same-sex sodomy was a particularly worrisome problem to the armed forces. Hillman notes a 1963 opinion by a military review panel that "described sodomy as loathsome, revolting, obscene, abominable, and detestable in the space of a few lines." Military courts tied themselves in desperate knots trying to understand sexual identity and behavior. What to make of the frequent defense, for example, that a witness had mistaken rough horseplay between men for a sexual act? Or what to make of people who engaged in both same-sex and opposite-sex relationships, or who claimed opposite-sex assault while apparently preferring same-sex activity?

In 1961, Master Sgt. Charles Chadd was convicted of beating and raping a Women's Army Corps private who is described in court records only as "A." But Private A was also suspected of lesbian activity, a matter that became a topic of Chadd's successful legal appeal. So were several of the witnesses who described her injuries, including an unnamed lieutenant who—as Chadd's lawyers put it—"was suspected of being a ringleader in the WAC homosexual group."

Old story: A private had been raped.

New story: A noncommissioned officer had been destroyed by the plot of a lesbian cabal.

The appeals court, Hillman concludes, assumed that A's female corroborating witnesses were actually her lovers; the subtext of their testimony was quietly rewritten in the act of assessing its text.

Another disputed topic in Chadd's legal appeal was the effect of Private A's sexual preferences on the sergeant's claim that she had consented to have sex with him. Conceding her participation in homosexual acts, the government argued that the evidence of those acts proved the fact of rape: A woman who had sex with women couldn't have wanted to have sex with a man. But that claim, the Court of Military Appeals concluded, was false; "while we do not pretend to psychiatric expertise, we call counsel's attention to the fact that many persons so afflicted are bisexual in their practices." Military courts were trying to arrive at an understanding of sexual orientation through the exchange of legal briefs.

In a similar discussion, the military justice system also didn't know what to make of Sgt. John Mathis, an American soldier stationed in Germany in 1963. Mathis "did not object to oral sodomy" with a stranger, but beat and stabbed the other man to death when his interests "turned to anal sodomy." Finding himself engaged in horrible acts in the bushes near the NCO Club, Mathis told investigators, he had finally cried out that "God ought to kill us both" before unleashing a frenzied attack on the man he would describe as his assailant. "At times during the fight," Mathis testified in a manic rush of recollection, "he'd feint before I would stab, and he'd lay still, and he'd get up, but he'd come back, like when he fell back dazed I got the rock and I came back. . . ."

The rock, the Army Board of Review would note of the trial

evidence, "weighed some 35 pounds and was carried in the dark of night from a point 90 feet from the location of the victim." Mathis hadn't just been defending himself in a relentless close-quarters fight; he had wandered away looking for another weapon after breaking off the blade of his knife in the attack. Mathis finally stopped bringing the rock down on the other man's head, "sitting on his chest, or on his stomach," when he heard "bubbling sounds, like water coming through a pipe or something." Then he dragged the body into the woods, "covered it with moss and leaves, went back and hid the rock, retrieved the pieces of his knife and his hat, and returned to his billets."

Through his trial and a series of appeals, no one knew what to make of the killing or the killer. It was a desperate act of self-defense that required the man defending himself to walk away a good distance, get a heavy rock, and carry it back; it was a horrified lashing-out against homosexual perversion by a man who had "reached a climax" after willingly going into the bushes with another man and unbuttoning his pants. Was Mathis homosexual, or had he been assaulted—like Fred Chewning's accusers—by a man who somehow got him to do a thing he hadn't really wanted to do? Was he a *victim* who had crushed his attacker's skull? Legal conclusions grew from social knowledge, or from its absence.

Convicted twice of murder, Mathis had both court-martial convictions thrown out in legal appeals. Testimony established that Mathis himself had been trying to get the military to cure him of his homosexual urges, which—as he told an army doctor—were causing a "desire to kill." The law officers at his courts-martial struggled and failed to find proper instructions to the court. When a soldier was both homosexually inclined and repulsed by homosexuality, where did his consent and desire end, and his right to defend himself against unwanted perversion begin? Military courts were engaged in great acts of legal shrugging and the jurisprudence of helpless guessing: *What is this? How does it work?*

New legal developments underlie that social confusion. Soldiers like Chadd and Mathis were making arguments they wouldn't have been able to make just a few years before, in a forum that hadn't existed. Military sex-crime convictions were taken before *appellate courts* that considered the *rulings of law officers.*

A series of fundamental things had changed in the system of military justice. But an underlying series of fundamentals remained very much the same: Culture still powerfully influenced the application of a more formalized system of law. The urgent debates taking place in American society also took place in military courtrooms.

IN THE IMMEDIATE AFTERMATH of World War II, Americans had widespread and highly public evidence of the wreckage of military justice. A series of committees in the armed forces churned through wartime court-martial records, decrying procedural injustice and remitting or reducing tens of thousands of sentences. Court-martial punishments, one army board found, were consistently excessive—"sometimes fantastically so."

Faced with such clear signs of a problem, Congress and the military began a years-long postwar effort to revise the nation's military law. They instead ended up entirely replacing its existing forms. The Articles of War and the separate Articles for the Government of the United States Navy became one system of law, the Uniform Code of Military Justice, or the UCMJ.

The consolidation of military law reflected the consolidation of the military, as the National Security Act of 1947 took the separate departments for land and naval forces and placed them under the unified command of the new Department of Defense.

The same law vindicated Billy Mitchell, who didn't live to see the change: The Army Air Force became simply the Air Force, organized with the other services under the unified command of the Secretary of Defense. Separate congressional committees for the land and naval services became the House and Senate Armed Services Committees we have now. A diffuse structure of power was pulled together into one military. And one military soon had one law.

The consensus about the changes produced by postwar political debate is that they made military courts look more like civilian courts. As legal historian Michael Scott Bryant describes it, military justice was making "the hard journey from command authority to due process." Legal scholar Edward Sherman similarly once described "a continuous civilianization of military justice, with particular acceleration in the post–World War II period and the present Vietnam War era." But command authority was still the foundation of a military that remained deeply connected to its institutional traditions and cultural expectations. A dramatic change in law was a surprisingly less dramatic change in practice; the UCMJ was a moment of significant evolution, not the arrival of wholly new law.

The creation of the UCMJ wasn't inevitable. In the postwar atmosphere of organized outrage over wartime failures of military justice, Congress first did the thing it was used to doing: It just revised the Articles of War. But it was real revision, with serious changes that reflected the depth of the prevailing concern about the fairness of military justice. The moment was eclipsed by a bigger change, and we can barely see it now for what it was at the time. But if the UCMJ had never been created, we would regard the changes of 1948 as a very big deal.

Among other things, the Elston Act of June 1948 codified the reform Judge Advocate General Enoch Crowder had regarded as "bolshevism" when it was proposed during World War I: It required that at least one-third of the members of courts-martial convened for the trial of enlisted soldiers be enlisted themselves, "when requested in writing by the accused." No longer would privates only be tried by officers. Military justice was democratized: Privates and sergeants had a vote.

Also, precisely as Samuel Ansell had wanted, legal professionals took some of the power that had been concentrated in the hands of line officers. "The new bill provided for greatly increased participation by lawyers at all stages and in all roles," historian William Generous writes. "For the first time, counsel was available for an accused during the pretrial investigation," and the law member of a general court-martial had to actually be a lawyer. No longer would men on trial for their lives be defended by infantry lieutenants. Defense counsel, for the first time, had to have legal qualifications of some kind, at least equal to the legal credentials of the prosecutor, though neither was required to be a member of the bar. For the first time, soldiers being questioned about an offense were guaranteed a warning about their right to avoid self-incrimination. Coerced confessions were barred from use before courts-martial.

The Elston Act also expanded the independent legal review of cases tried before courts-martial. A judicial council of general officers "would review cases involving sentences of life imprisonment and dismissal of officers or cadets," and any other cases the judge advocate general wanted to refer for review, with the power to throw out procedurally defective convictions and grossly unfair sentences.

Finally, the Elston Act is also the origin of an important idea that has grown to be military gospel: "unlawful command influence," language added to the Articles of War for the first time at the historically late moment of 1948. Like the 1920 reforms that changed the Articles of War, the revision is especially striking for the fact that it was new. For the first time in American military history, a convening authority could no longer say out loud *I'm putting this private in front of a court-martial, and I want the son-of-a-bitch convicted.* In theory, at least, commanders had to leave the task of judgment to the courts they called into being.

One proposed reform didn't make it into the new law, and it's a change that's still being debated seven decades later. As Generous notes, the Special Committee on Military Justice of the American Bar Association had suggested all of the changes implemented in the Elston Act, and also one more: The committee had recommended the complete separation of convening authority from the power of command. Like civilian prosecutors, only military lawyers would have the power to assemble a court-martial and put a soldier or sailor in front of it. For officers throughout the armed forces, the idea was a nonstarter—an obvious assault on command authority itself.

But officers in the navy didn't have to worry about that change, or any other. A similar bill to revise the code informally known as "Rocks and Shoals," the laws governing naval forces, never made it out of committee. And for a brief moment before the creation of the UCMJ, it wasn't clear what set of laws would apply to the newly independent Air Force; it seemed that Congress had created a service without a legal code to govern it. The Air Force Military Justice Act fixed the problem in June of 1948—the day after President Harry Truman signed the Elston Act—by extending the Articles of War to the new branch of the armed forces.

A great burst of military reform, in structure and in law, exploded in several directions and with limited organization. The army had new law, built on the scaffolding of its existing code; the navy, along with its Marine Corps, "was still operating under a court martial system that, in essence, was three hundred years old," having long ago been derived from the codes of the Royal Navy; and there was a long moment when no one was sure what was going on in the Air Force.

The mess metastasized. A month after Truman signed the Elston Act into law, Generous writes, "the Department of Defense began laying the foundation for its repeal." Even as they worked to complete a new set of legal reforms, the leaders of a newly consolidated military system recognized the absurdity of having multiple forms of military law.

Once again, personal choice shaped an institutional response. Looking for someone to lead an effort that would produce a uniform legal code for every branch of the military, the new secretary of defense, James Forrestal—who had also been the last person to serve as secretary of the navy when it was still a cabinet-level position—asked around for advice about an expert who could do the job. Forrestal didn't know the distinguished Harvard Law School professor Edmund M. Morgan, but the new general counsel of the Department of Defense did: Morgan had been Marx Leva's law professor. Choosing a professor to organize a deep revision of military law, the government wasn't merely turning to a resident of an ivory tower. Morgan was a former army officer, and spent World War I working in a very particular setting: He had worked in the office of the judge advocate general, where he was a protégé of Samuel Ansell. The person leading the effort to reform military justice after World War II carried the legacy of the person who most wished to reform military justice after World War I. And he was chosen for the job by people who knew exactly what his background was.

And yet the result wasn't simply a renewal of Ansell's activism, and the Morgan Committee was never just an instrument of a leftover set of ideas from an earlier reformer. As Generous notes, Morgan led one of three parallel efforts, part of a set of complementary boards and committees that all worked toward the same goal. The law professor and a team of other prominent reformers led the committee at the top of the project, but a "working group" of field-grade officers "from all three services" contributed ideas and analysis. A third panel, the "research group," was just the staff from the office of Felix Larkin, the assistant general counsel to the Defense Department. Morgan led a thing that couldn't just be led; he ran a project composed of a complex chain of institutional actors who all had a voice in a difficult process.

The project revealed by its written record was lawyerly, precise, and meticulous in the extreme—a work of analysis, not only of activism. Morgan, Larkin, and the other members of the three reform committees set out to understand the thing they proposed to fix, working point by point through existing military law and examining precisely how it was built, from the opening analysis of the *Comparative Studies Notebook*: What do the Articles of War mean when they refer to an "officer," and how do the Articles of the Government of the United States Navy define the same word? How do we want to define those terms in the UCMJ?

And then they kept going, issue through carefully studied issue, pulling apart the existing codes and comparing them both to one another and to the institutional ideals they hoped to achieve.

The center of the problem the reformers faced is revealed by the fact they started with comparison. They were trying to write unified law for branches of the armed forces that had gone their own way for 175 years. "The Articles of War and the Navy Articles were laid out in completely dissimilar fashions," Generous writes. "The services had different ideas about any number of aspects of military justice." Adding to the complexity of the problem, the cluster of wartime and postwar committees on military justice reform had all offered their own list of suggestions—and no list was the same.

Revisions of the Articles of War had started with a complete legal code, and changed pieces here and there; the drafting of the UCMJ started with a blank piece of paper and a set of ideas, starting over from the first word. In practice, this choice meant that settled questions were reopened: Should enlisted personnel serve on the courts-martial of fellow enlisted personnel? Should there be an appellate panel? Should military courts have a law *member*, or a separate law officer who issued legal rulings but didn't vote on a verdict and sentence?

Much of the code was successfully drafted by discussion and concurrence, but Larkin had been shrewd enough to secure a set of promises from Forrestal in exchange for his agreement to work on the project. First, to protect reform from a "'studied-to-death' fate," agreement on the reform committees was final; the army, for example, couldn't decide after a piece of the UCMJ was done that it had new objections or further thoughts. Second, as Generous summarizes it, "if the representatives could not agree on certain issues, then Forrestal himself would hear their arguments and decide, and his ruling would be final." Congress would get a draft of a new military code made up of every provision the services could agree on plus every provision the secretary of defense had been forced to finalize in the face of failed discussions.

On January 7, 1949, Forrestal met with the Morgan Committee and heard arguments about the last three "insoluble points." He announced his decision exactly a month later, on February 7. "In each case," Generous writes, "he approved the position taken by Morgan. Incorporated into the UCMJ, then, were provisions for a civilian Judicial Council, a law officer at general courts-martial, and eligibility of enlisted personnel to sit on courts as members." Samuel Ansell was there in spirit; the lawyerly process ended with a deadlock on the reforms that had always been the most contentious proposals in the arena of military justice, and the erstwhile lieutenant colonel from Ansell's staff was there to give them their final, successful push.

The completed code was simultaneously introduced as a House bill and a Senate bill, "the very day after Forrestal's final decisions"—and the reactions to its introduction reveal the moderation of the reform committees and their result. As Congress debated, two equally disappointed camps of critics emerged: very roughly, lawyers versus soldiers.

Committees heard testimony from whole lists of bar associations, as a representative of the American Bar Association sat next to a representative of the New York City Bar Association (who sat next to a representative of the War Veterans Bar Association). The proposed code didn't go nearly far enough, the lawyers argued. Command authority lived on. Commanders would still convene courts-martial. The lawyer from the New York City bar asked a congressman who was a lawyer "whether he would like to defend a criminal case before a jury that had been selected at the sheriff's office or by the district attorney." In the *New York Times*, a story announced the considered opinion of yet another lawyer's organization, an association of county attorneys: "The association said that no fundamental reform had been accomplished in the legislation pending before Congress." For lawyers, the UCMJ was no "civilianization" of military law; it was a continuation of all the old problems of martial justice, decorated in a pretty new package.

But for at least some soldiers, past and present, the proposed code was the very opposite thing, an assault on the military and its ability to protect the nation. The traditionalists tried to kill the UCMJ altogether, introducing alternative legislation that would have just extended the 1948 revision of the Articles of War to the navy; it quickly stalled, despite "considerable support at the Pentagon for such a measure." As Generous notes, the most formidable of the military traditionalists was a towering figure in American military law, Frederick Bernays Wiener. Like Morgan, Wiener was a distinguished lawyer who understood courts-martial from his direct experience, having spent World War II in the army's Office of the Judge Advocate General. "You cannot maintain discipline by administering justice," he told a House subcommittee; a balanced approach that assured due process for the accused was precisely not the point.

Wiener was particularly distressed by the proposed structure of the judicial council, the unified appellate panel that would have the power to review and throw out court-martial convictions. As proposed, he argued, the judges of the court would be civilians, with no requirement that they have a military background; they would simply not understand cases arising from the armed forces.

Pro-reform lawyers knew beyond a shadow of a doubt that the UCMJ was still far too military in its structure; traditionalists were absolutely certain that the UCMJ turned military courts into a sorry echo of the civilian justice system.

In limited ways, the larger debate produced changes in the work the reformers had done. The Morgan Committee's "Judicial Council" survived, and was created by the new law, but with one change: The name sounded too small, as if the military justice system would be overseen by some small-town city council. It became the court we know today as the Court of Military Appeals.

Other questions were left unanswered, acts of creation done in outline and handed back to the military for completion. The UCMJ created the new position of a law officer on courts-martial, but didn't define the duties and limits of the position. And so Congress passed the law; the Uniform Code of Military Justice went into effect on May 31, 1951—and then the military began the process of trying to figure out how it would work.

In part, that meant a new collaborative effort to write a new *Manual for Courts Martial*, a book of rules and definitions that would, for example, spell out the authority of the law officer. But as Generous writes, "the battles had already been fought." The manual put the UCMJ into practice, and the UCMJ was already the project of extensive negotiation and analysis. So the manual was largely "an exercise in familiarity," and completed in a few months.

The appearance of ease was entirely deceptive.

ARTICLE 46 OF THE UCMJ guarantees that a court-martial defendant will have the same opportunity to "obtain witnesses" as the prosecution and the court; one side doesn't get to have an advantage over the other in finding and calling people who can provide testimony beneficial to their cases. One of the central rights in questioning witnesses is the right of a defendant to question the witness who started the matter that led to a trial in the first place—the accuser. And so, when the military's new legal code took effect in 1951, an accuser had to sign a "charge sheet," a form describing what violations of the law he or she alleged, with a set of specifications precisely describing the reasons the person being accused had supposedly violated the law. The charge sheet would be clear and permanent, the root of the case: *Here's who accused you, here's what they accused you of, here are the basic facts they allege in support of the accusation.*

In 1951, Maj. Gen. Robert Grow was the American military attaché to the Soviet Union, assigned to the US embassy in Moscow. Like many senior officers in the armed forces, he kept a personal diary, and recorded his thoughts about the politics and military affairs of the day. And he didn't always keep it locked away in a safe place. While he was visiting Frankfurt, a Soviet agent managed to enter his guesthouse and photograph pages of private political analysis written in the general's own handwriting. Excerpts soon appeared in a book written by a British defector, Richard Squires, and then in Eastern Bloc newspapers.

The Soviets stretched their material beyond its apparent usefulness: After showing that they had pages in Grow's own hand,

and printing inflammatory excerpts, they began to invent new passages that had supposedly come from the same diary. The American general they invented was foaming at the mouth: He wanted the United States to attack the Soviet Union right away, and to "hit below the belt." His diary described his mental calculations as he tried to figure out which Soviet targets should be bombed and in which order. Squires made sure readers couldn't miss the point. In a passage highlighted by historian George Hofmann, the British defector wrote that Grow "knows nothing but gratification of his insatiable craving for blood and destruction." For ordinary Soviet readers, he became the sadistic monster trying to figure out which of them to kill and which of their neighborhoods to burn.

American newspapers discovered the material in Soviet and East German publications, and it quickly became a scandal about a reckless military officer who had carelessly given secrets to the enemy: "Red Agents Reveal U.S. General's Diary," read a *Washington Post* headline in March 1952. Investigations—and arguments—followed. The State Department and the still fairly new CIA weighed in, trying to decide how to contain American embarrassment and respond to Soviet propaganda.

In that climate, the question of how to handle Grow's indiscretion became a deeply political problem. "The State Department, like the CIA, was opposed to court-martialing Grow because of the possible international implications of such an action," Hofmann writes. Grow delivered his diary to the army, and the army read it. Now they knew the Soviets were using "excerpts" that didn't exist, but they weren't sure how to respond. For one thing, they had already made the mistake of telling the *Washington Post* that the excerpts were real, and walking back that authentication would just cause further embarrassment and skepticism.

The leadership of the army was distressed by the crisis over Grow's diary, for parallel reasons: It was a risk to national security, and a risk to their careers. Hofmann describes the agitated debate at the top of the army as a half dozen senior officers tried to decide what to do about Grow. They were very much thinking about their political audience. Lt. Gen. Alexander Bolling, the assistant chief of staff for army intelligence, argued that "the American public and the Congress will be satisfied with nothing less than a trial by court-martial for General Grow."

The brand-new UCMJ was supposed to have meant that it no longer mattered what Congress or any other political entity wanted, because charges of military wrongdoing were governed by clear law and an ordered procedure; there were lawyers in the room. The year after the code took effect, that already wasn't true. Unlawful command influence was strictly forbidden—and was the driving force behind the charges Grow would soon face.

This is where the problem of a charge sheet appears. "On April 19," Hofmann writes, "an urgent top army staff meeting was held . . . regarding the disposition of the Grow incident." The room held more stars than a planetarium: Bolling was there, and so was Lt. Gen. Maxwell Taylor, the deputy chief of staff for operations and administration, and so were generals and colonels from a half dozen army offices, including the army's liaison to Congress. The collection of officers emerged with an agreement to investigate the matter, "with a view to a trial by general court-martial." The army chief of staff, Gen. J. Lawton Collins, and Secretary of the Army Frank Pace Jr. agreed, and a JAG colonel prepared a draft of the charge sheet, which was handed around and revised by the top leaders of the army.

But then someone had to sign the charge sheet. And no one knew who it should be, because the charges were being orchestrated at the top of the organization. It should be *the accuser*, instead—whoever that was. Finally, because he was ordered to, Col. C. Robert Bard signed the charge sheet and became the accuser. Bard led the Military Justice Division of the army JAG office; he was a legal technician, chosen by his superiors to pretend to be the security expert who could accuse a general officer of violating security regulations.

Then a team of officers, "following Taylor's instructions," personally delivered the charge sheet and a bundle of supporting documentation to the headquarters of the 2nd Army, with Taylor's private instructions to the commander: Lt. Gen. Edward Brooks was to act as the convening authority for a court-martial, and order that it be held in secret. The army's deputy chief of staff was effectively convening a court-martial himself, but ordering a proxy to mask the effort.

The UCMJ contains another important procedural protection, contained in Article 32: "No charge or specification may be referred to a general court-martial for trial until a thorough and impartial investigation of all the matters set forth therein has been made." Grow's Article 32 hearing was also heard in secret, and Hofmann concludes that its outcome had been determined before it even began. "Command influence was overwhelming and positioned for a quick conviction even before the pretrial investigation of facts," he concludes; senior army officers "preordained guilt."

When he finally came to trial, Grow faced a court hand-chosen at army headquarters, in still another violation of court-martial procedure, and was convicted by a court that barely took an hour to deliberate. Facing two charges and a total of five specifications that described the allegations, Grow was found guilty of all but a single specification.

The court sentenced the major general to be reprimanded and suspended from command for six months, and Brooks—the putative convening authority—approved the sentence. The case went automatically to the Army Board of Review, housed in the Judge Advocate's Office. In Grow's case, then, the first appellate review of his conviction took place in one of the offices where his court-martial had been orchestrated. Headquarters got its court-martial back, so it could approve its own creature.

Grow got the message, and filed his retirement papers. In the years that followed, the officers who had orchestrated his court-martial carefully forgot their role. "I was not involved in the court martial of General Grow," Taylor would say, a claim he repeated; he "never got into it because of command influence." But he *had* gotten into it, and it was precisely an example of the unlawful command influence the UCMJ had been intended to stop.

WHERE THE UCMJ forced procedural changes in a court-martial to prevent unlawful command influence, it could still escape into the courtroom. The Ribbon Creek incident offers one of the best-known instances of exactly that occurrence.

On a late Sunday evening in April 1956, a Marine Corps drill instructor led his platoon into a creek, impulsively trying to get the full attention of men who hadn't developed habits of military discipline after many weeks of boot camp. But the salt-water creeks on Parris Island run with the ocean tide; as the platoon waded into Ribbon Creek, the tide was receding—so the creek was running out to sea, fast. And many of the men couldn't swim.

The drill instructor, Staff Sgt. Matthew McKeon, stayed close enough to shore to keep his feet on the creek's muddy bottom, but he was at the head of the column. Some of the young men behind him wandered out farther, stepped off an underwater ledge, and found themselves in deep water and a strong current. Many fought their way back to shore; some linked arms and dragged others out of the water. But several were swept away in the darkness.

As the sun rose the next day, the local sheriff arrived with hooks and nets to trawl the creek bed for the six privates who were still missing. Later that morning, with no sign of the missing men, Lt. Gen. Joseph Burger made the necessary phone call from his office at Parris Island to Marine Corps headquarters.

We have a detailed account of these moments because of the work of historian Keith Fleming, and because of the more recent efforts of John Stevens III. Stevens, a retired judge and former marine who went through boot camp on Parris Island in 1957, went back four decades later to dig more deeply into the events that had cast a long shadow over his training as a new marine. In a precisely constructed account, he puts the events on the banks of the creek alongside the things that happened in Washington, DC, after Burger made his phone call.

It was bad timing: In 1956, Marine Corps boot camp was already a controversial topic; hardened combat veterans of World War II and Korea trained new recruits with an informal routine of mental and physical abuse that went well beyond the toughness officially expected by the institution. In May 1956, a new commander at Parris Island would discover ten recruits sitting in the base hospital "with broken noses"; their drill instructors broke them. Reporters and members of Congress were already asking if the Corps had lost control of its DIs. Now one of those same men had probably—the bodies were still missing—gotten some of his recruits killed.

And so, as marines and the sheriff's volunteers dragged the creek for bodies, a Marine Corps colonel in DC "jumped into a car and went directly to Capitol Hill." Col. James Hittle raced through the Capitol and its office buildings on Monday morning looking for supporters, getting the news to allies before it could reach the Corps' critics—shaping the congressional response.

At the creek, the first body was found just after noon: in the words of a witness, "a tall husky Negro boy . . . in grotesque rigor mortis." Three more bodies were pulled up over the next hour. Back in Washington, one o'clock in the afternoon was the moment when the staff working the crisis at Marine Corps headquarters believed they had spread the news widely enough among congressional supporters to let it go wide. "Six Marines are missing from the Marine Recruiting Depot at Parris Island, South Carolina, following a night training exercise conducted last evening," went the entire announcement released to the wire services. Three hours later, the fifth body was found.

Later that afternoon, Marine Corps Commandant Randolph Pate reached Parris Island and briefed the large crowd of reporters who had already arrived in the wake of the vague announcement on the wires. Subordinate officers tried to prepare him for his encounter with the press; Maj. Duane Faw, the senior legal officer at the training depot, "urged Pate to address the factual issues but to express no opinion as to McKeon's guilt or innocence." Burger had already issued orders for a court of inquiry, not long after his phone call to headquarters. An investigation was about to begin, a recruit was still missing in the creek, and there was nothing else to say.

But Pate felt political pressures at the top of the Marine Corps that a major at Parris Island did not. Back in Washington, Stevens writes, "a strategy was formulated at headquarters to avert a congressional investigation: the Marine Corps would conduct its own full-scale inquiry, publicize the results, and make a number of substantive and visible changes in the training regimen."

And one other thing.

A reporter asked the commandant if the drill instructor had violated regulations. No one had investigated much of anything. The court of inquiry had been appointed, but wouldn't assemble until the following morning. Still, Pate answered the question as if he had an answer to give. "It would appear so," he said. But not to worry: He promised the drill instructor would be fully and vigorously punished.

With a body still missing and an investigation about to begin, the senior member of Matthew McKeon's service had pronounced his guilt in public, court-martial to follow. It was the first in a series of maneuvers intended to show that precisely one person was responsible for six training deaths in the Marine Corps: A single staff sergeant did it, and so the institution didn't, and Congress doesn't need to intervene.

On Tuesday afternoon, a Marine Corps diver found the sixth and final body. Pvt. Thomas Hardeman had been trapped in his boots by the deep mud at the bottom of the creek. Hardeman's body was pulled onto a boat; a photographer from *LIFE* magazine got the shot.

Since Pate had offered a public opinion about the case, neither he nor any of his subordinates could convene a court-martial; they would, after all, taint it with unlawful command influence, as members of the court learned what the convening authority or his own superior had said about the appropriate verdict. So the secretary of the navy became the convening authority, ordering first a court of inquiry and then a court-martial on that court's recommendation. But the idea that it was possible to remove command influence from a Marine Corps trial after the commandant had pronounced his verdict was absurd no matter who convened the court.

McKeon would be defended at his court-martial by a team of lawyers that was led by Emile Zola Berman, a celebrated civilian attorney mostly known for his personal-injury practice. Berman was a showman; he would push back against the spectacle of a trial preceded by the commandant's improper pronouncement of an expected verdict by arranging a bigger spectacle. He called Pate himself as a defense witness, bringing the man who had declared McKeon's guilt into the courtroom to declare the same person's innocence—meeting command influence with command influence. Pate was trapped in an untenable position he had built for himself with his own mouth. Stevens writes that the commandant entered the courtroom with "a feigned air of jocularity," wearing sunglasses that he never took off.

No one wanted to interrupt a man who outranked everyone in the room, and Berman ran straight into the space created by that awkwardness: He "audaciously began to ask a series of highly improper questions," ending with one about what course of action he would have taken if he had been permitted to handle the matter of McKeon's actions on his own. This is command influence with flashing lights and fireworks, directly asking the highest-ranking person in the service what he would do to the defendant if it were his decision to make. And amazingly, Pate answered. The whole thing was "a little fuzzy and hazy to me as to just what transpired," the commandant told the court, but it didn't seem like such a big deal in the end. "I think maybe I would take a stripe away from him," Pate declared, and "have him transferred away for stupidity." The man who declared that McKeon would be harshly punished declared that McKeon should be lightly punished; problem solved.

Soon after, Berman called a truly extraordinary witness in McKeon's defense, in a choice obviously made for the effect it would have on the members of the court rather than the information the witness could provide. The witness was Lt. Gen. Lewis Puller, known universally to marines as Chesty Puller—as the *New York Times* described him in its story on his testimony, "the most decorated and revered of living Marines." No one will ever know what Chesty Puller was thinking as he offered testimony to the court, because his first declared sentiment upon meeting the prosecution team was that "that son of a bitch ought to be shot." But at trial, questioned by Berman, Puller said exactly the opposite: He agreed with Pate, he said, and "regrets that this man was ever ordered tried by a general court martial."

The commandant of the Marine Corps and the most revered

general in its history agreed in court that McKeon shouldn't even be on trial.

It didn't work, though; the members of the court stood firmly against the obvious presence of command influence, convicting the drill instructor on multiple counts of involuntary manslaughter and drinking in the barracks. They sentenced him to nine months imprisonment at hard labor, reduction to private, the forfeit of $30 a month in pay, and a bad-conduct discharge. The political crisis settled by the public trial, the secretary of the navy remitted the sentence. McKeon stayed in the Marine Corps as a private—and left with an honorable discharge.

IN THE 1950s, the Supreme Court was busy limiting the reach of the nation's new military laws. In 1955, in *Toth v. Quarles*, the court struck down the conviction of a former member of the Air Force who had been convicted by a court-martial, after his discharge, for an earlier murder he had committed while still on active duty in Korea. The decision would cast a long and dark shadow.

Two years later, the court freed military families from court-martial jurisdiction. That decision set a pair of murderers free: In October of 1952, Dorothy Smith had stabbed her husband to death in Tokyo. A few months later, Clarice Covert had killed her sleeping husband with an ax, then spent the night in bed with his body. That murder happened in England, but it wasn't an English crime. Aubrey Smith was a colonel in the US Army, Edward Covert was a master sergeant in the US Air Force, and both were killed on American military posts. Both women were tried by courts-martial, and convicted; in Covert's case, a first court-martial verdict was overturned by the Court of Military Appeals over a mishandling of her insanity defense, and she was awaiting a new trial by court-martial in the United States when the Supreme Court took up her petition for habeas corpus. *Reid v. Covert* is a strange case in American legal history, heard twice and reversed by the court after Clarice Covert's lawyer—Frederick Bernays Wiener, who had argued in 1950 that the UCMJ went too far in weakening military authority—successfully petitioned for a rehearing in 1957.

"In essence, these tribunals are simply executive tribunals whose personnel are in the executive chain of command," wrote Justice Hugo Black in the majority opinion. But Clarice Covert wasn't in any chain of command anywhere. "The wives of servicemen are no more members of the 'land and naval Forces' when living at a military post in England or Japan than when living at a base in this country or in Hawaii or Alaska." Covert and Smith were released.

And then, a few years after it freed former service members and the families of military personnel from court-martial jurisdiction, the Supreme Court even limited the reach of military justice into the off-duty lives of active-duty armed-forces personnel.

In the summer of 1956, James O'Callahan was a sergeant in the army, and stationed at Fort Shafter, on the island of Oahu. He was drinking at a hotel bar when two friends told him about the girl they had seen on the balcony near their own room. At the sergeant's court-martial, one of those friends would remember his reaction: "He made a statement to the effect that he intended to have a woman that night before he went back to the barracks . . . even if he had to beat one on the head, or something to that effect." He did just that, forcing his way into the room of the girl his friends had seen. She was fourteen years old, and taking a nap while her parents were out. She woke to the weight of O'Callahan's body; he told her he had a knife, punched her in the face, and put a gag in her mouth. But then, probably drunk, he had to use the bathroom, and she took her chance. "I got up, opened the door leading into the hall and ran down the hall and then to the next floor," she told O'Callahan's court-martial. "Then the gag fell out of my mouth and I started to yell for help and a woman heard me and I went into her room."

In the security office, hotel guard Herman Oliviera responded to a phone call about a screaming woman by instantly locking the hotel elevators and sending other guards to cover the stairwells. He was waiting for O'Callahan on the ground as the sergeant scaled down the balconies in front of the hotel. Caught, O'Callahan confessed—in detail, describing exactly how he tied and gagged his victim, how he struck her in the face, how he threatened to cut her throat. The court-martial came to its obvious conclusion, and the sergeant was convicted, with a sentence of ten years' imprisonment at hard labor and a dishonorable discharge.

But then, having confessed to military police and been tried by a military court, O'Callahan filed a petition for a writ of habeas corpus from his prison in Pennsylvania. His crime, his lawyers argued, was not subject to military jurisdiction; it had been committed by a sergeant in the army, but not while he was on duty, not while he was in uniform, not against another soldier, and not on a military post. Some guy went drinking in a hotel and did something horrible, but nothing that he did had anything to do with the fact that he was a soldier. O'Callahan did poorly through many steps of the judicial process: The Army Board of Review and the Court of Military Appeals affirmed his conviction, and the federal district and circuit courts denied his petition for habeas corpus.

But then the Supreme Court agreed to hear his appeal— thirteen years after the crime. The court's 1969 decision caused an instant wave of law-review articles that tried to make sense of what had just happened to courts-martial; an essay in the *Duke Law Journal* pronounced the case a "millstone" around the neck of military justice.

The most remarkable fact about the opinion that Justice William Douglas wrote in *O'Callahan v. Parker*—Parker being the warden of the former sergeant's prison—is the degree to which it dismisses the significance of the postwar reforms in military justice. Military traditionalists like Frederick Bernays Wiener had been appalled by the UCMJ, a nasty piece of civilianization that assaulted the purpose of military discipline; Douglas wrote as if no reform at all had ever taken place.

"We find nothing in the history or constitutional treatment of military tribunals which entitles them to rank along with Article III courts as adjudicators of the guilt or innocence of people charged with offenses for which they can be deprived of their life, liberty or property," Douglas wrote. In fact, he added, "it still remains true that military tribunals have not been and probably never can be constituted in such way that they can have the same kind of qualifications that the Constitution has deemed essential to fair trials of civilians in federal courts."

And so, the court concluded, trial by military courts had to be limited to military matters; outside the aegis of martial discipline and the effectiveness of armed forces, soldiers were entitled to the benefits of trials in civilian courts. "There was no connection—not even the remotest one—between his military duties and the crimes in question," Douglas wrote. The conviction was overturned.

In a harshly worded dissent, Justice John Harlan wrote, "This Court has consistently asserted that military 'status' is a necessary *and sufficient* condition for the exercise of court-martial jurisdiction." A soldier is a soldier, and subject to military jurisdiction.

The Supreme Court covered different pieces of the same ground over and over again during the years after the creation of the UCMJ, narrowing the reach of courts-martial in ways that still reverberate in our own historical moment. It was a different forum for the question Robert Cranston had asked in 1817 after he was brought before a court-martial for insulting the governor of Rhode Island at a private reception: When is a soldier a soldier, and when can he be put on trial as one?

Members of the armed forces went on discovering that military justice could reach into parts of their lives that they wanted to hold apart from military authority. In 1952, Pfc. Allen McQuaid knew with perfect confidence that the Cold War he was serving as an airman was a capitalist effort undertaken on behalf of the banking industry. He put those sentiments on paper and "posted them in writing on the front door of the officers' club" at Elmendorf Air Force Base.

His First Amendment defense failed; he was not merely a citizen speaking his mind to some government officials. The Air Force Board of Review concluded that McQuaid's statement was "disloyal and disaffecting," writes the army lawyer John Kiel, because "it falsely portrayed the aims and objectives of the defense effort, it unjustly maligned the American economic system, and it tended to discourage faithful service to the United States by members of the armed forces." Members of the armed forces had only a limited free-speech right when they talked about military topics.

And then came the war in Vietnam.

12

"MY GOD, HE'S FIRING
INTO THE DITCH"

Vietnam, the Hollow Army, and the End of the Cold War

AT THE BEGINNING OF NOVEMBER 1965, THE EL PASO CITY council told the organizers of a planned antiwar protest that they wouldn't be permitted to march in the city-owned San Jacinto Plaza. And so, on November 6, an antiwar protest became an antiwar and pro–First Amendment protest. The demonstration had been organized by students and professors at what was then Texas Western College, but Henry Howe wasn't one of them. For a while, he just watched, a rolled-up piece of cardboard in his hand, not joining a group of people who were still just preparing to march against the war. But then, as the Court of Military Appeals would describe it, the protesters formed up and began to actually march in a line. Howe "joined the same at the rear thereof, unrolled the cardboard which he carried and held it before him as he walked, reversing the same from time to time so that each side was visible to the assembled crowd."

For a recently graduated political science major, Howe's spelling was pretty dismal. On one side of his sign: LET'S HAVE MORE THAN A 'CHOICE' BETWEEN PETTY, IGNORANT, FACISTS IN 1968. On the other: END JOHNSON'S FACIST AGRESSION IN VIETNAM. Howe had worked his way through the University of Colorado with a little help from the Reserve Officers' Training Corps; in November of 1965, he had been on active duty for about a year. He was in the area because El Paso borders on the army's Fort Bliss. For the same reason, military police had showed up in support of the local force. When 2nd Lt. Henry Howe, Headquarters Company, 31st Engineer Battalion, wandered by with a sign denouncing the commander in chief of the armed forces, the MPs walked up and placed him under arrest. He was charged under Articles 88 and 133 of the UCMJ: using contemptuous words against the president of the United States, and conduct unbecoming an officer and a gentleman.

At his court-martial, echoing an argument that has often been made in the American military, Howe argued that he'd been engaged in off-duty political activity, offering opinions that were protected in their expression by the First Amendment. It was true, and still is, that military officers have a right to their own political opinions, and they have a right to say what they think. But the tone and scope matter. As the army lawyer John Kiel wrote a few years ago, "the *Manual for Courts-Martial* specifically states that officers may not be prosecuted for adversely criticizing a designated official or legislature if the criticism itself was not personally contemptuous and it was done during the course of a political discussion." Howe had crossed that line into personal contempt, and it cost him a two-year prison sentence.

As soldiers had for more than two centuries, many more Vietnam-era service members would insist upon Howe's distinction between off-duty political speech and a soldier's obligation to obey.

In 1967, for one of the most famous examples, an army dermatologist was tried by a court-martial after he refused to provide medical training for Special Forces soldiers who were about to deploy to Vietnam. Capt. Howard Levy told his commanding officer, Col. Henry Fancy, "that he did not feel he could ethically conduct this training because it was against his principles, or words to that effect."

There was an obvious subtext at the trial. Other officers testifying at Levy's court-martial found their memories growing hazy when they were asked if they had felt a general distaste for the captain; Col. Chester Davis couldn't remember if he had called Levy a "pinko." But the ten Special Forces witnesses called by the prosecution did remember exactly what Levy had said to them. "Each of them testified that Levy had told them the Green Berets was a barbarous outfit, and they should refuse to go to Vietnam," writes journalist Joseph DiMona. Despite the testimony of Seymour Levy, the defendant's father, who "came to the witness stand clutching a small American flag, a Bible, and a framed copy of the Gettysburg Address," the captain was convicted on multiple charges, and sentenced to three years in prison at hard labor and a dishonorable discharge.

Levy's trial became a political symbol of the growing national opposition to the Vietnam War, and he became a hero to the antiwar movement. But pro-war sentiment also found its own symbol at the center of a court-martial, and invested it with a meaning it didn't have.

In the early months of 1968, a battalion-sized task force pieced together from scattered infantry companies set out to defeat the 48th Local Force Battalion, a Vietcong guerilla warfare unit in the Quảng Ngãi province of South Vietnam. Among the companies that made up Task Force Barker—named for its commander, Lt. Col. Frank Barker—was C Company, 1-20 Infantry, a part of the Americal Division's 11th Brigade.

Charlie Company's first platoon was led by 2nd Lt. William Calley, who had received his commission six months before the events that would lead to his court-martial. Calley joined the army after receiving a draft notice, and trained as a clerk at the Adjutant General School before being accepted for Officer Candidate School at Fort Benning, Georgia. Desperate for officers in a war that chewed through platoon leaders at a rapid pace, the army had substantially increased its class size and acceptance rate for OCS, and sharply increased the graduation rate for officer candidates. A school that had turned out an average of 300 new lieutenants a month began to produce 1,500 a month, and then 3,000 a month between the summer of 1966 and the summer of 1967. Quickly, suddenly, it became much easier to get a second lieutenant's gold bar, at a moment when second lieutenants assigned to combat-arms units had an increasingly dangerous and challenging job.

Calley graduated in the bottom quarter of his OCS class, in a school that had until recently had a washout rate close to 50 percent; he was one of the men who would not have been given the responsibility of leadership under less desperate circumstances. Slightly built, nervous, distinctly lacking in command presence, and persistently hopeless with a map and compass, Calley was soon sent to Vietnam to lead men in combat. His company commander, Capt. Ernest Medina, addressed him in front of enlisted soldiers as "sweetheart" and "Lieutenant Shithead." To the men he led, Calley was mercurial, excitable, incompetent—"a kid trying to play war."

In March of 1968, Charlie Company was being torn apart in a war against an enemy they couldn't find. The 48th Local Force Battalion fought with the quickness and quietness of guerilla war, striking and vanishing; American soldiers were killed by land mines, booby traps, and snipers, never finding a decisive battle against an enemy that would stand and fight. It had been eighty years since American soldiers had fought this kind of war. The army had no institutional memory to help with the task. Soldiers often responded the way 1st Lt. Preston Brown had to an unseen enemy in the Philippines, striking at the targets they could find. On March 14, a booby trap killed Sgt. George Cox, and horribly maimed other Charlie Company soldiers. "Another GI lost his eyes, and a third lost his arms and legs," Michael Belknap writes. The survivors were enraged, horrified, and understandably frightened.

The next day, the company held a memorial service for Cox—followed immediately after by Medina's briefing on their plans for the following day, a moment of mourning turning into a moment of planning. They would assault a hamlet, designated "My Lai (4)," within the village of Son My, where they would find and destroy the bulk of the 48th Local Force Battalion. My Lai would be full of weapons and enemy combatants, the men who had just killed George Cox. It would be the company's chance to take its revenge against the men who had struck at them with such horrible success. No one there would be a noncombatant, Medina said; they would all be gone by the time the assault began, having left for the marketplace and the tasks of the day. The company would land under heavy fire, and hurl itself into its enemy. Defeating the opposing force, they would also destroy the foundation of its combat strength; they would "burn hooches, kill livestock, close wells, and destroy food crops." No enemy would survive in the area, and no base of support would allow them to rebuild.

On the morning of March 16, Calley led first platoon into My Lai by helicopter, preceded by artillery fire, securing it so the rest of the company could land safely and join the fight. No one fired at them as they landed, around seven thirty in the morning, but their briefing had warned them that they were flying into the teeth of an enemy battalion. Listening on the radio, Medina heard a report from scouts flying overhead that "several armed men in black pajamas" had run from the village as the assault began. He had radioed his platoon leaders that the landing zone was "cold," not under active fire; now he apparently got back on the radio and told them the landing zone was "hot," though an army investigation would raise doubts about that change. In either case, Calley's platoon laid down heavy fire as they jumped off the helicopters and moved into the village.

First Platoon soldiers later testified at Calley's court-martial that they hadn't come under fire as they landed, but many weren't sure at the moment of their arrival. Their own heavy fire masked the silence of My Lai; firing, they heard gunfire. As they searched the hamlet, though, they found women, children, and the elderly, none armed. It was wartime; the hamlet had bunkers, and had contained at least a few armed Vietcong soldiers, but those men had already run away. Some arms remained, mostly not inside the village. A helicopter, flown by Warrant Officer Hugh Thompson, discovered a nearby cache of 60mm mortar rounds, and directed an infantry platoon to their location. Thompson and his crew also helped to capture two men who ran from the village, and then flew away to refuel. Second Platoon moved into My Lai to the left of 1st Platoon, and members of both began to kill villagers.

"As the 1st Platoon moved into the hamlet," an army investigation would conclude, "its soldiers began placing heavy fire on fleeing Vietnamese, throwing grenades into houses and bunkers, slaughtering livestock, and destroying foodstuffs. Several witnesses testified to having observed an old Vietnamese man being bayoneted to death by a member of the Platoon and to having seen another man thrown alive into a well and subsequently killed with a hand grenade."

Second Platoon did much the same, and possibly on a larger scale, at least at first. "Members of the 2d Platoon began killing Vietnamese inhabitants of My Lai (4) as soon as they entered its western edge," the army report would say. "In at least three instances inside the village, Vietnamese of all ages were rounded up in groups of 5–10 and were shot down. Other inhabitants were shot down in the paddies bordering the northern edge of the hamlet while attempting to escape. Women and children, many of whom were small babies, were killed sitting or hiding inside their homes."

Charlie Company was surrounded by its chain of command, arrayed all around and above them as they went through a village killing unarmed people. Medina stood at a command post near the landing zone throughout much of the four-hour operation, though his direct involvement in the killing would later be the source of considerable controversy. The company's brigade commander, Col. Oran Henderson, flew overhead in a helicopter. So did Lt. Col. Barker. So, at some point, did Maj. Gen. Samuel Koster, the commander of the American Division. The men killing unarmed villagers weren't alone in the wilderness; they were deeply enmeshed in the authority of the army and their company, battalion, brigade, and division.

As the killing went on, the men leading it began to develop a system and an order to the task. Calley directed men from his platoon to lead villagers into a ditch, concentrating them in a helpless position and killing them from above with rifle and machine-gun fire. They settled methodically into their work.

And then an intervention descended from the sky, an actual and physical arrival from above. Thompson had flown his helicopter away from My Lai to refuel. Shortly before nine o'clock, he returned, and spotted wounded women and children on the ground around the hamlet. As he radioed for medical aid, his crew chief, Spc. Glenn Andreotta, spotted more wounded villagers in the ditch where they had been taken to be killed. Thompson's door gunner, Spc. Lawrence Colburn, later described the moment when the men on the helicopter realized what was happening on the ground: "As we watched from about 15 feet off the ground, back maybe 20 meters, we saw this captain approach the woman, look down at her, kick her, step back and then blow her away. It all crystallized in that moment. In unison, all three of us shouted, 'You son of a bitch!' That was Captain Ernest Medina."

Thompson stopped trying to get someone else to help, and started doing it himself. He landed, putting his helicopter between the ditch and the soldiers, and got out to discuss the matter with 1st Platoon directly. Exactly how that conversation went was disputed in many ways during later testimony, but Thompson would say that he had told a sergeant the wounded people in the ditch needed help. "Thompson testified that the sergeant's response to his question about helping the wounded was to the effect that the only way he could help them was to kill them," the army report would say.

Thompson also spoke directly with Calley at some point in the morning, but "the recollections of those involved are inconsistent, and while the two clearly had a heated discussion, it is not clear whether this happened before the chopper took off or the next time it touched down." In either case, as Thompson returned to his helicopter and took off again, Andreotta shouted about a soldier on the ground: "My God, he's firing into the ditch." They could see, now, that the killing of unarmed people was methodical and sustained.

Soon after, Thompson landed again and had another conversation with a soldier about a group of women and children he had seen looking out from a bunker. He had a replay of his earlier conversation, telling a soldier—possibly Calley, though that would be disputed—that they needed to get the people out and move them to safety. The reply was that they could only be removed "with a hand grenade." So Thompson walked to the bunker and led them out himself; joined by other helicopter pilots, a US Army warrant officer flew Vietnamese villagers away from their homes, saving them from his own fellow soldiers.

And he had done one other thing: In one of the most extraordinary moments of the morning, Thompson had ordered Colburn "to train his machine gun on the American troops surrounding the bunker," and to be prepared to fire on them if they kept killing unarmed villagers.

While Thompson and his crew were flying villagers to safety—and then returning yet again so Andreotta could carry a wounded boy out of a ditch—Medina was beginning to bring the killing to a close. By nine thirty, the captain had ordered his 2nd Platoon to "cease fire" or "stop the killing." But it was only a transition in the direction of restraint, not a full stop; while Medina toured the area and looked at the dead, the army report would note, "a member of his command group also shot and killed a small child who was standing, crying, in the midst of the group of bodies." An hour later, a major from Task Force Barker headquarters ordered Medina by radio to "stop the killing." The captain "ordered a lunch break, and called a meeting with his Platoon leaders." The major, Charles Calhoun, arrived at My Lai by helicopter and directly gave orders "to make sure there was no unnecessary killing/burning or words to that effect." The killing stopped, fully and finally, with between 175 and 200 dead villagers. Charlie Company had one casualty, a soldier who accidentally shot himself in the foot with a pistol.

Disgusted, Thompson had reported the killing while it was still under way, starting with his immediate superior, Capt. Barry Lloyd. "It's mass murder out there," he told Lloyd. "They are rounding them up and herding them in ditches and then just shooting them." Lloyd took Thompson to see their commanding officer, Maj. Frederic Watke, and Watke reported the allegations of mass killing directly to Barker. Soon after, Calhoun flew to My Lai, probably in response to Thompson's report.

But the matter ended there. From Task Force Barker through the Americal Division, no commander acted on Thompson's report that soldiers had deliberately and systematically killed unarmed people. War went on; soldiers died. Among them were Lieutenant Colonel Barker, killed in June in a helicopter crash, and the helicopter crew chief Glenn Andreotta, who had waded into a ditch full of bodies to save an injured child. Second Lt. Stephen Brooks, Calley's counterpart in 2nd Platoon, was killed in combat. It was entirely possible that the killing at My Lai would have remained a story told by soldiers to other soldiers—except that one of those soldiers was Ron Ridenhour.

Ridenhour, a helicopter door gunner, had friends in Charlie Company. In April 1968, he sat down to drink beer with one of those men, Pfc. Charles Gruver, who eventually asked him a question: "Hey man, did you hear what we did at Pinkville?" Ridenhour hadn't heard anything, so Gruver told him: "Yeah, we massacred this whole village. We just lined them up and killed them . . . Men, women and kids, everybody, we killed them all." Knowledge of the event made Ridenhour feel complicit, even without having participated. He began to ask around, seeking out friends who would have been there. "And it would be like lancing a boil," he would explain, nearly thirty years later. "I mean, if you asked them, they were compelled to talk. They couldn't stop talking. They were horrified that it had occurred, that they had been there, and in the instances of all of these men, that they had participated in some way."

After a year of investigation and thought, Ridenhour decided what to do with the things he'd learned. On March 29, 1969, back home in Arizona, he wrote a five-page letter describing what he knew about My Lai, and sent it to a long list of officials: twenty-three members of Congress, "the secretaries of state and defense, the secretary of the army, and the chairman of the Joints Chiefs of Staff." By mid-April, the army had opened an investigation into Ridenhour's claims, and quickly found them to be credible.

But the shadow of *Toth v. Quarles* reached My Lai. The ranks of the army that fought the war in Vietnam were filled with short-term conscripts, men drafted for two years and then returned to civilian life. Men spent months in training, then went to Vietnam for a year, then rotated stateside and quickly left the military. Riden-hour sent his letter a year after the events it described; most of the men who had participated in the deliberate killing of unarmed people at My Lai were no longer subject to the UCMJ and military courts. Thirty-one years later, Congress would extend the jurisdiction of federal courts to former military personnel who commit war crimes overseas, but no such law existed in 1969. And Barker and Brooks were dead. There was no way to bring most of Charlie Company, or its battalion commander, to trial.

That left Medina, Calley, Henderson, and a few others. Bizarrely, absurdly, Calley would matter the most.

A little more than a century before the deliberate act of mass killing at My Lai, a regiment of Colorado volunteers had gone out looking for the armed bands of Cheyenne warriors who were inflicting real harm on settlers in the territory; instead, they found the peaceful settlement at Sand Creek, and destroyed it. After attacking and killing invented adversaries, Col. John Chivington returned to Denver a hero, bragging about the great danger he had faced and defeated. Capt. Silas Soule, a warrior of proven courage who had refused to join in a morally cruel and strategically meaningless attack on noncombatants, returned to the ridicule and disgust of neighbors and colleagues who thought he had tried to shelter their enemy.

It happened again. As he awaited trial, William Calley became the warrior he had never been, celebrated as the rare soldier who really dared to take the fight to the enemy. He had groupies. Ensconced in bachelor officer quarters at Fort Benning, Calley "often entertained well-wishers there, pouring drinks behind a padded bar and cooking elaborate meals." A writer on assignment for *Esquire* magazine, John Sack, brought a tape-recorder and his girlfriend, and took Calley to a lakeside cabin to record interviews. "They would tape in the morning, tape in the afternoon, and go water skiing and slalom skiing and ski jumping in between," Carol Polsgrove would write in a history of *Esquire* in the 1960s.

Calley's court-martial opened in November of 1970; after a process of selection and challenges, it was made up entirely of combat veterans. Testimony turned into a parade of horrors, as the men of 1st Platoon "tied Calley directly to the killings." Their platoon leader had personally herded women and children into a ditch, personally fired at them, and personally given direct and explicit orders to subordinates to kill unarmed people. Calley's radio operator, Spc. Charles Sledge, had watched as the lieutenant shot an old man, "who was wearing the robes of a priest," in the face; he had seen Calley throw a child into a ditch and fire into its body. Granted immunity to testify against his platoon leader, Pvt. Paul Meadlo tried to back out and refuse to answer questions; forced to take the stand, he spoke in a "lifeless voice," describing the moments when Calley had turned to him for help at the side of the ditch. "He ordered me to help kill the people. I started shoving them off and shooting."

Unable to seriously challenge any of the testimony about what had happened at My Lai, Calley's lawyers built a defense around the testimony of a series of psychiatrists, who argued that stress and fear "acted to limit his volition, his ability to make a choice, to decide." The court hearing that testimony was made up entirely of men who had been in combat.

Taking the stand himself, Calley offered a weak soup of wandering testimony in which he hadn't done anything wrong, but he was also following orders and anything he did was Captain Medina's fault. Under cross-examination, he acknowledged firing a few rounds into the ditch, but "claimed not to know whether he had hit anyone."

After five months of testimony from 104 witnesses, Calley's court began its deliberations. The lieutenant "waited in his apartment," surrounded by supporters, "pouring them one bourbon after another." On March 29, 1971, the court delivered its verdict: Calley was guilty of premeditated murder, having killed "an unknown number," but at least twenty-two people. The court heard additional testimony in a brief sentencing phase, and then pronounced its sentence: Calley, the court told the defendant, was to be "confined at hard labor for the rest of your natural life."

His heroism instantly became more pronounced. An Alabama DJ and musician, Terry Nelson, recorded a spoken-word ballad, "The Battle Hymn of Lieutenant Calley," recounting his heroism in a fierce battle; it sold 2 million copies. Alabama governor George Wallace promised that, if he were elected as president, he would pardon the martyred lieutenant. Veterans' groups promised to raise money for his legal appeals, and demanded meetings at the White House to lobby for clemency. By mid-May, Michael Belknap writes, President Richard Nixon had received "260,000 letters and cards and approximately 75,000 telegrams. Over 99 percent of correspondents continued to oppose the verdict." Members of Congress joined the carnival, demanding that Nixon act to help Calley. A grateful nation rushed to the defense of a wartime hero, unjustly convicted for fighting the enemy.

Trained as a clerk, a white-knuckle graduate of an Officer Candidate School that had aggressively lowered its standards, the Charlie Company commander's "Lieutenant Shithead" had become the very symbol of American military prowess, the bold warrior betrayed by a nation gone soft. It had nothing to do with the man himself, who offered no substance to support the weight of the meaning he was assigned. In 1971, deep into a ghastly war and an increasingly ugly national divide between pro-war and antiwar sentiment, Americans needed someone as a symbol of military courage and honor. William Calley stumbled into the moment, and the laurels landed on his head. They didn't belong there, and they didn't stay.

Nixon ordered the army to transfer Calley from the post stockade to his own quarters, where he remained confined under house arrest until he was paroled in 1974. Medina and Henderson were acquitted; Calley was the only soldier convicted on any charges related to the mass killing of unarmed people at My Lai. He married, settled down in Columbus, Georgia—a few miles outside Fort Benning—and went into the jewelry business.

Hugh Thompson went to work for the Veterans' Administration, occasionally answering the phone to hear death threats for his supposed act of betrayal. The army awarded Thompson a medal for his efforts to stop the killing at My Lai.

In 1998.

EVEN AS COURTS-MARTIAL struggled with the Vietnam War, the civilization of military law continued. The Military Justice Act of 1968 created military judges, a long step away from the law members and law officers that appeared in the preceding structure of military justice. The law also "broadened the right of an accused to counsel, established procedures for pretrial release (a military version of bail), and enhanced appellate review opportunities," Elizabeth Lutes Hillman writes.

But the end of the Vietnam War led to a strange absence, as a nation tried to look away from its military. Two world wars earlier in the century had produced urgent debate over the nature of military justice, and Vietnam appeared for a moment to be having the same effect. After the war, law reviews were briefly swamped with articles pointing out failures and proposing reforms. As always, critics targeted command influence, the feature of courts-martial that seems to be the most stubbornly resistant to reformers. And then came nothing much. The post-war environment of the 1970s wasn't the postwar environment of 1919, or of the late 1940s; this time, the debate faded away without having an effect, as an exhausted society declined to take up a topic centered on the management of armed forces.

Even before the United States had withdrawn from Vietnam, the American military had entered a decade of crisis. An investigative series in the *Washington Post*, "An Army in Anguish," described an organization beleaguered by "a breakdown in spirit, in ethics, and in discipline." Crime plagued military posts; soldiers feared the social conditions they saw inside decaying barracks. "Drug abuse, burglaries, acts of violence, and racial conflict were a part of daily life," writes historian Alexander Vazansky.

In January of 1973, the end of the draft turned the armed forces into all-volunteer services—with unintended effects. The armed forces struggled to fill the ranks. As the army chief of staff, Gen. William Westmoreland "ended reveille formations, sign-out policies, bed checks, and travel restrictions, and he approved, on a trial basis, beer in mess halls and the installation of beer vending machines in barracks." Still falling behind in recruitment and retention, the army lowered personnel standards. A new policy adopted in July 1973 allowed half of all new enlistees to be "non–high school graduates," even as the officials making the change acknowledged that dropouts in the ranks had significantly more frequent disciplinary problems.

By 1980, a decade of social conflict, ruined standards, and postwar budget reductions had deeply harmed the American military. In testimony before a congressional committee, the army chief of staff, Gen. Edward "Shy" Meyer, blurted out that he ran a "hollow army." News stories throughout the postwar decade reflected the degree to which military courts had been forced to contain the damage inflicted on their institutions: "GI Sentenced in Heroin Death," for an example from 1973, or the story about the sailor who was discharged that same year for falsely testifying during a court-martial that he saw a black sailor "hit a white three times during a wild melee at sea last October."

In the 1980s, improved budgets and changes in personnel policies began to improve the quality of the armed forces. Modest legal change came from within, not from the strong public pressure and political debate that had given motive force to earlier reforms in military justice. In 1983, for the first time, Congress gave military personnel the right to be represented by a lawyer during general and special courts-martial, and during pretrial Article 32 hearings. It also became easier for people convicted by courts-martial to appeal directly to the Supreme Court from the Court of Military Appeals.

Meanwhile, the Supreme Court gradually reversed itself on the question of "crimes unrelated to military service." By the 1980s, "military crimes no longer had to be 'service connected'" to be tried by a court-martial. The reach of military courts grew, while their procedural rules became more elaborate.

As the Soviet Union collapsed and the Cold War ended, military justice was again faced with a series of scandals over sexual identity and sexual aggression. It was still a struggle.

In September 1991, the annual convention of the Tailhook Association, a private club for naval aviators, was held in Las Vegas. On one hand, the Tailhook convention offered "symposia on aviation issues"; on the other, it featured "hospitality suites" with strippers and open bars. Drunk and wild by Saturday night, aviators formed a "gauntlet" in a hallway and forced women to run it, "fondled and groped as they walked past the men." Like the men forming the gauntlet, many of the women at the convention were active-duty military personnel; one, Paula Coughlin, was an admiral's aide.

As the story of the Tailhook gauntlet exploded into the news, overwhelming the navy's early efforts to downplay it, political reaction was loud and fierce. Careers slammed to a halt. As legal scholar Kingsley Browne has written, the Senate Armed Services Committee "put a hold on promotions of about 4,500 Navy and Marine Corps officers until it could be determined which ones were associated with the Tailhook convention." But there weren't 4,500 men in one hallway, and many of the damaged careers shouldn't have been damaged. Their ability to gain promotions and assignments sharply limited, some officers retired, abandoning their military careers before being exonerated. Aggressively political demands for punishment prevented successful discipline, as pressure from navy commanders led to "a series of ham-fisted prosecutions." No successful court-martial trials resulted.

"Of the 140 cases referred by the [navy inspector general] for disciplinary action," Browne has written, "a majority of them (and almost all of the most serious ones) were dropped due to insufficient evidence. Twenty-eight cases were dealt with by Admiral [J. Paul] Reason at non-judicial 'admiral's masts,' with sanctions generally being limited to fines, reprimands, and some non-punitive actions." Serious misconduct went formally unpunished, or minimally punished, as political influence warped investigations and prosecutions. In the end, several hundred naval aviators saw their military careers limited by a sloppy legal process that mostly functioned as a public-relations effort.

Six years later, allegations regarding the sexual assault of female recruits by army drill sergeants at the Aberdeen Proving Ground led army investigators to interview every woman who had trained there since 1995. One drill sergeant, Delmar Simpson, was sentenced to twenty-five years in prison for the sexual assault of six soldiers he had been responsible for training. Eight others were administratively punished.

Military justice had gone through many rounds of reform, becoming more rational, systematic, and formally structured. But command influence and political climate still mattered. The

Tailhook scandal ended with chaos, slipshod justice, and a mix of fairly and unfairly ruined careers; the Aberdeen scandal ended with one serious conviction and a relative sense that the crisis had been met and handled.

Looking back, the twentieth century had seemed to be a march of legal progress on paper—and radically uneven practical results. But as the century ended, it was easy to overlook the uneven patches and focus on the progress. The American armed forces were strong and well ordered, with relatively few serious problems in the arena of discipline. Rebuilt, reinvigorated, and decisively at peace, the world's remaining superpower stood triumphant on the winning end of a long twilight struggle with a global adversary that had disappeared. The future seemed to promise a sustained calm, and few serious challenges for the military or its justice system.

The Living Past

The Court-Martial in Contemporary America

For a society that had gone two generations without experiencing a sustained war, the savage shock of 9/11 was followed by a long series of hard surprises. Some of the nation's soldiers objected to their orders, argued against the wars they were sent to fight, publicly criticized their chain of command, and leaked damaging information about military operations. Enemy combatants of ambiguous status, captured on a poorly delineated battlefield, challenged the structure of military justice. It all seemed like uncharted territory—the very thing that it most certainly wasn't. Our experiences of the last fifteen years reflect our long history; they are marked by continuity far more than they are defined by sudden change.

In the spring of 2012, a sergeant assigned to the Marine Corps Recruit Depot in San Diego posted a series of strongly worded comments to a Facebook group, the Armed Forces Tea Party Patriots page. Sgt. Gary Stein "said he would not follow unlawful orders from President Obama such as ordering the killing of Americans or taking guns away from Americans." Stein's battalion commander ordered an investigation, and the sergeant soon found himself in front of an administrative separation board. News stories said that Stein had unambiguously broken the law:

"The Uniform Code of Military Justice prohibits uniformed personnel from making comments critical of their chain of command, including the commander in chief."

It doesn't. Article 88 of the UCMJ forbids the use of "contemptuous words against the President," but it only applies to commissioned officers—and Stein was a noncommissioned officer, not covered by the article. Military personnel often criticize their chain of command in considered and respectful ways, as when seven soldiers who had fought in Iraq published a serious critique, "The War as We Saw It," in the August 19, 2007, edition of the *New York Times*—without being punished.

Stein routinely adopted a more aggressive tone, and his chain of command might have been able to bring him before a court-martial under Article 134 of the UCMJ, which prohibits "all disorders and neglects to the prejudice of good order and discipline in the armed forces" and "all conduct of a nature to bring discredit upon the armed forces." But those charges wouldn't have been a slam-dunk, since they would have required military prosecutors to argue that it brings discredit upon the armed forces for a marine to say he would disobey unlawful orders. It wasn't an accident that Stein's aggressively political comments, and his aggressively political page, were handled by an administrative hearing rather than a trial in front of a court-martial.

No reporters noticed. They routinely said that Stein had violated the UCMJ; none identified the article that defined his transgression, or apparently thought to ask.

Stein's conflict with his chain of command was one of several instances of political speech by members of the armed forces that led to angry debate in a nation divided by a long war and bitter politics. In January of 2007, another Marine Corps sergeant on active duty had visited Capitol Hill to present Congress with the "Appeal for Redress," a petition signed by active-duty military personnel who wanted the war in Iraq brought to an end. Writing in the *Atlantic*, retired army colonel Andrew Bacevich complained that the petition delivered by Sgt. Liam Madden "heralds the appearance of something new to the American political landscape: a soldiers' lobby." Worse, Bacevich warned, the appeal "was the brainchild of enlisted personnel—of Madden and Jonathan Hutto, a young seaman stationed at Norfolk, Virginia. Although the appeal's signers today include several hundred junior officers, the majority are sergeants, petty officers, and ordinary GI's. In an arena where things typically start at the top, here the impetus comes from below."

The appeal, Bacevich concluded, threatened to "crack open the door to praetorianism"; it offered "further evidence of advancing constitutional decay."

It didn't. There are many signs of advancing constitutional decay in the contemporary United States, and Bacevich has spoken clearly and well on many of those problems. But the fact that sergeants have opinions and wish to make them public isn't one of them.

In our contemporary discourse, every development represents a new reality; every soldier who speaks in the political arena is the first one who ever did such a thing. But the past exists, whether we notice it or not. For two and a half centuries, Americans have fought to define their social and political place as soldiers. Far more aggressively than the men and women who signed the Appeal for Redress, members of the armed forces have often debated, resisted, refused, and—often, but not invariably—taken their punishment.

The Kentish Guards declined, as gentlemen, to submit to a militia draft in 1808. Tennessee militiamen serving under Andrew Jackson in the Creek War announced that their term of service had expired, and they went home—after an open debate with their commanders. In Rhode Island in 1821, Col. Leonard Blodget told a brigadier general that he couldn't give an order his men wouldn't agree to obey; then his regiment marched off the field, shouting, "Fix bayonets!" to prevent obedience to the brigadier's assault on the social custom that governed their training days. During the Civil War, soldiers frantically and brutally policed the politics of the 1864 presidential election, destroying Democratic ballots in army camps and purging anti-Lincoln soldiers from the ranks. And in the Vietnam War, junior enlisted personnel circulated petitions and sent letters of support to Capt. Howard Levy, celebrating his "courageous stand against America's dirty imperialist war." We have done this before.

Soldiers have also often fought to set aside some piece of themselves from the reach of military hierarchy, in an exchange that began in 1775 and continues today. In 1817, Capt. Robert Cranston was charged with insulting the governor of Rhode Island, his commander in chief as a member of the state's military forces; his court-martial refused to hear the case after he warned them that doing so would subject them all to "martial law" at every moment of their lives. Col. Thomas Butler went to his grave in 1805 wearing the powdered queue of a Federalist gentleman; he was sure the army couldn't tell an officer how to wear his hair, a matter of purely personal business.

Gary Stein believed, comparably, that he could obey his chain of command at work but express himself in a public forum as a citizen protected by the First Amendment. He thought there was a part of him that lived separately from his military identity, a citizen breathing and speaking from its place alongside the marine. He wasn't the first member of the armed forces to have that thought.

History is a cycle. We ask a question, settle it, put it aside for a while—and then rediscover it, asking it again as a new question. The courts-martial of Howard Levy and William Calley became political referenda on the Vietnam War; the courts-martial of army lieutenant Ehren Watada, who refused orders to deploy to

Iraq, and Pfc. Bradley Manning, who leaked classified Iraq War material to the whistleblower site WikiLeaks, became political referenda on the war both set out to expose and criticize.

The cycle also returns us to a place where we see the conscience of soldiers in moments of extraordinary difficulty. In Vietnam, the young soldier Ron Ridenhour struggled with the story he'd heard about the mass killing at My Lai, and he finally insisted that his government take notice. In Iraq in 2008, Pfc. Justin Watt knew that other soldiers from his platoon in the 101st Airborne Division "had raped a 14-year-old girl and then killed her and her family" at their home in Mahmoudiyah. He called his father, who had also been a soldier, and asked him what he should do; then he reported the crimes to his chain of command. At the Abu Ghraib military prison, Spc. Joseph Darby slipped a compact disk full of now-infamous photos depicting the abuse of detainees under the door of a CID investigator's room.

At both Mahmoudiyah and Abu Ghraib, crimes exposed by soldiers resulted in several court-martial convictions—and one set of convictions in federal court, since one of the perpetrators, Steven Green, left the military and escaped court-martial jurisdiction before being caught. Unlike many of the soldiers at My Lai, who had been released from legal jeopardy by the Supreme Court's decision in *Toth v. Quarles*, Green found that he could still be brought to justice after he took off his uniform; Congress had assured that possibility with the Military Extraterritorial Jurisdiction Act of 2000, which granted federal courts the authority to try ex-military offenders for crimes they had committed in uniform without being discovered in time to be brought before a court-martial. Green committed suicide in 2014 while serving a life term in federal prison.

At Guantánamo Bay, we labor over the fate of non-state detainees held by the military and tried by military commissions. In 2006, the Supreme Court ruled, in *Hamdan v. Rumsfeld*, that the use of military commissions to try those detainees was unconstitutional. In response, Congress passed the Military Commissions Act of 2006, and the commissions resumed—slowly, haltingly, with continuing uncertainty and political controversy. A provision of the law forbade the Article III courts from hearing habeas corpus petitions from detainees; in 2008, in the case of *Boumediene v. Bush*, the Supreme Court struck down that limit on judicial authority.

Compare our recent political debate and legal exchange over detainees to Winfield Scott's entirely uncontested use of military commissions in Mexico in the 1840s, or the nineteenth-century trial by military commissions of Dakota and Modoc warriors who were quickly convicted and rushed to the gallows. Legal scholars and erstwhile government officials Jack Goldsmith and Cass Sunstein have argued that a "ratchet effect" in American political discourse has led governing elites to adopt an ever more expansive vision of wartime civil liberties. The shock of 9/11, and its resulting effects in the growth of the national-security state, make that argument hard to accept on a first reading—but it's equally true that no one would have expected the Modoc defendants to successfully pursue habeas corpus litigation in federal courts after killing Maj. Gen. Edward Canby. Khalid Sheikh Mohammed has legal rights that Captain Jack couldn't have imagined.

AMERICAN MILITARY PERSONNEL of our own moment also have legal rights that their nineteenth-century predecessors couldn't have imagined, the result of a long series of reforms in the conduct of courts-martial: 1916, 1920, 1948, 1950, 1968, 1983. A steady march toward the civilianization of military courts has given soldiers due-process protections that are, in their historical context, stunning. There are no American soldiers, sailors, airmen, or marines who now have to worry that they'll be shot by a firing

squad in the immediate aftermath of a hurried court-martial conducted in the field. The twenty-first century is a different political
universe for military personnel, and another place we can argue
for a ratchet effect in the expansion of personal rights.

Remarkably, though, the ratchet in military justice may not
hold. The armed forces have been caught in a larger political
debate in which due-process protections for the accused are
understood to be unfair to the victims of sexual assault.

The military has been pulled into a larger discussion. In
the summer of 2014, Sen. Kirsten Gillibrand signed on as a
co-sponsor of the Campus Safety and Accountability Act,
a bill to change the way publicly funded universities police
and report sexual assault on campus. "We will not allow these
crimes to be swept under the rug any longer," she said. "Students deserve real safety and accountability instead of empty
promises." The bill, and Gillibrand's advocacy of it, represented
an ongoing debate—a cultural contest as much as a political
one—over the scope of an American "rape culture." Colleges
have felt the pressures of the political moment, adopting new standards for adjudicating on-campus sexual-assault allegations that
increase protections for accusers and sharply reduce the due-process
rights of the accused. Students charged with sexual offenses by campus panels can be questioned without legal representation—and
found guilty, or its administrative equivalent, by sharply reduced
standards of proof. A flood of lawsuits has followed, as students
condemned by campus disciplinary panels accuse universities of a
deeply flawed rush to judgment.

As she argued for reform in the handling of campus sexual
assaults, Gillibrand was also working for the passage of another
piece of legislation, the Military Justice Improvement Act, that
would change the way the armed forces police and report sexual
assault in the ranks. "The brave survivors of sexual assault are
our sons and daughters, husbands and our wives, and they have

been betrayed by the greatest military on earth," she wrote in an op-ed piece. "We in Congress owe it to them to make things right." Gillibrand's legislation was one of a small flood of bills on the topic of military sexual assault, joining Rep. Jackie Speier's Sexual Assault Training Oversight and Prevention Act and Sen. Claire McCaskill's Victims Protection Act.

As it has been for two and a half centuries, the American military is America; debate in the narrower sphere is inextricably connected to debate in the larger sphere. Congress took up military sex crimes as a topic of debate at exactly the moment it took up sexual assault on college campuses. When we talk about courts-martial, we're often talking about ourselves—our culture, our politics, our society, and our government.

But military justice also remains a separate creature. Its complexity and historical particularity have led reformers into a series of unintended consequences that were sometimes deeply unfortunate. Gillibrand proposed to do a portion of the thing that earlier reformers like Samuel Ansell had wanted to do: She argued that the presence of command authority in military justice distorted its outcomes, and should be removed in some instances. In particular, sexual assault charges should be brought by neutral outsiders, the equivalent of a district attorney for each military post, and commanders should have no role in convening or reviewing courts-martial in those cases. Though the precise forms of the proposals have varied, some version of this is exactly the thing that reformers have tried to do in America for an entire century: They have tried to take control of military justice out of the hands of commanders, and move it into the control of lawyers.

But the new reformist view of command influence also flips a century of history on its head. Ansell, and many other critics, had argued that the role of commanders in convening and reviewing courts-martial cost military personnel the due-process rights that

American civilians had always expected; justice tainted by the effects of command was arbitrary and dangerous to the accused. In the twentieth century, the complaint about military justice was always that it was far too easy for the accused to be convicted and harshly punished. Now, though, the ongoing attack on command influence in courts-martial is based on a demand for more convictions, harsher punishments, and an end to the possibility that commanders will mitigate sentences.

Some reform has already been passed into law. After an air force commander overturned the sexual assault conviction of Lt. Col. James Wilkerson, a fighter pilot, Congress made modest changes to Article 60 of the UCMJ, instituting new rules to regulate the way convening authorities evaluate court-martial verdicts and sentences. The effect of those legal revisions remains unclear, and at least some military lawyers are underwhelmed; a 2014 law-review article by Marine Corps Reserve Capt. Zachary Spilman was titled "Not Helping: How Congressional Tinkering Harms Victims During the Post-Trial Phase of a Court-Martial."

In any event, change never moves in a straight line, and our own recent political contretemps over sexual assault in the armed forces has created some darkly ironic consequences. The problem with the attempt to reform military justice is precisely that Congress has reformed military justice. In 1950, Edmund Morgan sawed out a piece of the floor under our own contemporary political debate—and at least one military leader sprinted into the hole Morgan had opened, as if he didn't know it was there. Article 37 of the UCMJ defines and forbids unlawful command influence. No commander, it says, "may attempt to coerce or, by any unauthorized means, influence the action of a court-martial or any other military tribunal or any member thereof, in reaching the findings or sentence in any case."

In October 2012, a Marine Corps recruiter, Staff Sgt. Stephen Howell, was convicted by a Parris Island court-martial on a laundry list of charges: rape, forcible sodomy, adultery, and other crimes against a young woman who had been trying to enlist. He was sentenced to nearly twenty years in the military prison at Fort Leavenworth. Two years later his conviction evaporated, thrown out by the Navy–Marine Corps Court of Criminal Appeals—itself a creation of the UCMJ.

The irony of Howell's appeal was that it had to do with precisely the thing Gillibrand and other reformers object to in the military justice system—but for exactly the opposite of the reason they object to it. In the spring of 2012, seeing political sentiment building in Congress for an attack on command authority in military justice, Marine Corps commandant James Amos had made a sweeping tour of the country, personally delivering a harsh message to marines about the need to crack down on rape in the ranks. On April 19, Amos spoke at the Marine Corps Recruiting Depot Parris Island, where Howell was about to be put on trial. Of the eleven marines who served on Howell's court-martial, eight were in the audience to hear Amos's comments. In effect, the commandant was speaking to the majority of what we would consider the jury in a civilian trial. And his message was painfully clear.

"I see this stuff in courts-martial, I see it in the behavior and just for the life of me I can't figure out why we have become so ecumenical, why we have become so soft," Amos told the marines gathered to hear him speak at Parris Island. "If you have a Marine that is not acting right, you've got a Marine that deserves to leave the Corps, then get rid of them; it is as simple as that."

Shortly before a court-martial, then, the commandant of the Marine Corps told the members of the court that he expected convictions and discharges. In an institution that operates on the principles of command and obedience, the top uniformed leader of the institution stood in front of men who would very

soon be called upon to offer their independent judgment on sexual assault charges—and all but ordered them to convict marines
brought up on sexual assault charges. "Amos is essentially directing potential jurors to start with the presumption of guilt and
that, if they do find guilt, dictating that the punishment should
be dismissal from the service regardless of other mitigating fac-
tors," writes political scientist James Joyner, who teaches at the
Marine Corps Command and Staff College. "There's simply no
escaping that this is unlawful command influence."

It's a circle: As reformers have tried to remove command
authority from military sexual assault cases to ensure the aggressive punishment of rapists, the political pressure on the armed
forces led the uniformed leadership to pressure subordinates to
deliver court-martial convictions—an injection of unlawful command influence into military sexual assault cases, which caused
convictions to be overturned and prevented the trials of military
personnel accused of sexual assault.

But Amos isn't the only leader to have made this mistake.
"Obama Delivers Blunt Message on Sexual Assaults in Military,"
read a headline on a May 2013 story in the *Washington Post*. Speaking at a White House press conference, the president had indeed
been blunt: "If we find out somebody's engaging in this stuff,
they've got to be held accountable, prosecuted, stripped of their
positions, court-martialed, fired, dishonorably discharged—
period," he said.

Two months later, another headline described the effect
of those comments: "Remark by Obama Complicates Military
Sexual Assault Trials." The commander in chief had publicly
demanded more court-martial prosecutions and dishonorable
discharges, effectively directing the outcomes of military trials.
"In at least a dozen sexual assault cases since the president's
remarks at the White House in May," the *New York Times* reported,

"judges and defense lawyers have said that Mr. Obama's words as commander in chief amounted to 'unlawful command influence,' tainting trials as a result."

The damage, the newspaper added, was just starting; the president's comments "were certain to complicate almost all prosecutions for sexual assault."

And so the political effort to make the prosecution of military sexual assault more effective had the immediate effect of making it far less successful. Over the longer term, it's impossible to say what will happen; as I write this, several reform efforts continue. But for much of American military history, the demands for court-martial convictions from Amos and Obama wouldn't have complicated any subsequent prosecutions. Demanding harsh discipline from military courts was just something that commanders did—until Congress made it illegal. Today's attempt at military justice reform tripped over its predecessors.

THE HISTORICAL SEPARATENESS of American military justice has made it neither better nor worse than civilian justice. It's just *different*, in good ways and bad. Many competing values have pushed and pulled at courts-martial, forcing them into an endless effort to find balance. Our current political debate on the topic has made a rich history into a dark cartoon. There is so much more depth and complexity to this separate justice than we have chosen to see.

Whatever rules and structure govern them, and however our arguments about military-justice reform play out, courts-martial and military commissions will go on confronting fundamental questions about the course of American society. Military courts have always been a place where Americans have worked to identify their values, and the future won't change a reality established by two and a half centuries of our history. In our military justice system, we will go on arguing about the meaning of America, defining ourselves by the acts we punish and the choices we tolerate. Disagreeing, arguing, and exploring the values that make sense of our actions, we will discover the country that we mean to become.

Acknowledgments

The publication of a book involves more people than I can properly thank. First, though, I have to offer my thanks to the small army of archivists and librarians who have made it possible to research the topic of military justice, starting with the staff of the Charles E. Young Research Library at UCLA. I spent many productive hours at the American Antiquarian Society; the Huntington Library; the state archives in Connecticut, New Hampshire, and Rhode Island; the historical societies of Connecticut, Rhode Island, Massachusetts, New Hampshire, and Newport; and (especially) the Massachusetts National Guard Museum and Archives in Worcester.

I am particularly grateful to Keith Vezeau at the Massachusetts National Guard Museum and Archives, Jeannie Sherman at the Connecticut State Archives, Frank Mevers at the New Hampshire State Archives, and Kenneth Carlson at the Rhode Island State Archives. The director of the Massachusetts National Guard Museum and Archives, Len Kondriatuk, offered years of encouragement and insight. I owe them all many thanks.

A similar army of professors have offered their guidance and support throughout the years. My thanks to Stuart McConnell,

Rita Roberts, Andre Wakefield, Jonathan Petropoulos, and Albert Wachtel at the Claremont Colleges. At UCLA, Joan Waugh began to guide my course as a graduate student before I even arrived on campus, and was generous with her time and insight for many years. My thanks also to Michael Meranze and Geoffrey Robinson. John Hall at the University of Wisconsin offered important early encouragement, and the late Ralph Luker was an endless source of support and inspiration, as was Bill Deverell at USC.

When it came time to think about writing a book, my long-time newspaper and magazine editor Chris Lehmann guided me to my literary agent, Melissa Flashman, at Trident Media Group. At W. W. Norton, Matt Weiland's thoughtfulness and endless patience made this a far better book than I could have written alone. Rachelle Mandik's exceptional skill as a copyeditor helped to produce a clear and coherent manuscript, and Helene Berinsky turned that manuscript into a beautifully designed book. My thanks also to Remy Cawley for her generous help with the work of getting a book into print.

I was a soldier before I was a historian, and I couldn't begin to mention everyone in the US Army who deserves my thanks. But Drill Sgt. Rodney Flores and Command Sgt. Maj. George Stopper showed me what it means to have integrity and a work ethic, and I'm grateful, especially when I fall short of their examples.

Finally, and most importantly, I thank my family for their love and patience.

Notes on Sources

EPIGRAPH

The quote from William Tecumseh Sherman, often repeated in government reports and hearings, is from his 1879 treatise, *Military Law*, published in 1880 and available for free on Google Books.

The quote from Capt. Alpheus Shumway is from his Connecticut militia court-martial, the records of which can be found in the Connecticut state archives, Record Group 13, Box 48.

INTRODUCTION

Regarding the theme of civilianization, an early example is Edward F. Sherman, "The Civilianization of Military Law," which was published in the *Maine Law Review* in 1970. A few years later, an article in the *Texas Tech Law Review* by army judge Charles Schiesser and law professor Daniel Benson suggested its premise in the title: "A Proposal to Make Courts-Martial Courts: The Removal of Commanders from Military Justice." Military courts wouldn't even be fully courts until they weren't convened by commanders, the very heart of military justice.

More recently, on similar themes, see Michael Scott Bryant, "American Military Justice from the Revolution to the UCMJ: The Hard Journey from Command Authority to Due Process," in the *Creighton International and Comparative Law Journal*, and David A. Schlueter, "The Military Justice Conundrum: Justice or Discipline," in the *Military Law Review*. Both articles appeared in the spring of 2013.

The "bitch the thing up" quote from Edmund M. Morgan is taken from an essay by the legal scholar Jonathan Lurie, "The Military in American Legal History," which appears in volume 2 of *The Cambridge History of Law in America*, edited by Michael Grossberg and Christopher Tomlins.

Morgan's "a court martial was not a court" quote is taken from a 1921 essay he wrote, titled simply "General Samuel T. Ansell." It appeared in the January–February edition of *The Lawyer & Banker and Southern Bench & Bar Review*, and can also be found online through the Yale Law School Legal Scholarship Repository: http://digitalcommons.law.yale.edu/fss_papers/4017/.

Readers interested in a detailed and lawyerly overview of court-martial structure and procedure have an excellent resource in Lawrence J. Morris, *Military Justice: A Guide to the Issues.*

1. "ALMOST A BLASPHEMER":
Citizen-Soldiers as Neighbors in the Early United States

The records of the court-martial that tried Ens. Thomas Bevins in 1814 can be found at the Connecticut State Archives, in Record Group 13, Box 46. Bevins was convicted and cashiered, but testimony during his trial established that he had insulted Beach in the middle of the duty day; when the captain insisted on a personal inspection of a man claiming exemption from training due to a testicular injury, Bevins made a circuit through the company to announce that its commander had become the "bollux master general" of the Vermont militia.

The records of the Maryland court of inquiry convened to examine Jonathan Meredith's toast to the damnation of democracy were printed for the public in 1808 by a Baltimore publisher, G. Dobbin and Murphy, supplemented with related material like his letter of resignation. Titled, *Proceedings of the Officers of the Thirty-Ninth Regiment of Maryland Militia, on an Inquiry into the Conduct of the Adjutant*, copies can be found at the American Antiquarian Society, or online at the subscription-only Archive of Americana.

Regarding the purges of Loyalist officers and the creation of militias of association, see David Hackett Fischer, *Paul Revere's Ride*. The quotes about militiamen gathering around Capt. John Parker on the Common are from the same book.

Regarding the committee of privates in Pennsylvania, see Steven Rosswurm, *Arms Country, and Class: The Philadelphia Militia and the "Lower Sort" during the American Revolution*, and Richard Alan Ryerson, *The Revolution Is Now Begun: The Radical Committees of Philadelphia, 1765–1776*.

An important discussion of late-colonial American military discipline appears in Chapter Four, "There Is No Spare Here of the Whip: Interactions Between Provincial and Regular Troops," of Fred Anderson's 1984 book, *A People's Army: Massachusetts Soldiers & Society in the Seven Years' War*. When provincial troops fell under the same British military code as regular troops, provincial officers manipulated their reporting of offenses to assure lesser punishments for their men.

George Washington tried to impose stern discipline in the Continental Army, often with limited success. For the attempt to impose harsh discipline, see Harry M. Ward, *George Washington's Enforcers: Policing the Continental Army*. Regarding the limits of harsh discipline in the Continental Army, see, for example, Richard Kohn's discussion of the Newburgh Conspiracy in *Eagle and Sword: The Federalists and the Creation of the Military Establishment in America, 1783–1802*; and Carl Van Doren's 1943 book about the large-scale revolts in the Pennsylvania and New Jersey lines, *Mutiny in January*. During the revolt of the Pennsylvania line, mutineers—who had killed an officer as they marched out of camp—appointed a committee of sergeants to negotiate the resolution of their mutiny.

The records of the court-martial that tried Robert Cranston were printed for the public by a Providence publisher, Jones and Wheeler, in 1817: *Proceedings of a general court-martial: holden at Newport, August 1, 1817, for the trial of Captain Robert B. Cranston of the Newport Artillery as officially reported by the Judge Advocate Providence*. Many copies are archived in collections around the country, including the Harvard Library and the American Antiquarian Society. An electronic edition recently became available through the Gale Digital Collections "Making of Modern Law: Trials, 1600–1926" database. I first found a copy of the Cranston record in the records of another trial: the 1817 court-martial of Lt. Joseph Peabody. The lieutenant submitted Cranston's court-martial record to his own court, arguing that it supplied a precedent the court could use to dispose of his case. The records of Peabody's court-martial can be found at the Massachusetts National Guard Museum and Archive, Courts Martial boxes, Vol. 7.

Regarding the courts-martial of Col. Thomas Butler, see Donald R. Hickey, "The United States Army Versus Long Hair: The Trials of Colonel Thomas Butler, 1801–1805," in *The Pennsylvania Magazine of History and Biography*, October 1977.

Vermont's military records were mostly lost in a 1945 fire, described here: https://vermonthistory.org/journal/70/vt703_405.pdf.

My account of David Whitney's court-martial is taken from *An Address of the Council of Censors, to the People of Vermont*, published in 1800 by the Bennington printer Anthony Haswell. It's available through the Archive of Americana, and was also reprinted in newspapers.

Regarding skimmington, see the essays in *Riot and Revelry in Early America*, edited by William Pencak, et al., especially Steven J. Stewart, "Skimmington in the Middle and New England Colonies."

Regarding the decline of wife-beating trials in post-Revolutionary civil courts, see Ruth H. Bloch, "The American Revolution, Wife Beating, and the Emergent Value of Privacy," in the Fall 2007 edition of *Early American Studies: An Interdisciplinary Journal.*

The courts-martial of officers from Connecticut's 17th Regiment can be found in that state's archives, Record Group 13, Boxes 46 and 47. Other courts-martial are interspersed through the set of folders that contain the records of related trials from the 17th Regiment. The relevant courts-martial are these:

Box 46
Trial of Ensign Robert H. Austin
Trial of Captain William Beebe
Trial of Ensign Luther Cook
Trial of Lieut. Julius Griswold
Trial of Lieut. Marvin Griswold
Trial of Capt. David Hall
Trial of Lieut. William Hall
Trial of Capt. Jeremiah Holt

Box 47
Trial of Lieut. Benoni Johnson
Trial of Lieut. Chester Loomis
Trial of Capt. Elisha Loomis
Trial of Ensign Reuben Loomis
Trial of Lieut. Warren Loomis
Trial of Capt. Joseph Mansfield
Trial of Lieut. Stephen Russell
Trial of Ensign Champion Scovill
Trial of Captain Zimri Skinner
Trial of Captain Uriel Tuttle
Trial of Ensign Henry Whittelesey
Trial of Ensign Samuel Wright

The conflict between the officers of the 17th Regiment and Lt. Col. Commandant Lucius Smith over the appointment of a regimental major is discussed throughout the court-martial records. See especially the defense statement of Capt. William Beebe. Also see, at the state archives, two hand-written legislative journals:

(1) *Journal of the House of Representatives, begun the 11th of Oct 1810.* On the second page of entries for Thursday, May 28, 1812, afternoon, two items: "Passed a bill appointing Aaron Smith Lieut Col of the 17th Regt of militia,"

and, "Passed a bill appointing Lucius Smith Majr of the 17th Regt of Militia."
Then, at the bottom of the third page of entries for Tuesday, June 2, 1812
P.M.: "Passed a Bill which came from the upper house appointing a Majr
of the 17th Regt of Militia, with alterations, by erasing the name of Morris
Woodruff and inserting in lieu thereof the name of Lucius Smith." Then, on
the third page of entries for Wednesday morning, June 3, 1812: "Appointed
[illegible] Sheppard + G Barr a committee of conference on the different votes
of the houses on the bill appointing a Majr of 17 Regt of Militia." Then, on
the fourth page of entries for Wednesday morning, June 3, 1812: "Passed a bill
appointing Lucius Smith major 17th Regiment." Then, the second entry for
Thursday afternoon, August 27, 1812: "Passed a bill appointing Lucius Smith
Esq a Major in the 17th Regiment of militia." Finally, on the second page of
entries for Friday morning, August 28, 1812: "Concurred with the upper house
in referring a bill appointing a major of 17th Regt to the Genl Assembly in
Oct next."

(2) *Journal of the House of Representatives, October Session A.D. 1812*. First entry
for Thursday, Oct. 15, 1812 A M · "Passed a bill appointing Lucius Smith Esq.
a Major in the 17th Regt of Militia." Then, the second entry for Friday, Oct. 16,
1812 A.M.: "Concurred with the Honl upper house in passing a bill appointing
Morris Woodruff a Majr in the 17th Regt of Militia."

The 1822 court-martial of Lt. Jacob Robinson can be found at the Connecticut State Archives, Record Group 13, Box 48.

The record of the extralegal "court-martial" of Pvt. Richard Hazard Jr. can
be found at the Newport Historical Society, in Box NA1: Records of the Newport Artillery Company. In the handwritten company journal titled, "Records,
Newport Artillery, Vol. 2: 1794–1825," see the entry of October 20, 1814.

Regarding the death of Richard Hazard Jr., see the death notices on page
1 of the *Independent Chronicle and Boston Patriot*, August 2, 1823, which is available through the America's Historical Newspapers database.

The document founding the Kentish Guards, signed by fifty-four subscribers, can be found as Agreement of Organization, East Greenwich Kentish Guards, 1774, in the Rhode Island Militia Records, MSS 673, SG7, Box 1,
Folder 36, Rhode Island Historical Society.

The record of the court-martial that tried Col. David Pinniger and the
other officers of the Kentish Guards was published by the Warren, Rhode
Island, printers Nathaniel and John F. Phillips in 1808, and is available
through the Archive of Americana database. The original trial record is available at the Rhode Island State Archives.

The record of the court-martial that tried Col. Leonard Blodget was published in 1821 by the Providence printers Miller & Hutchens, under the title,
Report of the Trial of Leonard Blodget, Colonel of the Second Regiment, on Charges

Preferred Against Him by Joseph Hawes, Brigadier General of the Second Brigade of the Rhode-Island Militia, Before a General Court Martial, Holden by orders from the Major-General, Which Convened at the State House in East-Greenwich, October 23d, 1821. Copies are archived in several collections; I read the copy at the Huntington Library. The original trial record is available at the Rhode Island State Archives. Blodget was convicted, and sentenced to be "broke"—stripped of his commission and discharged from the militia. But the major general reviewing his sentence revised the sentence, and Blodget returned to his command after a brief and functionally meaningless wintertime suspension.

I discuss all of these cases in more detail in my 2012 UCLA dissertation, *Disobedience, Discipline, and the Contest for Order in the Early National New England Militia.* It's available online, and easily found at the University of California's escholarship.org website by searching for the title with any search engine.

2. "A BLIND LOTTERY":
Discipline and Justice in the Old Navy

Much of this chapter is drawn from James E. Valle's magnificent 1980 book, *Rocks and Shoals: Order and Discipline in the Old Navy, 1800–1861,* which has sadly gone out of print. I hope to see it reissued.

The flogging of Thomas Ayscough, described by Valle in *Rocks and Shoals,* is covered in slightly more detail in Christopher McKee's *Edward Preble: A Naval Biography 1761–1807.* Ayscough was soon subjected to several more rounds of serial flogging.

Also useful for a detailed description of the early navy is Christopher McKee, *A Gentlemanly and Honorable Profession: The Creation of the U.S. Naval Officer Corps, 1794–1815.*

Herman Melville's autobiographical novel *White-Jacket; or, the World of a Man-of-War* was first published in 1850. Mad Jack's moment of defiance in the storm while transiting Cape Horn is described in Chapter 26, "The Pitch of the Cape." The aftermath of that act is described in Chapter 27, "Some Thoughts Growing Out of Mad Jack's Countermanding his Superior's Order." Melville's thoughts on flogging are expressed throughout the book, but especially important are Chapter 33, "A Flogging"; Chapter 34, "Some of the Evil Effects of Flogging"; Chapter 35, "Flogging Not Lawful"; Chapter 36, "Flogging Not Necessary"; Chapter 67, "White-Jacket arraigned at the Mast"; Chapter 86, "The Rebels Brought to the Mast"; Chapter 87, "Old Ushant at the Gangway"; and Chapter 88, "Flogging Through the Fleet."

Note that the chapter on the flogging of the sailor named Ushant presents a theme quite similar to the real case of Col. Thomas Butler in the early US Army. Ushant, a petty officer on the *Neversink,* refuses an order from Captain

Claret to shave his thick beard, and Claret orders him flogged. Bound for flogging, a defiant Ushant tells his captain that he is trying to regulate another man's body, which is beyond the reach of his proper military authority: "My beard is my own, sir!" Moments later, he repeats the theme, concluding, "you . may flog me, if you will; but, sir, in this one thing I can *not* obey you." Ushant wears his beard in the ship's brig, resolutely refusing to shave it, until his term of service expires and the ship returns to port. He is rowed to shore with his beard intact, "amid the unsuppressible cheers of all hands."

In *White-Jacket*, the description of officers turning away in disgust and refusing to hear complaints about sexual misconduct aboard the ship appears in Chapter 89, "The Social State in a Man-of-War."

Regarding Capt. James Sever's poor seamanship during the 1800 voyage of the warship *Congress*, see George C. Daughan, *If by Sea: The Forging of the American Navy—From the American Revolution to the War of 1812*. Also useful are Daughan's *1812: The Navy's War*, and *The Shining Sea: David Porter and the Epic Voyage of the U.S.S. Essex During the War of 1812*.

My account of the thwarted mutiny on the *Somers* is taken from Buckner Melton's *A Hanging Offense: The Strange Affair of the Warship Somers*.

Regarding abolitionists and the campaign against navy flogging, see Myra C. Glenn, "The Naval Reform Campaign Against Flogging: A Case Study in Changing Attitudes Toward Corporal Punishment, 1830–1850," which was published in the *American Quarterly* in the Autumn 1983 edition.

3. "A LAWFUL GOING HOME":
Conflict and Coercion in the Jacksonian Military

Regarding the execution of the six Tennessee militiamen, and the courts-martial of the officers who didn't prevent them from deserting, see, "On the proceedings of a Court-Martial Ordered for the Trial of Certain Tennessee Militiamen in 1814," February 11, 1828. *American State Papers, Military Affairs* 3, no. 371.

The Library of Congress has put the American State Papers online, so you can easily find this report here: http://memory.loc.gov/ammem/amlaw/lwsplink.html.

You can also find this report on Google Books; try searching for "John Harris, to whose name such remarkable notoriety has been attached." Like Joseph Hawes in his conflict with Leonard Blodget, members of Congress treated the matter as the simple application of statutes to facts—a choice contemporary historians follow.

Copies of the Coffin Handbills can be easily found online; just search for the phrase. The handbills were widely distributed and often reprinted during the nineteenth century, and some archived copies have been found to be later reproductions. See the February 15, 2012, post by Lydia Blackmore, "Some Account of 'Some Account of some of the Bloody Deeds of Gen. Jackson,'" on the museum blog *Winterthur Unreserved.*

Two volumes of James Parton's *Life of Andrew Jackson* are available as free ebooks on Google Books, and easily found there with a simple search. Volume 2, from which this account is drawn, is the only volume not available as a Google ebook. Still, an awkwardly formatted copy of Volume 2 can be found here: https://archive.org/details/lifeandrewjacks03partgoog.

Compare the account of this nineteenth-century writer who knows the militia traditions of the early century with the account of a twentieth-century Jackson biographer. "These men were charged with mutiny, desertion, inducing others to desert, and stealing military supplies," Robert Remini flatly declares. "They were tried, found guilty, and executed." And yet, despite the trials and convictions, he concludes, anti-Jackson newspapers still "saw the incident as savage brutality."

Missing from this kind of account is any sense of a competing tradition—which Parton identified without difficulty, and discussed in detail. Remini's Whiggish account of the Coffin Handbills can be found in the first volume of *History of American Presidential Elections, 1789–2008*, volume 1, 4th edition, edited by Gil Troy, Arthur M. Schlesinger Jr., and Fred L. Israel.

Remini's view has become the established one, eliding an important tradition and several decades of urgent debate in our past. For an example of the way that the Coffin Handbills have become viewed as an uncomplicated piece of empty mudslinging, see Steven A. Seidman, *Posters, Propaganda, and Persuasion in Election Campaigns Around the World and Through History*, footnote 11, chapter 2: "Jackson biographer Robert Remini concluded that these six militiamen, who were executed during the Creek War in 1813 [sic], were guilty of the crimes for which they were executed." Like Joseph Hawes, historians see just the text of the law, and assume that it offers the final word.

Robert Remini's description of Andrew Jackson being "honored above all living men" is the opening sentence from *Andrew Jackson: The Course of American Empire, 1767–1821*, the first volume of his three-volume Jackson biography.

The reference to Jackson's "ubiquitous rage" is from Michael Paul Rogin, *Fathers and Children: Andrew Jackson and the Subjugation of the American Indian.*

The Fremont court-martial, and the "I looked him down" incident, were widely discussed in newspapers all over the country. For an example that can be found on the newspapers.com website, see "The Fremont Trial—A Scene" on page 3 of the *Greensboro Patriot*, Saturday, January 22, 1848.

The commentary on the Fremont trial from *The Farmer's Cabinet* is from the January 20, 1848, edition, page 2, under the headline, "What Is Greatness?" It can be found using the America's Historical Newspapers database.

A detailed and balanced account of the meeting between Andrew Jackson and William Weatherford can be found in H. W. Brand, *Andrew Jackson: His Life and Times.*

Regarding the summary executions of the Creek leaders Josiah Francis and Homathlemico, see Frank L. Owsley Jr., "Prophet of War: Josiah Francis and the Creek War," which was published in *American Indian Quarterly* in the summer of 1985.

Regarding filibusters, see Robert E. May, *Manifest Destiny's Underworld: Filibustering in Antebellum America.* A good account of earlier filibusters is Frank L. Owsley Jr. and Gene A. Smith, *Filibusters and Expansionists: Jeffersonian Manifest Destiny, 1800–1821.*

Two vivid research articles describe the reluctance of government officials to interfere with filibusters, and the moments when that reluctance shaded into active assistance. Both appear in a volume of essays edited by Samuel Watson, *Warfare in the USA, 1784–1861*: Robert E. May, "Young American Males and Filibustering in the Age of Manifest Destiny: The United States Army as a Cultural Mirror," and Durwood Ball, "Filibusters and Regular Troops in San Francisco, 1851–1855." May's essay can also be found in the *Journal of American History*, and Ball's essay also appeared in *Military History of the West.*

My account of Andrew Jackson's actions in New Orleans is mostly drawn from Matthew Warshauer's definitive 2006 book, *Andrew Jackson and the Politics of Martial Law.*

Frank L. Owsley Jr. discusses the execution of Robert Ambrister and Alexander Arbuthnot in a 1985 research article, "Ambrister and Arbuthnot: Adventurers or Martyrs for British Honor," which can be found in the *Journal of the Early Republic.*

The full transcript of the Ambrister and Arbuthnot court-martial can also be read on Google books, in a record that includes both the revision of Ambrister's sentence and the order from Jackson for his execution. See chapter 5 of S. G. Heiskell, *Andrew Jackson and Early Tennessee History*, volume 1, second edition, which is available here: https://books.google.com/books?id=LPqZ80I8pfgC.

My account of the US Army's Irish immigrant deserters in Mexico is mostly drawn from Peter F. Stevens, *The Rogue's March: John Riley and the St. Patrick's Battalion, 1846–1848*, as is some of my discussion of Martin Tritschler and his military trial.

Regarding Winfield Scott's use of military commissions in Mexico, see Haridimos Thravalos, "The Military Commission in the War on Terrorism," which (despite the title) discusses the use of such commissions throughout American history. It was published in the *Villanova Law Review* in 2006. Also important is Erika Myers, "Conquering Peace: Military Commissions as a Law-fare Strategy in the Mexican War," which was published in the *American Journal of Criminal Law* in 2008.

PART TWO

The full text of the Lieber Code is available online at the website of the Yale law school's Avalon Project: http://avalon.law.yale.edu/19th_century/lieber.asp.

Quotes from the legal historian John Fabian Witt are taken from his recent and important book, *Lincoln's Code: The Laws of War in American History*, which discusses the Lieber Code in depth.

Robert Penn Warren's description of the "secret school" for the mass war-fare of the twentieth century is from *The Legacy of the Civil War*, a 1961 essay later reprinted as a short book.

Robert Wiebe's description of "island communities" and the transition to a bureaucratic national system appear in his 1967 book, *The Search for Order, 1877–1920*.

4. "I WON'T BE QUIET":
Force and Consent in the Civil War

The title of Elizabeth Samet's book reflects her theme: *Willing Obedience: Citizens, Soldiers, and the Progress of Consent in America, 1776–1898*.

Field-officer courts have been the subject of little serious study, and two different historians have drawn two different conclusions about them. In 2004, Joseph C. Fitzharris concluded that many regiments ignored the new law and continued to conduct regimental courts-martial. See his article, "Field Officer Courts and U.S. Civil War Military Justice," in *The Journal of Military History*. But Lorien Foote, in the book discussed immediately below, concluded more recently that "implementation of field officer courts was in fact widespread in the Union Army and was enforced through orders descending from the War Department and issued through brigade and division headquarters." In any event, note that the most common form of armed forces tribunal in the Civil War has drawn little attention from scholars, a sad reflection of the attention historians give to the topic of military justice.

Confederate courts-martial have been the subject of little scholarship, and many records that would help in that scholarship have been lost. But the Confederate Congress made a similar attempt to ease the burden of courts-martial on commanders in the field: an October 1862 law that created standing military courts, attached to army corps in the field. But the Confederate govern-ment struggled to find officers who would serve as members, slowing military justice and creating a serious backlog of cases. Under those circumstances, "men awaiting trial were kept under arrest for long periods, contrary to the articles of war." See Jack A. Bunch, *Military Justice in the Confederate States Armies.*

Also useful regarding Confederate military justice is Aldo S. Perry, *Civil War Courts-Martial of North Carolina Troops.*

The incidents involving Bernard McMahon, Jefferson C. Davis, and Charles Horton, and the general discussion of dueling in the Civil War army, are taken from Lorien Foote's important 2010 book, *The Gentlemen and the Roughs: Violence, Honor, and Manhood in the Union Army.*

Regarding the long confinement without trial or charges of Brig. Gen. Charles Pomeroy Stone, see James T. Currie, "Congressional Oversight Run Amok: Ball's Bluff and the Ruination of Charles Stone," which was published in the Autumn 1993 issue of *Parameters*; and Stephen W. Sears, *Controversies and Commanders: Dispatches from the Army of the Potomac.*

The court-martial of Maj. Gen. Fitz John Porter is discussed in many sources; see, for example, Donald R. Jermann, *Fitz-John Porter, Scapegoat of Second Manassas.*

James McPherson's description of Southern war-weariness in 1864, and the vote for Lincoln among Union soldiers voting by absentee ballot, is taken from his highly regarded book *The Battle Cry of Freedom: The Civil War Era.*

Jonathan W. White discusses the use of military punishment to shape the wartime politics of Union Army soldiers in his extraordinary 2014 book, *Emancipation, the Union Army, and the Reelection of Abraham Lincoln.* The portions of this chapter that discuss the examples of Maj. John Key, Maj. Charles Whiting, Col. John Warner, and Lt. John Garland; Pvts. Mack Ewing and Rufus Miller; and Lt. Edward Austin are taken from this book, as is the quote from Col. Thomas Bennett.

The incident involving the 7th New York at the end of the war is also described by Lorien Foote in *The Gentlemen and the Roughs.*

Regarding the Confederate general Edmund Kirby Smith and the disappearance of his army at the end of the war, see Mark A. Weitz, *More Damning Than Slaughter: Desertion in the Confederate Army.*

For an example of the way earlier historians discussed Civil War courts-martial, see the late Bell Irvin Wiley's important 1952 book, *The Life of Billy Yank: The Common Soldier of the Union,* later editions of which can be partially read on Google Books. Chapter VIII, "Toeing the Mark," opens with several pages describing extraordinarily brutal and arbitrary examples of Civil War military punishment, after which Wiley writes this: "Courts-martial and military commissions followed a well-defined procedure designed to assure a full hearing and a fair trial for the accused." A few pages later, Wiley writes that "the failure to bring offenders promptly to trial violated fundamental principles of justice," while circumstances were "further complicated by the dearth of officers skilled in court-martial procedure." A respected and highly knowledgeable historian wrote an essentially self-refuting description of military justice, a sign of prevailing assumptions that overwhelm the attempt at analysis. It is not the case that Civil War courts-martial reliably followed established and thorough court-martial procedures. Strangely, Wiley's book was published very shortly after a massive national attempt at military-justice reform, which had grown from the premise that the laws and legal systems of the armed forces had old, deep, and obvious defects.

5. "AMENABLE TO MILITARY LAW":
Policing Civilians with Military Authority

The arrest of the reporter Lawrence Mathews is described in Mark A. Neely, *Southern Rights: Political Prisoners and the Myth of Confederate Constitutionalism*, which I use as a source throughout this chapter.

Also useful is Kenneth J. Radley, *Rebel Watchdog: The Confederate States Army Provost Guard*.

My account of John Merryman's arrest, and the events surrounding it, are taken from Jonathan W. White, *Abraham Lincoln and Treason in the Civil War: The Trials of John Merryman*.

The full title John F. Marszalek's book on the events described here is *Sherman's Other War: The General and the Civil War Press*.

Regarding Lambin Milligan, see Frank L. Klement, *Dark Lanterns: Secret Political Societies, Conspiracies, and Treason Trials in the Civil War*. The 1865 book released by the recorder appointed to Milligan's army trial is Benn Pitman, *The Trials for Treason at Indianapolis, Disclosing the Plans for Establishing a North-Western Confederacy*. It can be downloaded free from Google Books. The timing of the Supreme Court's decision and opinion are discussed in John Fabian Witt's *Lincoln's Code: The Laws of War in American History*.

6. "ALL THAT SAVORED OF THE OVERSEER":
Black Soldiers in the Nineteenth Century

Jim Downs describes the ordeal of Joseph Miller and his family in *Sick from Freedom: African-American Illness and Suffering During the Civil War and Reconstruction*. Also useful is Richard D. Sears, *Camp Nelson, Kentucky: A Civil War History*.

The full text of Miller's statement to army officials regarding his family is available online at the website of the Gilder Lehrman Institute of American History: https://www.gilderlehrman.org/sites/default/files/inline-pdfs/Nov64.pdf.

The portion of the Militia Act of 1862 that authorizes the recruitment of black soldiers—and requires their lower pay—is available online: http://www .freedmen.umd.edu/milact.htm.

The quote from Sgt. Maj. James Trotter is taken from Keith P. Wilson, *Campfires of Freedom: The Camp Life of Black Soldiers During the Civil War.*

So is the relevant portion of General Order 111: http://www.freedmen .umd.edu/pow.htm.

P.G.T. Beauregard's refusal to execute black prisoners of war is described in many sources. See, for example, Howard C. Westwood, "Captive Black Union Soldiers in Charleston: What to Do?" in *Black Flag over Dixie: Racial Atrocities and Reprisals in the Civil War*, edited by Gregory J. W. Urwin; Charles W. Sanders, *While in the Hands of the Enemy: Military Prisons of the Civil War*; and Linda Barnickel, *Milliken's Bend: A Civil War Battle in History and Memory.*

Barnickel also examines in detail the possibility that Confederate soldiers murdered prisoners after the Battle of Milliken's Bend; see especially chapter 0, "'A Disagreeable Dilemma': The Fate of Union Prisoners, Black and White."

Harry C. Westwood also discussed General Order 111, and Lincoln's response, in a 2008 book, *Black Troops, White Commanders, and Freedmen During the Civil War.*

For another example of Confederate soldiers killing black Union army soldiers they held as prisoners, see Linda Barnickel, "'No Federal Prisoners Among Them': The Execution of Black Union Soldiers at Jackson, Louisiana," in the February 2010 edition of the magazine *North & South.*

Edmund Kirby Smith's letter about the "disagreeable dilemma" is widely quoted. See, for example, Hondon B. Hargrove, *Black Union Soldiers in the Civil War*, and an essay by James G. Hollandsworth Jr., "The Execution of White Officers from Black Units by Confederate Forces During the Civil War," in *Black Flag over Dixie*, cited above.

The Fort Pillow massacre is discussed in *Black Flag over Dixie*. See also Andrew Ward, *River Run Red: The Fort Pillow Massacre in the American Civil War.*

The court-martial statements of Lt. Col. Augustus Bennett and Sgt. William Walker appear in a 1982 collection, *Freedom: A Documentary History of Emancipation 1861–1867, Series 11: The Black Military Experience*, edited by Ira Berlin. The statements can be found by searching within the book on Google Books.

Regarding the mutiny in the 3rd South Carolina Colored Infantry, see also David W. Blight, *Frederick Douglass' Civil War: Keeping Faith in Jubilee*. Blight calls Walker's execution "one of the ugliest episodes of the war."

Also important regarding Walker and the 3rd South Carolina is Christian G. Samito, "The Intersection Between Military Justice and Equal Rights: Mutinies, Courts-Martial, and Black Civil War Soldiers," an article published in the journal *Civil War History* in June 2007. This article is also my source for the incidents involving Pvt. Sampson Goliah and Pvt. Wallace Baker.

Thomas Wentworth Higginson's book *Army Life in a Black Regiment* can be read online as a free ebook: http://www.gutenbcrg.org/files/6764/6764-h/6764-h.htm.

Regarding the execution of black soldiers at Camp Shaw in 1864, and the examples of Lt. Col. Augustus Benedict and Lt. Henry Cady, see John F. Fannin, "The Jacksonville Mutiny of 1865," in the Winter 2010 issue of *The Florida Historical Quarterly*.

Many books address "redemptionist" violence during Reconstruction, including attacks on Freedmen's Bureau teachers and black voters. See, for example, LeeAnna Keith, *The Colfax Massacre: The Untold Story of Black Power, White Terror, and the Death of Reconstruction*; Charles Lane, *The Day Freedom Died: The Colfax Massacre, the Supreme Court, and the Betrayal of Reconstruction*; Nicholas Lemann, *Redemption: The Last Battle of the Civil War*; and a vivid political biography by Stephen Kantrowitz, *Ben Tillman and the Reconstruction of White Supremacy*. Most important among recent titles is Michael W. Fitzgerald, *Splendid Failure: Postwar Reconstruction in the American South*.

Regarding Ku Klux Klan trials in federal courts, see, for example, Lou Falkner Williams, *The Great South Carolina Ku Klux Klan Trials, 1871–1872*, and Jerry Lee West, *The Reconstruction Ku Klux Klan in York County, South Carolina, 1865–1877*.

Regarding trials by military commissions during Reconstruction, see Detlev F. Vagts, "Military Commissions: The Forgotten Reconstruction Chapter," which was published in the *American University International Law Review* in 2007.

Charles L. Kenner examines the service of black soldiers after the Civil War in his 1999 book, *Buffalo Soldiers and Officers of the Ninth Cavalry, 1867–1898: Black and White Together*.

John Marszalek discusses the early history of black cadets at the United States Military Academy in his 1972 book, *Assault at West Point: The Court-Martial of Johnson Whittaker*. After being thrown out of the West Point, Whittaker went home to South Carolina and built careers as a lawyer and a teacher. His sons were commissioned as army officers. For a discussion of his later life and legacy, see "Seeking 'Fair Deal' for a Black Cadet," *New York Times*, January 31, 1994.

The transition to rigid and invariable segregation in the South was most memorably described by C. Vann Woodward in his 1955 book, *The Strange Career of Jim Crow*.

For an example of an account that puts black cavalrymen ahead of the Rough Riders at San Juan Hill, see Gary Gerstle, *American Crucible: Race and Nation in the Twentieth Century*.

Garna Christian's book is *Black Soldiers in Jim Crow Texas, 1899–1907.* Also useful is James N. Leiker, *Racial Borders: Black Soldiers Along the Rio Grande.*

7. "MANIACS OR WILD BEASTS":
Military Justice and American Expansion

My description of the Dakota trials and executions draws heavily from Carol Chomsky, "The United States–Dakota War Trials: A Study in Military Injustice," which was published in the *Stanford Law Review* in November 1990.

A "Famous Trials" website hosted by the University of Kansas–Missouri City School of Law includes a few trial transcripts and an eyewitness account of the executions: http://law2.umkc.edu/faculty/projects/ftrials/dakota/dakota.html

The quote regarding Chaska is taken from Micheal Clodfelter, *The Dakota War: The United States Army Versus the Sioux, 1862–1865.* (Clodfelter's first name is spelled correctly.) The woman who tried to save Chaska was Sarah Wakefield. Another account of her attempts to prevent Chaska's death appears in Duane P. Schultz, *Over the Earth I Come: The Great Sioux Uprising of 1862.* A book by Hank H. Cox, *Lincoln and the Sioux Uprising of 1862,* describes Lincoln's struggles to puzzle through Dakota names and ensure he was pardoning the men he intended to pardon; see the opening of chapter 14, "I Could Not Hang Men for Votes."

Regarding the Sand Creek massacre, see Duane Schultz, *Month of the Freezing Moon: The Sand Creek Massacre, November 1864,* and Patrick M. Mendoza, *Song of Sorrow: Massacre at Sand Creek.* The proclamation from Gov. John Evans "To the friendly Indians of the Plains" is reprinted in many government reports, and is available on a National Park Service website: http://www.nps.gov/sand/learn/news/proclamation-to-the-friendly-indians.htm.

The testimony of soldiers who were present at Sand Creek is widely reprinted in government reports. See, for example, *Condition of the Indian Tribes: Report of the Joint Special Committee,* published by the Government Printing Office in 1867 and available for free on Google Books. The quote that describes a lieutenant killing and scalping women and young children appears on page 61.

Capt. Silas Soule is buried at Riverside Cemetery in Denver. The unincorporated village of Chivington is described on a website about ghost towns, with pictures of what little is left: http://www.ghosttowns.com/states/co/chivington.html.

An important study of the aftermath of the Sand Creek massacre examines the later hearings as a contest over the meaning of the event. See Ari Kelman, *A Misplaced Massacre: Struggling over the Memory of Sand Creek.*

Regarding the Modoc War executions, see Doug Foster, "Imperfect Justice: The Modoc War Crimes Trial of 1873," which was published in the *Oregon Historical Quarterly* in the Fall 1999 issue, and Boyd Cothran, *Remembering the Modoc War: Redemptive Violence and the Making of American Innocence.*

Today, some Modoc live in Oregon, as members of the Klamath Tribes. Captain Jack's band -the portion of the Modoc people who fought the US government—were removed to Oklahoma. The Modoc Tribe of Oklahoma website contains a page on Modoc history: http://www.modoctribe.net/history.html.

American military commissions in the Philippines are described by David Glazier in "Precedents Lost: The Neglected History of the Military Commission," which was published in the *Virginia Journal of International Law* in Fall 2005.

The incident involving 1st Lt. Preston Brown is taken from Louise Barnett, *Atrocity and American Military Justice in Southeast Asia*, and Meredith Mason Brown, "A Killing in the Philippines, 1900: A Kentuckian Faces Insurgency and Military Justice." The latter was published in the Winter 2006 issue of *The Register of the Kentucky Historical Society.*

Regarding the court-martial of Maj. Littleton Waller, see Barnett's *Atrocity and American Military Justice in Southeast Asia.*

PART THREE

Regarding high modernism and twentieth-century bureaucratic culture, see Zygmunt Bauman, *Modernity and the Holocaust*, and James Scott's indescribably important *Seeing Like a State: How Certain Schemes to Improve the Human Condition Have Failed.*

The quote from Jennifer Keene is taken from her 2011 book, *World War I: The American Soldier Experience.*

8. "WE RETURN FIGHTING":
Black Soldiers in the Jim Crow Era

Many books describe the "Double V" campaign, though they tend to focus on World War II veterans. See, for example, Christopher S. Parker, *Fighting for Democracy: Black Veterans and the Struggle Against White Supremacy in the Postwar South.*

The full text of W.E.B. Du Bois's famous 1919 "we return fighting" declaration is available online: http://www.yale.edu/glc/archive/1127.htm.

The revolt of the 3rd Battalion 24th Infantry is described in Robert V. Haynes, *A Night of Violence: The Houston Riot of 1917*, and is also discussed in Garna L. Christian's *Black Soldiers in Jim Crow Texas, 1899–1917.*

Several sources describe the court-martial of Lt. Jack Robinson, and the events leading up to it. My account relies on an article by Jules Tygiel, "The Court-Martial of Jackie Robinson," in the August/September 1984 issue of *American Heritage* magazine; a book by Arnold Rampersad, *Jackie Robinson: A Biography*; and a book by David Falkner, *Great Time Coming: The Life of Jackie Robinson from Baseball to Birmingham.*

Tygiel's article is available here: http://www.americanheritage.com/ content/court-martial-jackie-robinson.

Also, an essay by John Vernon on the National Archives website includes the images of several documents relating to Robinson's court-martial: http://www.archives.gov/publications/prologue/2008/spring/robinson.html.

The *Chicago Tribune* article on Yeoman First Class Barbara Foss, "Girl Deserter Ties Navy's Red Tape in a Knot," appeared on page 7 of the August 10, 1918, issue.

My account of the general strike by black women assigned as WAC medical technicians at Fort Devens is taken from Leisa Meyer, *Creating GI Jane: Sexuality and Power in the Women's Army Corps During World War II.*

See also two stories in the New York Times, neither of which named the writer: "Sentence Four Negro WACs Who Protested Taking Menial Jobs," March 21, 1945, and "Negro WACs Back on Duty," April 4, 1945.

Regarding the Port Chicago mutiny and the resulting trial, see Robert L. Allen, *The Port Chicago Mutiny: The Story of the Largest Mass Mutiny Trial in U.S. Naval History.*

Journalists Jack and Leslie Humann describe the Fort Lawton incident in their 2005 book, *On American Soil: How Justice Became a Casualty of World War II.*

For an example of another protest by black officers over segregation on military posts, with resulting courts-martial, see Lawrence P. Scott and William M. Womack Sr., *Double V: The Civil Rights Struggle of the Tuskegee Airmen.*

9. "AN EMERGENCY CONDITION":
World War I and the First Debate over Reform

William T. Generous Jr. describes the debate over court-martial reform between World War I and the adoption of the Uniform Code of Military Justice in a 1973 book, *Swords and Scales: The Development of the Uniform Code of Military Justice.* My description of the Ansell-Crowder debate draws heavily from this source.

The postwar Associated Press story describing soldiers' complaints about courts-martial to the military newspaper *Stars and Stripes* was widely reprinted. A version that can be found online without a database subscription appeared on the front page of the Marine Corps *Chevron* on March 28, 1946, and can be found on the website of the Princeton University Library, within the Princeton Historic Newspapers Collection: http://historicperiodicals.princeton.edu.

The quote from Jennifer Keene is taken from *World War I: The American Soldier Experience*, cited above.

Much of the exchange between Crowder, Ansell, March, Baker, and other adversaries in the debate over military reform is contained in a bound volume from the Government Printing Office, *Establishment of Military Justice*, that was printed in 1919. This volume is available for free download on Google Books: https://books.google.com/books?id=bSsuAAAAYAAJ&.

Quotes from John Lindley are taken from his 1990 book, *A Soldier Is Also a Citizen: The Controversy over Military Justice, 1917–1920*, which is also my source for much of the information in this chapter about the trials of Privates Cook, Sebastian, Ledoyen, and Fishback.

Also useful is Jonathan Lurie, *Military Justice in America: The U.S. Court of Appeals for the Armed Forces, 1775–1980*, which contains several chapters on the Ansell-Crowder dispute; and an article by Maj. Terry W. Brown, "The Crowder-Ansell Dispute: The Emergence of General Samuel T. Ansell," which appeared in the *Military Law Review* in 1967.

A brief biography of Gen. Peyton March appears on the website of the US Army Historical Foundation: https://armyhistory.org/general-peyton-c-march/.

The full text of Baker's letter to Wilson on the four death sentences imposed by courts-martial in Europe appears in a February 21, 1919, story on page 4 of the *New York Times*, "Baker's Own Plea Saved Four Soldiers."

The court-martial of Billy Mitchell is discussed in an article by Rebecca Maksel, "The Billy Mitchell Court-Martial," that appeared in the July 2009 issue of *Air & Space Magazine*. The article is available online: http://www.airspacemag.com/history-of-flight/the-billy-mitchell-court-martial-136828592/.

My account of the Billy Mitchell trial is also drawn from a 1972 book by Joseph DiMona, *Great Court-Martial Cases*.

10. "WE'VE GOT TO LIVE WITH THIS THE REST OF OUR LIVES": *The Deadly Justice of World War II*

The story of the German saboteurs landing on American beaches in 1942 is told by Michael Dobbs in a 2007 book, *Saboteurs: The Nazi Raid on America*. The subsequent legal battle is best described by the lawyer Pierce O'Donnell in a lively and detailed book, *In Time of War: Hitler's Terrorist Attack on America*. Also useful is Louis Fisher, *Nazi Saboteurs on Trial: A Military Tribunal and American Law*.

French L. MacLean's important book on the men buried in Plot E at Oise-Aisne is *The Fifth Field: The Story of the 96 American Soldiers Sentenced to Death and Executed in Europe and North Africa in World War II*.

The op-ed piece by Alice Kaplan, "A Hidden Memorial to the Worst Aspects of our Jim Crow Army," appeared in the September 25, 2005 issue of the *Chicago Tribune*, and is available online: http://articles.chicagotribune .com/2005-09-25/news/0509250486_1_jim-crow-army-till-official-army.

Kaplan also discusses World War II military justice in her 2007 book, *The Interpreter.*

The quote regarding William Harrison Jr. is from J. Robert Lilly and J. Michael Thomson, "Executing U.S. Soldiers in England, World War II: Command Influence and Sexual Racism," which was published in *The British Journal of Criminology*, Spring 1997.

The material about a postwar criminology study is taken from William Generous, *Swords and Scales: The Development of the Uniform Code of Military Justice.*

Regarding the desertion and execution of Pvt. Eddie Slovik, William Bradford Huie's 1954 book, *The Execution of Private Slovik*, remains the most significant source, and is also the source of the information about the number of men excused from service "for reasons other than physical." In *The Fifth Field*, French MacLean also provides an important discussion of the Slovik court-martial.

As Huie writes, the army had about 40,000 battlefield deserters in Europe during World War II, narrowly defined to exclude "those charged with the relatively minor offenses of overstaying leave, drunkenness, [and being] AWOL from training camps."

See also a recent book by Charles Glass, *The Deserters: A Hidden History of World War II*, which puts the total number of American deserters at closer to 50,000.

Ross Henbest's actions outside Bastogne are described by Peter Schrijvers in *Those Who Hold Bastogne: The True Story of the Soldiers and Civilians Who Fought in the Biggest Battle of the Bulge*. Henbest survived; Sgt. Bill Korte responded to the lieutenant colonel's order to leave him behind with, "Hell no, Colonel."

Back home after the war, Henbest started a PhD program at the University of Michigan. In 1948, at the age of forty-three, he died of a sudden illness. Regarding his career as a history teacher, and his sudden death after the war, see "Short Illness Is Fatal to Ross Henbest," March 31, 1948, on page 7 of the *Northwest Arkansas Times*.

The sinking of the *Indianapolis*, and the court-martial and political controversy that followed, are described in detail on a website: http://www .ussindianapolis.org. Several books are also useful, including Doug Stanton, *In Harm's Way: The Sinking of the U.S.S. Indianapolis and the Extraordinary Story of Its Survivors*; Dan Kurzman, *Fatal Voyage: The Sinking of the U.S.S. Indianapolis*; and Raymond B. Lech, *The Tragic Fate of the U.S.S. Indianapolis: The U.S. Navy's*

Worst Disaster at Sea. The quote from the Navy JAG regarding public interest is taken from the latter. "The American people were astonished at the number of fatalities," Lech writes, "and demanded that they receive answers about the cause of this disaster and who was to blame. The Navy decided to point to Charles McVay as the culprit."

A list of US Navy ships sunk during World War II is available here: http://www.navsource.org/Naval/losses.htm.

For the two *New York Times* editorials on the *Indianapolis* and the Office of Censorship, see page 16 of the August 17, 1945, issue.

President Franklin Roosevelt's Proclamation 2561, "Denying Certain Enemies Access to the Courts," July 2, 1942, declared that captured enemy spies and saboteurs would be tried by military tribunals. The text of the order is available online: http://www.presidency.ucsb.edu/ws/?pid=16281.

Army JAG Myron Cramer's legal advice about civilian trials for the German saboteurs is described in "Sitting in Judgment: Myron C. Cramer's Experiences in the Trials of German Saboteurs and Japanese War Leaders," which appeared in the Summer 2009 issue of *Prologue*, the magazine of the National Archives and Records Administration. The same article describes the fears within the government that a trial in open court would reveal military ineptitude and the limits of the FBI's investigative magic. It's available here: http://www.loc.gov/rr/frd/Military_Law/pdf/Sitting-in-Judgment.pdf.

Regarding damaging information and the risk of a civilian trial, see also Jonathan Lurie's discussion of *Quirin* in *The Supreme Court and Military Justice.*

The *New York Times* story on the bravery of the Coast Guard and the brilliance of the FBI in capturing the German saboteurs appeared in the July 16, 1942, issue, page 1.

Regarding the Supreme Court's decision in *Ex Parte Quirin*, see Robert E. Cushman, "Ex Parte Quirin ct al: The Nazi Saboteur Case," which was rushed into the *Cornell Law Review* in November 1942; Andrew Kent, "Judicial Review for Enemy Fighters: The Court's Fateful Turn in *Ex parte Quirin,* the Nazi Saboteur Case," which was published in the *Vanderbilt Law Review* in 2013; and Jonathan Lurie, *The Supreme Court and Military Justice.* The description of the meeting on the farm is drawn from Michael Dobbs, *Saboteurs: The Nazi Raid on America.* My discussion of the resulting legal battle is drawn in significant part from Pierce O'Donnell's excellent book *In Time of War: Hitler's Terrorist Attack on America.*

A brief summary of *In Re Yamashita* can be found on the PBS website: http://www.pbs.org/wnet/justice/world_issues_yam.html.

For a detailed discussion of the Yamashita trial, see Philip R. Piccigallo, *The Japanese on Trial: Allied War Crimes Operations in the East, 1945–1951.*

Regarding the reexamination of World War II courts-martial by the American military, see William T. Generous Jr., *Swords and Scales: The Development of the Uniform Code of Military Justice.*

11. "YOU CANNOT MAINTAIN DISCIPLINE BY ADMINISTERING JUSTICE":
The Cold War and the UCMJ

The events involving Capt. Fred Chewning are described by the Army Board of Review in its opinion on *United States v. Captain Fred Chewning*, which was dated April 14, 1953. Elizabeth Lutes Hillman briefly mentions the case in the notes to chapter 2 of *Defending America: Military Culture and the Cold War Court Martial.*

The court-martial of Capt. Edward Geddes is brilliantly described by Louise Barnett in *Ungentlemanly Acts: The Army's Notorious Incest Trial.* A radio interview with Barnett describes the case in detail: http://www.ttbook.org/listen/37611.

Regarding the focus of Cold War military justice on sexual behavior, see Elizabeth Lutes Hillman, *Defending America: Military Culture and the Cold War Court Martial,* and an unpublished dissertation by Kellie Wilson Buford, *Policing Sex and Marriage in the American Military: The Court-Martial and the Construction of Gender and Sexual Deviance, 1950–1975.*

David Johnson's book is *The Lavender Scare: The Cold War Persecution of Gays and Lesbians in the Federal Government.*

The courts-martial of Master Sgt. Charles Chadd and Sgt. John Mathis are both discussed by Hillman in *Defending America.* My account also draws from the opinion of the Court of Military Appeals in *United States v. Charles D. Chadd,* which was dated January 25, 1963; and an opinion of the Army Board of Review in *United States v. Sgt. John P. Mathis,* which was dated January 30, 1964. The recorded testimony is that the man Mathis beat to death would "feint" and recover during the attack, but in context it appears more likely that the other man was fainting from loss of blood and struggling not to lose consciousness.

In his book *Swords and Scales: The Development of the Uniform Code of Military Justice,* William T. Generous Jr. describes the committees in the armed forces that reviewed wartime court-martial records: "These included, in the Navy, the two Ballantine committees, 1943 and 1946; the Taussig study in 1944; the McGuire committee of 1945; the Keefe General Court-Martial Sentence Review Board, 1946; and Father White's study of prisoners, 1946. Similar bodies worked on Army problems: the Roberts board on clemency, 1945–47, the Vanderbilt committee and the Doolittle board, both 1946."

The quote from Michael Scott Bryant comes from the title of a 2013 research article, "American Military Justice from the Revolution to the UCMJ: The Hard Journey from Command Authority to Due Process," which was published in the *Creighton International and Comparative Law Journal*.

Edward F. Sherman's article, "The Civilianization of Military Law," was published in the *Maine Law Review* in 1970.

The full text of the Elston Act is available online at the website of the Library of Congress: http://www.loc.gov/rr/frd/Military_Law/pdf/act-1948 .pdf. The first part of the law deals with Selective Service requirements; scroll down to Title II.

Lawrence J. Morris discusses the major provisions of the Elston Act in *Military Justice: A Guide to the Issues*, and William Generous covers the act in a chapter of *Swords and Scales*. Both sources also provide important discussion of the development of the UCMJ.

My discussion of the case involving Maj. Gen. Robert Grow is taken from George F. Hofmann, *Cold War Casualty: The Court-Martial of Major General Robert W. Grow*.

My discussion of the Ribbon Creek incident is taken from John C. Stevens III, *Court-Martial at Parris Island: The Ribbon Creek Incident*. Keith Fleming's book on the incident is *The U.S. Marine Corps in Crisis: Ribbon Creek and Recruit Training*.

Regarding Dorothy Smith and Clarice Covert, see Capt. Brittany Warren, "The Case of the Murdering Wives: Reid v. Covert and the Complicated Question of Civilians and Courts-Martial," which was published in the *Military Law Review* in 2012.

The court-martial and legal appeal of Sgt. James F. O'Callahan is discussed by the journalist Joseph DiMona in *Great Court-Martial Cases*. Regarding the degree to which the Supreme Court's majority opinion in the case ignored military justice reform, see Robinson O. Everett, "*O'Callahan v. Parker*—Milestone or Millstone in Military Justice?" which appeared in the *Duke Law Journal* in October 1969. The Supreme Court's decision in the case was dated June 2, 1969.

Regarding the case of Pfc. Allen McQuaid, see John Loran Kiel Jr., "When Soldiers Speak Out: A Survey of Provisions Limiting Freedom of Speech in the Military," which appeared in the US Army War College journal *Parameters* in 2007.

12. "MY GOD, HE'S FIRING INTO THE DITCH":
Vietnam, the Hollow Army, and the End of the Cold War

John Loran Kiel Jr., "When Soldiers Speak Out: A Survey of Provisions Limiting Freedom of Speech in the Military," also discusses the Vietnam War courts-martial of Lt. Henry Howe and Capt. Howard Levy. The Levy court-martial is also discussed in Joseph DiMona's *Great Court-Martial Cases*.

Also useful regarding the Howe and Levy trials is Leonard B. Boudin, "The Army and the First Amendment," which was published in a 1971 book, *Conscience and Command: Justice and Discipline in the Military*, edited by James Finn.

The classic account of the pain and loss that new army officers faced in the late 1960s is Rick Atkinson, *The Long Gray Line: The American Journey of West Point's Class of 1966*.

A massive body of literature describes the My Lai massacre and the court-martial of William Calley. My account is taken from four sources:

(1) Michal R. Belknap, *The Vietnam War on Trial: The My Lai Massacre and the Court-Martial of Lieutenant Calley*.

(2) The report of the army investigation led by Lt. Gen. William Peers, available online, especially this detailed timeline of events: http://law2.umkc .edu/faculty/projects/ttrials/mylai/Ccompany.html.

Most of the report is also available on the website of the Library of Congress: http://www.loc.gov/rr/frd/Military_Law/Peers_inquiry.html.

(3) The rest of the "My Lai Courts-Martial 1970" website maintained by Professor William Eckhardt, the chief prosecutor in the My Lai cases, at the website of the University of Missouri–Kansas City law school: http://law2 .umkc.edu/faculty/projects/ftrials/mylai/MYLAI.HTM (and http://law2 .umkc.edu/faculty/projects/ftrials/mylai/myl_bcalleyhtml.htm).

(4) From 2011, "Interview—Larry Colburn: Why My Lai, Hugh Thompson Matter": http://www.historynet.com/interview-larry-colburn-why-my-lai-hugh-thompson-matter.htm.

Sources vary significantly in their estimate of Vietnamese dead. The Peers report puts the number at "175–200"; Michael Belknap puts the number at "as many as 500."

William Eckhardt's "My Lai Courts-Martial 1970" website contains two statements from Hugh Thompson and Ron Ridenhour, both from a conference at Tulane University in 1994. Ridenhour's statement describes the conversation with a friend in which he learned about the killing at My Lai: http:// law2.umkc.edu/faculty/projects/ftrials/mylai/Myl_hero.html.

The quote from Carol Polsgrove regarding William Calley and John Sack is taken from her book, *It Wasn't Pretty, Folks, but Didn't We Have Fun?: Esquire in the Sixties*.

Hugh Thompson Jr. died in 2006. His obituary appeared in the *New York Times* on January 7 of that year, and described the death threats he received after the war. In 1999, Thompson was invited to speak at Fort Benning, appearing on a panel at the School of the Americas during Human Rights Week.

Army officers in the audience gave him a standing ovation. That appearance is described by Leslie Gill in a 2004 book, *The School of the Americas: Military Training and Political Violence in the Americas*. I was an infantryman at Fort Benning in 1999, and met Thompson that day.

Ron Ridenhour died earlier, in 1998, at the age of fifty-two. His obituary appeared in the *New York Times* on May 11 of that year.

The Military Justice Act of 1968 is discussed generally in Lawrence J. Morris, *Military Justice: A Guide to the Issues*. Regarding the creation of military judges, and the limits on their practical independence, see Frederic I. Lederer and Barbara S. Hundley, "Needed: An Independent Military Judiciary—A Proposal to Amend the Uniform Code of Military Justice," which appeared in the *William & Mary Bill of Rights Journal* in 1994.

Elizabeth Lutes Hillman discusses the wave of post-Vietnam law-review articles calling for military justice reform in the "Afterword" section of *Defending America*.

The "Army in Anguish" series in the *Washington Post* was written by Haynes Johnson and George C. Wilson. It opened on September 12, 1971, with an article titled "The U.S. Army: A Battle for Survival," which described an unnamed seventeen-year-old soldier in army barracks in Germany who "has been beaten twice by fellow soldiers in senseless acts of violence. . . . Part of his fear stems from the organized drug traffic within his barracks." The series closed on September 20 with an article titled "The Army: Its Problems Are America's."

The quote regarding drug abuse and burglaries in the barracks is from Alexander Vazansky, "'Army in Anguish': The U.S. Army, Europe, in the Early 1970s," which appears in *GIs in Germany* (volume 1), edited by Thomas W. Maulucci Jr. and Detlef Junker.

The quote regarding William Westmoreland's changes to army policies on reveille formations, bed check, and other features of daily soldier life is taken from Meredith H. Lair, *Armed with Abundance: Consumerism & Soldiering in the Vietnam War*.

Regarding the July 1973 army policy allowing 50 percent of new recruits to be high school dropouts, see "Manpower Shortage Forces Army to Lower Standards," *Washington Post*, July 28, 1973, page A2; and Bernard D. Rostker, *I Want You!: The Evolution of the All-Volunteer Force*.

The story "GI Sentenced in Heroin Death" appeared in the *Washington Post* on December 18, 1973, page A13; Pfc. Vance A. Gibson was sentenced to six years in prison at hard labor after the death of Pvt. Edward G. Monk. Regarding false testimony in a navy court-martial about racial violence, see "Sailor Discharged," *Washington Post*, September 22, 1973, page A22.

Lawrence J. Morris discusses the Military Justice Act of 1983 in *Military Justice: A Guide to the Issues*. Also useful is "Highlights of the Military Justice Act of 1983," a brief article by Maj. John S. Cooke, which appeared in the journal *The Army Lawyer* in February 1984.

Regarding the Tailhook scandal, see Kingsley R. Browne, "Military Sex Scandals from Tailhook to the Present: The Cure Can Be Worse Than the Disease," which appeared in the *Duke Journal of Gender Law & Policy* in 2007.

The sexual-assault allegations at the Aberdeen Proving Ground, and their aftermath, are described in Jackie Spinner, "In Wake of Sex Scandal, Caution Is the Rule at Aberdeen," *Washington Post*, November 7, 1997.

EPILOGUE: THE LIVING PAST:
The Court-Martial in Contemporary America

The quotes describing Stein's Facebook posts, and saying that the UCMJ bans criticism of the chain of command by military personnel, are taken from a story in the *Los Angeles Times*: "Marine Faces 'Administrative Action' over Obama Facebook Post," March 22, 2012: http://articles.latimes.com/2012/mar/22/local/la-mc-0322-obama-marine-20120322.

The Armed Forces Tea Party page is still online, and still being updated. Though it contains posts from Gary Stein, the original comments that led to his discharge appear to have been removed: https://www.facebook.com/REALAFTP.

For another example of a news story that says Stein violated the UCMJ—without saying which article he violated—see ABC News, "Marine Sgt. Gary Stein Gets 'Other Than Honorable' Discharge over Anti-Obama Facebook Comment," April 25, 2012: http://abcnews.go.com/US/marine-sgt-gary-stein-honorable-discharge-anti-obama/story?id=16216279.

The essay by Andrew Bacevich, "Warrior Politics," appeared in the May 2007 issue of the *Atlantic*, and describes Liam Madden and the Appeal for Redress: http://www.theatlantic.com/magazine/archive/2007/05/warrior-politics/305764/.

Like Stein, Madden was investigated by the Marine Corps after wearing part of his uniform to an antiwar protest as a member of the Individual Ready Reserve, and threatened with an other than honorable discharge. The Marine Corps ultimately abandoned that effort. See Heather Hollingsworth, "Marines Drop Case Against Iraq Veteran," in the *Washington Post*, June 29, 2007.

Regarding antiwar petitions and GI support for Capt. Howard Levy, see this chronology listing acts of resistance at the website *Sir, No Sir*: http://www.sirnosir.com/timeline/chronology_protests2.html.

May 1967, for example: "Six GIs (Sp/5 Paul J. Gaedtke, Pvt. A. D. Stapp, Sp/4 Richard Wheaton, Pvt. Stan Ingerman, PFC T. E. O'Reilly, and Pvt. J. R. Wood) send telegram of support which said: 'We support you in your courageous stand against America's dirty imperialist war in Vietnam. You have recognized that as a doctor your duty lies in healing the sick, not in training Gestapo-like Green Beret killers. We wish you luck in your trial and hope others will follow your example' to Dr. Howard Levy."

February 23, 1968: "Fort Ord - Pvt. Kenneth Stolte and PFC Daniel Amick distribute antiwar petition at Ft Ord, which says in part: 'We protest. We protest the war in Vietnam . . . Too many of our friends, not to mention the Vietnamese, are being killed for nothing . . . We are tired of it. We are tired of all the lies about the war. We are uniting and organizing to voice our opposition to this war. If you really want to work for peace and freedom, then join us in our opposition. We are organizing a union in order to express our dissension and grievances.' "

1st Lt. Ehren Watada's court-martial for his refusal to deploy to Iraq ended in a mistrial, after which he was discharged from the army. See, for example, Kim Murphy, "Army to discharge officer who refused to go to Iraq," *Los Angeles Times*, September 29, 2009: http://articles.latimes.com/2009/sep/29/nation/na-watada-discharge29.

Regarding the court-martial of Bradley Manning, see Chase Madar, *The Passion of Bradley Manning: The Story of the Suspect Behind the Largest Security Breach in U.S. History*.

Pfc. Justin Watt's decision to report the Mahmoudiyah rape and murders is described in Gregg Zoroya, "Soldier Describes Anguish in Revealing Murder Allegations," *USA Today*, September 13, 2006: http://usatoday30.usatoday.com/news/nation/2006-09-12-soldier-anguish_x.htm.

Regarding Spc. Joseph Darby's decision to report the abuse of detainees at Abu Ghraib, see John Shattuck, "On Abu Ghraib: One Sergeant's Courage a Model for US Leaders," *Christian Science Monitor*, May 16, 2005: http://www.csmonitor.com/2005/0516/p09s02-coop.html.

Steven D. Green's suicide in federal prison is described in "Convicted US War Criminal Steven Green Dead in 'Suicide,'" BBC News, February 19, 2014: http://www.bbc.com/news/world-us-canada-26265798.

Regarding the "ratchet effect" in wartime civil liberties, see Cass R. Sunstein and Jack L. Goldsmith, "Military Tribunals and Legal Culture: What a Difference Sixty Years Makes," a University of Chicago Public Law & Legal Theory Working Paper from 2002: http://chicagounbound.uchicago.edu/cgi/viewcontent.cgi?article=1190&context=public_law_and_legal_theory.

Sen. Kirsten Gillibrand's statement about campus sexual assault being swept under the rug can be found in a press release distributed by a colleague, Sen. Claire McCaskill: http://www.mccaskill.senate.gov/media-center/news-releases/campus-accountability-and-safety-act.

Gillibrand's op-ed essay on military sexual assault, "Sexual Assaults and American Betrayal," appeared in the *New York Daily News* on March 14, 2014: http://www.nydailynews.com/opinion/sexual-assaults-american-betrayal-article-1.1721007.

Capt. Zachary Spilman's law review article, "Not Helping: How Congressional Tinkering Harms Victims During the Post-Trial Phase of a Court-Martial," appeared in the online *Columbia Law Review Sidebar* on July 28, 2014: http://columbialawreview.org/not-helping_spilman/.

Regarding the court-martial conviction and successful legal appeal of Marine Corps Staff Sgt. Steve Howell, see Michael Doyle, "Marine's Sexual Assault Conviction Overturned Because of Commandant's Tough Talk," McClatchy Washington Bureau, May 22, 2014: http://www.mcclatchydc .com/2014/05/22/228240/marines-sexual-assault-conviction.html.

The Parris Island comments from Marine Corps Commandant James Amos that caused Howell's conviction to be overturned are described in detail by James Joyner, a former soldier who now teaches at the Marine Corps Command and Staff College, in a June 8, 2014, post on the blog *Outside the Beltway*, "More on Unlawful Command Influence": http://www.outsidethebeltway. com/more-on-unlawful-command-influence/.

The *New York Times* story "Remark by Obama Complicates Military Sexual Assault Trials," appeared on July 13, 2013.

INDEX